Infant and Toddler Experiences

by

Fran Hast and Ann Hollyfield

Redleaf Press

Published by Redleaf Press
a division of Resources for Child Caring
10 Yorkton Court
St. Paul, MN 55117
Visit us online at www.redleafpress.org

Redleaf Press books are available at a special discount when purchased in bulk for special premiums and sales promotions. For details, contact the sales manager at 800-423-8309.

Library of Congress Cataloging-in-Publication Data
Hast, Fran.
    Infant and toddler experiences / by Fran Hast and Ann Hollyfield.
        p.   cm.
    Includes index.
    ISBN 1-884834-57-4
    1. Day care centers—United States. 2. Infants—Care—United
States. 3. Toddlers—Care—United States. 4. Early childhood
education—United States. 5. Child development—United States.
I. Hollyfield, Ann. II. Title.
HQ778.63.H38   1999
362.71'2—dc21   99-30809
                                                                              CIP

Manufactured in the United States of America

Acknowledgments

This book is both our story and the story of the Palo Alto Infant Toddler Center (ITC), where we have worked together for almost twenty years. ITC is all of us who have participated in the center throughout the years; caregivers, children, and parents may recognize their names in this book. Their use is sentimental to us, but, more importantly, their inclusion should not be construed to represent involvement in actual happenings. The scenarios we present are real, but names and circumstances have been changed.

We are grateful for Janet Gonzalez-Mena and Dianne Widmeyer Eyer's book *Infancy and Caregiving, First edition*, which the center has used as a reference and standard. Some of its concepts have been invaluable to us. "For every no, give two yeses," "optimal stress," and teacher "facilitation" were first presented to us by Janet in a workshop in Palo Alto in 1980. These concepts were adopted as part of the ITC philosophy for caregiving and have been in continual use ever since. In addition, we appreciate Janet's most recent workshops, in which she models her evolution as a committed caregiver and human being.

We acknowledge our families here as well—a small salutation for all of their encouragement. In particular, we wish to thank our parents Jane, Bill, John, Trudy, Yvonne, Jean, and Skip, all of whom instilled in us a love of reading for information and for an appreciation of the ways people make connections with one another, which helped bring us to the point where we could share our professional experience in this book.

A special thank you to the current staff at ITC—Jill, Johanna, Katya, Marilyn, Maryann, Naomi, Nena, and Terry—for supporting our investment of time and energy in this endeavor with their own. We appreciate our friends' acknowledgement of the place writing the book has taken in our lives and the sincere interest that ITC parents have expressed. Palo Alto Community Child Care has supported our workshops and this book both materially and with much cheerleading. Thank you to Margo, Janice, Judy, Lisa, Lanie, and Jenny.

This book has evolved over years. Ro, our first center director, inspired the vision of infant/toddler child care as a community. We thank Lois at Addison-Wesley for her early interest and worthy suggestions. Beth, at Redleaf, has proved the perfect combination of gentle stretching and ready understanding.

We could not have done it alone. As it turns out, we would not have wanted to.

Ann and Fran
December 1998

To those who are committed to caring for children
and
To Mark, who supports in all ways

Infant and Toddler Experiences

Table of Contents

Introduction 1

Chapter 1: The Foundation 5

What We Believe about Infants and Toddlers in Child Care 7

Making the Commitment to Caring Interactions 23

Chapter 2: Being with Babies: Strategies for Caring for Infants and Toddlers 28

Observation and Optimal Stress 28

Modeling Behavior 32

Acknowledging Feelings 33

Anticipating Transitions, Unusual Events, and Changes in Routine 36

Helping Children Articulate Their Needs and Wants 37

Offering Real Choices 38

Setting Consistent Limits 40

Chapter 3: Supporting Curiosity 43

Helping Children Feel Comfortable 43

Strategies for Promoting Curiosity 44

Supporting Curiosity during Routines 50

Chapter 4: Playing with Curiosity **57**

Experiences for Infants 60

Experiences for Infants and Toddlers 68

Experiences for Toddlers 83

Chapter 5: Encouraging Connections **107**

It All Starts with Physical Connection 108

Connections in Child Care 108

Strategies Caregivers Use to Support Connections 110

Promoting Connection during Routines 121

Caring Responses to Hurtful Behaviors 126

Helping Toddlers Learn Manners 128

Chapter 6: Playing with Connection **132**

Experiences for Infants 133

Experiences for Infants and Toddlers 143

Experiences for Toddlers 157

Chapter 7: Fostering Coordination **185**

Coordination as a Way of Thinking about Physical Development 186

Strategies Caregivers Use to Promote Coordination 187

Using the Strategies during Caregiving Routines 194

Chapter 8: Playing with Coordination **202**

Experiences for Infants 203

Experiences for Infants and Toddlers 207

Experinces for Toddlers 210

Index **253**

Introduction

Finding quality child care for infants and toddlers outside the family continues to be a pressing need for today's working parents. In many communities, lack of available spaces, affordability, and quality care for the young ones are very real dilemmas. According to the Children's Defense Fund 1998 yearbook, *The State of America's Children,* six million infants and toddlers in the United States spend all or part of their day being cared for by someone other than their parents. Half of these families earn less than $35,000 a year and can ill afford the $4,000 to $10,000 annual costs of quality infant/toddler child care.

High cost, however, doesn't guarantee quality. National studies continue to reveal alarming deficiencies in the quality of care. The same Children's Defense Fund yearbook also reports that 40 percent of center-based infant/toddler programs provide care that could jeopardize children's safety and development. Moreover, relatively few child care centers meet the higher standards required for accreditation. In 1997 only 6 percent of all child care centers in the United States were accredited by the National Association for the Education of Young Children.

Lack of adequate education and compensation are the issues lying at the root of another significant blow to quality: low job satisfaction for caregivers. The Children's Defense Fund reports that low wages continue to be the norm for child care staff, just as they were twenty-five years ago. Even with their relatively higher level of education, child care teachers earn less per year than the average bus driver or garbage collector. Staff in child care centers typically earn $12,000 per year (only slightly above minimum wage) and receive no medical benefits or paid leave. As a result, turnover among caregivers is high, shattering any hope for building the stable relationships that infants and young children need to feel safe and secure.

In this book we offer a model of infant/toddler child care that makes the best use of these limited resources. Our nation's child care deficiencies still need to be addressed. But what caregivers can do now, today, is improve the quality of care for children through their commitment to the children and families with whom they work. This book, based on our work together in a nearly twenty-five-year-old tradition at the Palo Alto Infant-Toddler Center (ITC), will show you how it can happen.

Palo Alto Community Child Care

Since 1974 Palo Alto has offered uniquely organized child care programs. A small group of parents had the idea that while they worked their young children could be cared for in a community-based homelike setting. They had a

1

vision of a neighborhood center for young children that mirrored an extended family. Their vision became reality in 1975, when the ITC first opened its doors. From that beginning, the parents put together an umbrella organization, the Palo Alto Community Child Care (PACCC), which standardized care and administration throughout a system of child care centers serving families with infants, toddlers, preschoolers, and school-age children. In a unique partnership with the city of Palo Alto, this private nonprofit organization continues to provide subsidy and operating funds to fifteen child care programs. In an effort to retain staff and thus maintain the best quality care, PACCC provides a strong benefit package, including medical and dental insurance, paid leave, retirement, and tuition reimbursement for early childhood education classes. A board of directors, including parents and community members, oversees all functions.

The Mission of Palo Alto Community Child Care

Palo Alto Community Child Care is an advocate for and a provider of comprehensive child care and closely related services for families living or working in Palo Alto and surrounding communities. PACCC is a nonprofit corporation that strives to develop broad-based community support to meet the needs of families at all economic levels. (Adapted by the PACCC Board, March 19, 1992.)

Program Philosophy of Palo Alto Community Child Care

PACCC programs were created to provide comprehensive child care within the framework of quality developmental standards. While building a sense of community for all children and families, our goal is to enhance each child's self-concept. Age-appropriate experiences provide opportunities for independent decision making and social interaction while challenging both physical and cognitive skills. From this basic philosophy each individual program develops its own style with help from parents, staff, and children.

In 1975 the Palo Alto Infant-Toddler Center was set up in the classroom area of a neighborhood church for children four months to three years of age. In keeping with the parents' initial vision of an extended family, the children were not separated by age into "classrooms." Students and caregivers who worked at ITC became involved in the Demonstration Infant Program at the local Children's Health Council, which was codirected from 1972 to 1977 by Magda Gerber and Dr. Tom Forrest. The program introduced the caregivers to the philosophy of respect, responsiveness, and reciprocity in infant/toddler care, which was adapted from the ideas of Emmi Pikler in Hungary. Magda

Gerber continues to espouse this philosophy through Resources for Infant Educarers (RIE).

The first ITC staff of college-educated parents from the neighborhood and child development students from nearby universities worked cooperatively. Each was paid the same hourly wage, and all shared the tasks of caring for the children. This sharing of all tasks led to today's staff rotation system of organization. The system includes a teaching director who works alongside the staff and is a scheduled part of the staff-child ratio most of the day. Teaching directors continue to be a unique and strong component of each PACCC center in its efforts to support caregivers in forging a pattern of professional commitment to long-term quality care for children and their families.

How Did We Get Here?

Neither of us planned a career in child care. In 1976, after a short stint as an elementary reading group tutor, Fran came to ITC with a degree in psychology. Ann, who has a degree in elementary education, joined the staff in 1980. What we found at ITC was a community of staff members and families who cared for and learned from one another. We also found the opportunity to develop our interests and skills as caregivers of infants and toddlers, and to think through the ideas that are fundamental to caring interactions with very young children. We have stayed because of our strong connections to the families and our commitment to guiding meaningful interactions with infants and toddlers. We fell heir to a legacy of community and ideas about infant/toddler care that we want to pass on to other infant/toddler caregivers. We hope that from this book caregivers will gain a fresh perspective for approaching their work that will lead to job satisfaction and long-term commitment, ultimately improving the quality of infant/toddler care.

About This Book

Our purpose in writing this book is to offer caregivers, and interested parents, a repertoire of ways to respond to infants and toddlers that support individual development. We refer to planned curricula for infants and toddlers as "experiences" rather than "activities," in order to emphasize the importance of focusing on the *way* the children relate to the materials, the caregivers, and one another, instead of on what they make. The word "experience" implies being affected by what one encounters in the course of one's life. In speaking of infants and toddlers, we offer the idea of an experience as a free-form process of learning through repeated interactions and explorations. Some "activities" may fit this concept, but often the focus in an activity is on the product rather than the process. The planned experiences are described simply and include a list of materials as well as suggestions for setting up the experience and being with the children while they are exploring it.

As well as planned experiences, we also present practical strategies for approaching everyday interactions between infants, toddlers, and their caregivers. These strategies become foundations of practice for caregivers. When caregivers use these approaches, the quality of the child's experience makes a difference in her development. Both the strategies and the experiences are organized by what we call the "Three Cs": the *curiosity* of the child, the *connections* children make with other children and with adults, and the physical *coordination* necessary for skill integration. Children's curiosity ignites their learning. Their emotional connections allow them to explore their relationships with other people. Children's developing physical coordination gives them more opportunities for investigation. Of course, in the development of the whole child, all of these areas overlap. However, we have separated them here to make it easier for caregivers to think about one aspect of development at a time.

We want this book to be a practical resource for people who care about young children. While we suggest very specific approaches for interacting with infants and toddlers, we intend the strategies to be flexible. They are all based upon the principle of respectful care. We encourage you to use these approaches to inspire, to experiment, or to expand your own or another's expertise.

Terms

We use the terms *infants* and *toddlers* throughout the book. *Infants* include those children from birth to approximately twelve months of age who may be mobile but are not yet walking. *Toddlers* include those children who are walking to three years of age. The term *caregiver* refers to the adult in attendance. Parents are included in the *caregiver* designation. And, in turn, *parents* includes anyone who lives with or is responsible for a child.

Suggestions for Using This Book

Caregivers can use the book's strategies as a "hip-pocket" source of responses to infants and toddlers. After becoming familiar with the philosophy and practicing the strategies, a caregiver builds a repertoire of responses to everyday infant/toddler scenarios. Offering effective and caring responses to a variety of situations then becomes as straightforward as pulling them out of one's hip pocket.

People who are new to infant/toddler group care can use this book as an introduction to effective ways of being with young children. It can be a resource for on-the-job training in a center or family child care setting. The strategies and experiences can be introduced, practiced, and evaluated in an organized manner by the individual or center staff. For example, the strategies could be developed into a checklist for staff training and observation, or for planning and evaluating curricula. Of course, readers can also browse through the book, focusing specifically on topics that interest them such as "infants" or "connection" or "planned experiences for promoting toddler coordination."

Like many caregivers, we have chosen to care for young children because we want to make a difference. Please join us in this investigation of how we can do the job we want to do, making the difference we want to make.

Contact the Authors:

Fran Hast and Ann Hollyfield
Palo Alto Infant-Toddler Center
4111 Alma, Palo Alto, CA 94306
itexperience@aol.com

1

The Foundation

It is vital that a child care program have a written philosophy that reflects a consistent approach to caring for the children. A written philosophy tells parents how caregivers will care for their child and why caregivers respond to children the way they do. It helps parents understand that the care given to their child is purposeful and also provides a reference for discussion when parents have questions about ideas and practices unfamiliar to them. In addition, a written philosophy provides a foundation from which caregivers work. It guides how they respond to each child at any given moment and explains why children are approached in a particular way. When concerns or issues arise among staff, caregivers can revisit the written philosophy for clarification. In this way, a written philosophy helps the staff maintain a consistent approach to the children.

ITC's philosophy is based on our understanding of child development as represented in the theories of Piaget, Erikson, and others, and it is supported by the latest research in brain development. In this chapter we talk about the ITC philosophy, upon which this book is based.

Why Is It Important to Understand Infant/Toddler Development?

Caregivers must be able to recognize each infant and toddler's developmental level in order to care for them appropriately. Being knowledgeable about developmental theories gives meaning to the behaviors caregivers see every day. In addition, when caregivers understand a child's current level of development and respect it as "just fine," they can allow that child's development to unfold naturally.

If you have been caring for infants and toddlers for several months, you have observed patterns of behaviors. And you probably have formed ideas about the children you work with. When reference is made to a "five month old" or a "fourteen month old," an image pops into your head. Or you may see children at the grocery store and guess their ages. These images and ideas come from the observations you have made during caregiving. Developmental theories such as Piaget's theory about how children's thinking develops and Erikson's theory about emotional stages of development are simply observations just like the ones you make, written down and put in order over time.

Understanding child development affects caregivers' responses to individual children and overall curricula. For example, caregivers respond differently to the eighteen month old saying "No no NO" as they try to put on her socks when they know that soon she will say, "Help, please," and then, "Me do it." With practice she will be able to put on her socks by herself. When caregivers recognize that her saying no is a step in a predictable developmental sequence, they are more apt to be understanding and responsive to the child's growing independence.

Here is another example: Thirty-month-old Pablo says, "It's a dog because it's brown." The caregiver knows that Pablo's statement is not true—every brown animal is not a dog! However, knowing Piaget's theory that children learn by making generalizations and then refining them over time, the caregiver can respond, "You see a brown dog." This both honors Pablo's experience and respects his developmental stage.

Understanding child development enables caregivers to recognize the child as the active agent in the construction of her own knowledge and to see themselves as facilitators of this natural process, rather than the directors of it.

Brain Development in the First Three Years

Many of us in the child care profession were gratified when the results of recent infant brain research hit the media. The results confirmed our beliefs about the importance of caregiver relationships with infants and toddlers that build children's trust and respect their independence. Brain research tells us that a child's early learning in the stages of sensory and emotional development reflects her everyday experiences. For example, when an infant's needs are met in a predictable manner, she develops the physical foundation of trust: pathways in the brain are established from this experience that lead the infant to expect that her needs will be met. In turn, this expectation allows her to be more relaxed and to have more energy for exploring new experiences and integrating them into what she already knows.

Babies are born with great potential. Flexibility is the marvel of the human brain. Instead of being hard-wired for every possible eventuality, our brains are made to learn from experience. Children are born with areas in the brain specialized for different functions, such as language, movement, and processing messages from the senses. However, it is a young child's experiences that form the networks in the brain that determine how these functions are connected and how the child will be able to use them. Clearly, then, everyday experiences permanently affect the connections in children's brains.

Even more important than the simple experiences, however, is the emotional context within which they occur. As most people already know, memories are clearer when they are attached to feelings. This happens because the brain is chemically responsive to emotional experiences. Because of the way babies' brains are set up to respond to emotions, it is not possible to separate their development of logical thought from their emotional development. The emotions involved in individual interactions with caregivers are particularly important to very young children as they organize their experiences for future learning. So what happens when the emotional context of interaction with adults is neutral (for example, the adult doesn't express feelings or respond to the infant's feelings) or damaging (for example, the adult expresses mostly strongly negative feelings toward the infant)? Unfortunately, the qualities that expand the potential of the human brain also make it vulnerable. We know about the "failure to thrive" syndrome, which can cause death in infants deprived of touch and human interaction. But it appears that the *manner* of interaction also makes a difference. Neutral or uncaring interactions may meet babies' physical needs but can fail to give them the emotional nourishment they need to learn.

All this research points to the necessity of providing an environment rich in emotional support for infants and toddlers. It appears that human beings have evolved to build upon the kind of intimate emotional contact with other human beings available in an extended family. In such a setting, caring adults interact with infants to reflect their concerns, meet their needs, and provide experiences consistent with what we know about development. For further reading in this area, we recommend *The Growth of The Mind* by Stanley Greenspan.

What We Believe about Infants and Toddlers in Child Care

1. Center-based care of infants and toddlers is best organized to feel like a home as much as possible. To make the center feel more like a home, we organize space by function (instead of by age), use family age grouping (which allows children in a sibling-like age range to spend their day together in small groups), and rotate staff.

2. In order to learn and grow, children's developmental needs must be met in ways that respect them as individuals. We use the Ten Principles of respectful caregiving developed by Janet Gonzalez-Mena and Dianne Widmeyer Eyer.

3. The caregiving environment for infants and toddlers must foster independent learning and allow them to explore safely.

4. In order to respect and nurture infants and toddlers, it is necessary to respect and nurture their families as well. This means welcoming participation, acknowledging family cultures, and remaining open to each parent's perspective.

A Center That Feels like Home

At ITC, we imitate home care by the way we set up the environment, the way we group children, and the way we organize our staffing. We believe the most appropriate care for very young children occurs in an environment that looks and feels like a home. Such an atmosphere might feel similar to living with an extended family. This model of care encourages children to be self-directed. It also provides opportunities for intimate interactions between caregivers and children that a more rigid, stratified system may not. We're suggesting a "soft" environment, where meals are served family style, caregivers mingle with families and all ages of children, and children are not required to stand in line.

The traditional school model, in which children of the same age are grouped together for instruction and interaction, has become the model for child care in the United States. For example, in many centers siblings may not see each other at all during the day. Often room and caregiver changes are made for adult convenience, rather than to address a child's needs, interests, or development. These age-segregated settings are inherently less flexible for meeting the needs of children on the cusp of developmental milestones. For example, how does a newly walking infant get to be with the other toddlers—by the calendar, her age, or the timing of her development when she walks? Such decisions define a child care program's philosophy.

Planning the Environment by Function

Understanding how important children's emotional experiences are to their early development, we set up our environment to help caregivers focus on individual children. Instead of being assigned to a particular age group of children, each room in the center provides a place for a specific type of experience. These individual rooms suggest a home, where rooms are used for varying purposes by differing combinations of family members. At the same time, caregivers have latitude to meet children's needs because each room can function independently to provide food, diapers, or a quiet corner.

The flow between rooms offers children the flexibility to change their experience or caregiver. The children can have their individual needs met and feel at home in each room. For example, one large carpeted room functions like a family room, where different kinds of experiences may take place simultaneously. There is an indoor climbing structure designed to give mobile infants and toddlers a new perspective by allowing them to climb up platform steps to look at the room, out a high window, or down on others. The room also houses open toy shelves, a dramatic play area under the loft, a comfortable reading area, a family-sized love seat, cubbies for toddler belongings, toy storage cupboards, and an access door to the backyard. Snacks and lunch are eaten family style at two long tables with child-sized chairs.

This room therefore serves a wide range of functions for a family age group of children: stairs and couches for climbing; large floor space for infants to crawl and for toddlers to pull toys or build; scheduled toddler mealtimes; and care-

giving routines such as diapering and dressing. Caregiving needs are met individually during self-directed play so that routine experiences are nurturing and specific to each child.

The art room, on the other hand, provides space for small groups to engage in art and other small-motor experiences. In this room are art supplies, easels mounted on the wall, and an open toy shelf. There is opportunity for both ordered and messy play experiences here. A large picture window provides natural light. One table with child-sized chairs is used for serving snacks and lunch, as well as for some planned play experiences.

Children who are not yet walking are cared for in a separate infant room that toddlers may visit as the adult-child ratio allows. The infant room supports the individual scheduling and charting necessary to provide safe, nurturing care for infants. This large room has cribs, a rocking chair, a low table and cube chairs, a small refrigerator and a microwave, and storage shelves for food-related supplies. Lining the floor are numerous soft pillows and various shaped cushions that can be positioned for changing developmental needs. Open toy shelves offer toys and cruising support for infants. A closet for toy storage makes it easier to exchange the toys on the open shelves with toys that have been washed. There are large baskets for each infant to store personal belongings. A large bulletin board maintains charts of each infant's caregiving routines and developmental information. A door leads directly to the backyard, which the babies often visit.

The backyard offers diverse areas that appeal to the senses and provide large-muscle experiences: wooden climbing structures, sand, grass, concrete, and a woodsy area. Portable equipment can be set up for a wide variety of skill practice, including crawling, cruising, balancing, climbing, running, jumping on mats, throwing, and kicking. Also available outdoors are an A-frame building and slides; a loft for climbing and looking out; spring horses and belt swings; and push, pull, and wheeled toys.

Because we are in California, we can be outside almost every day of the year, but El Niño has enlightened us to the difficulties of wet, cold, or otherwise restrictive weather faced in other locales. Programs may need to brainstorm how to provide opportunities for fresh air, safe climbing, natural textures, and other physical activity when the weather restricts outdoor play. This can be done by rearranging rooms or parts of rooms, investing in foam mats, designating some toys for inside use or for rainy days, and assigning parts of the area for wheeled-toy use.

Family Age Grouping

To further emulate a home, we use an organizational system of family age grouping. Family age grouping allows children in a sibling-like age range to spend their day together in small groups. The children's experience is like being at home with brothers and sisters. Toddlers generally spend time in groups of four to six children, in various rooms and in "pockets of play" outdoors. At mealtimes, they may eat in a group as large as twelve. Three infants spend most of the day  together, with the company of visiting toddlers as time and ratio allows. Children move through the center based on their individual development and interests, rather than their chronological age. Because the children are grouped in this way, the relationships among children, caregivers, and parents are continuous; there is no caregiver or room change at preset times.

We strive for non-hierarchical, friendly, yet professional relationships among children, caregivers, and parents. Because we don't use a primary caregiving system, where each child has one caregiver who attends to her needs throughout the day, parents and children have access to all the caregivers. This expands the possibilities for relationship, support, and sharing specific child-related information.

Family age grouping dilutes the frustrations of some stages of development. In groups of very young children of similar developmental needs, interactions may be characterized by highly intense emotional responses. For example, two young toddlers may interact by grabbing, pushing, or pulling each other. In a mixed age group, however, it is more likely that an assertive action (grab, push, pull) will meet with a verbal response than with physical retaliation. The grabbing, pushing, pulling eighteen month old can practice her newfound assertiveness on and observe and learn from older toddlers who have already experienced that level of interaction.

In addition, when children are at different levels of development, there is less competition for the same kinds of toys and comfort. Because children of different ages and developmental levels need different kinds of support, caregivers are better able to offer each child cognitive, social-emotional, and physical strategies for entering play or approaching another child, for respecting one's own and others' possessions, and for practicing a problem-solving approach to conflicts. A useful source for more information about family age grouping is *The Case for Mixed Age Grouping in Early Education* by Lilian Katz et al.

Staff Rotation System of Organization

At ITC we use a staff rotation system rather than the more common approach of primary caregiving. A staff rotation system, also referred to as a "caregiving team," allows for staff duty changes and variety within a consistent routine. Such a system allows caregivers maximum undistracted time with the children. Household tasks are accomplished and shared by all. We offer a stable team of adult caregivers so that the children, caregivers, and parents can develop relationships spontaneously, rather than through stilted, arbitrary assignments.

In *Cross Cultural Child Development, A View from the Planet Earth* (Pacific Grove, CA: Brooks/Cole Publishing Company, 1979), Emmy Elisabeth Werner notes that only in the Western nuclear family model does the mother take primary care of her infant. American child care for infants and toddlers seems to be based on this primary care model. But many other cultures utilize a model of multiple caregivers for infants. In these cultures, other family members share the infant's care so the mother can complete her other tasks. Usually, this results in the baby being attached to its mother *and* to the other adults. This expands the opportunities for the infant to feel secure. Given the present high turnover of caregivers in American child care, the rotation system actually gives children and families the most continuity—an infant knows all the caregivers, and if one leaves, the child knows and can rely on the others.

In our rotation system there are four positions with specific responsibilities: outdoor caregiver, art room caregiver, floater, and infant room caregiver. Each caregiver performs the duties of one position for a week at a time and then moves through the other positions in a sequential order.

The staff rotation system requires extensive communication among caregivers, particularly about the infants, which promotes close collaboration. At the week's end, the infant caregivers make notes for the next week's caregivers regarding changes in infant diets, new skills, and parent requests. Naps, food intake, and diaper changes are charted individually, and the previous week's charts are available to help caregivers anticipate patterns and maintain consistency. In addition, information about infant care is exchanged at weekly staff meetings.

The rotation system is also flexible and can be adapted to different caregiver-to-child ratios and shift lengths. We are fortunate to have a teaching director, who does not take a rotation position during teaching hours but is counted in the ratio and can be where she is needed. As a regular member of the team, she cares for the children while modeling for and mentoring the staff.

The combination of family age grouping and the rotation system offers real advantages to children and families. A family entering ITC with a two-month-old child can expect care from the same group of caregivers until that child is three and leaves the program to go to

Here is an example of how the rotation system works from a child's perspective: Eleven-month-old Sascha arrives with her dad Monday morning. She greets Nena, the caregiver, who is the morning infant caregiver this week. Sascha recognizes Nena, because she helped with the infants last week, when she was the floater. Since Sascha is cruising capably, she spends time out of the infant room with the toddlers. When she goes outside this morning, she'll be greeted by Johanna (the morning outdoor person this week), who was infant person last week. Sascha's transition from the infant room has been discussed. She is eating table foods and will therefore be invited to share snack times with the toddlers. As Sascha moves to a midday nap, she will sleep in the crib room with other toddlers. As her skills increase, she will spend more and more time out of the infant room, until parents and staff collaborate on the decision to move her cubby to the loft room. All the staff will be familiar because they all care for all the children. Because the toddlers are family age grouped, there will not be a "room change" when she turns two. This continuity of caregivers and peers allows deep relationships to form naturally and will continue until Sascha turns three and leaves the center to attend preschool.

preschool. There is no division of walking children by age, and no room change at set times of year or by birth date. Siblings are delighted to spend part of their days together. The entire center functions as a whole, like a home, for the whole community of infants, toddlers, their parents, and the caregivers. We find that caregivers are willing to invest emotional energy in and make a commitment to children and families when they know that their connection to them will continue.

In Order to Learn and Grow, Children Must Be Respected as Individuals

Our program philosophy is further supported by the Ten Principles of respectful caregiving found in *Infants, Toddlers, and Caregivers* by Janet Gonzalez-Mena and Dianne Widmeyer Eyer (Mountain View, CA: Mayfield Press, 1997). These principles, developed and refined from the work of Dr. Emmi Pikler, summarize Gonzalez-Mena's experience at the Demonstration Infant Program of the Children's Health Council in Palo Alto from 1972 to 1975. We use them to accomplish the kind of emotionally authentic child-adult interactions that developmental theory and recent brain research confirm young children need to learn and grow best, as discussed in the Introduction. We encourage the reader to think of applying the principles by substituting the word *children* or *people* for the words *infants* and *toddlers*. In the real world everyone deserves such respectful attention!

The Ten Principles of Respectful Caregiving

1. Involve infants and toddlers in things that concern them. Don't work around them or distract them to get the job done faster.

2. Invest in quality time. Don't settle for supervising groups, without focusing (more than just briefly) on individual children.

3. Learn each child's unique ways of communicating (cries, movements, gestures, facial expressions, body positions, words) and teach them yours. Don't underestimate children's ability to communicate even though their verbal language skills may be nonexistent or minimal.

4. Invest in time and energy to build a total person (concentrate on the "whole child"). Don't focus on cognitive development alone or look at it as separate from total development.

5. Respect infants and toddlers as worthy people. Don't treat them as objects or cute little empty-headed dolls to be manipulated.

6. Be honest about your feelings around infants and toddlers. Don't pretend to feel something that you don't or not to feel something that you do.

7. Model the behavior you want to teach. Don't preach.

8. Recognize problems as learning opportunities, and let infants and toddlers try to solve their own. Don't rescue them, constantly make life easy for them, or try to protect them from all problems.

9. Build security by teaching trust. Don't teach distrust by being undependable or inconsistent.

10. Be concerned about the *quality* of development in each stage. Don't rush infants and toddlers to meet developmental milestones.

—from *Infants, Toddlers, and Caregivers*, 4th ed. by Janet Gonzalez-Mena and Dianne Widmeyer Eyer (Mountain View, CA: Mayfield Press, 1997).

Our goal is to respect the children in our care, so that they grow up respecting themselves and others. The Ten Principles provide practical guidelines for caregivers in the situations they encounter daily in an infant/toddler program. Because we use these principles to guide all our work with infants and toddlers, we have provided a closer look at each one of them, using real examples from our experience at ITC.

---

1. Involve infants and toddlers in things that concern them. Don't work around them or distract them to get the job done faster.

For example, one of the most common and necessary caregiving routines is nose wiping.

Fourteen-month-old Daniel stands next to a table in the sand area fingering and palming piles of sand. The caregiver, Ro, notices his runny nose and approaches him, saying "Daniel, I see your nose is running. I'd like to wipe it, please." He stops his hand motions and lifts his head toward Ro, who gently wipes his nose and says, "Thanks, Daniel, all done." Daniel resumes his sand play.

Rather than walk up to Daniel unannounced and wipe his nose hurriedly, Ro respectfully tells him what she sees and wants to do. Daniel is involved in this caregiving routine when he stops his actions and presents his nose for wiping. This approach is so simple and so respectful that eventually a two year old will initiate by saying "I have a runny nose" or "I need a tissue." A simple thank you acknowledges Daniel's participation.

What happens when Daniel says no?

Fourteen-month-old Daniel, who has been at the center since he was three months old, stands next to a table in the sand area fingering and palming piles of sand. Ro notices his runny nose and approaches him, saying "Daniel, I see your nose is running. I'd like to wipe it, please." Without taking his eyes from the sand, he says, "No." Ro answers, "I can see you're very busy. I need to wipe your nose. Do you want a tissue or shall I wipe it?" She waits patiently. After ten seconds, Daniel asks for a tissue.

Being clear about what needs to be done, and involving him by giving a choice as to *how* it can be accomplished, Ro respects Daniel as a person and accomplishes the goal.

---

2. Invest in quality time. Don't settle for supervising groups, without focusing (more than just briefly) on individual children.

Caregivers can validate children's sensory experience when they are available and responsive.

Kelly, who is two and a half years old, takes a caregiver's hand and leads him to a corner in the yard. "Spider," she says solemnly. "I see you found a spider," Raul responds. After a pause, he adds, "See its web?" "It's swinging!" Kelly observes. The two watch together in silence.

Raul takes the time to respect Kelly's interest in finding a spider and its web. Her curiosity and observation of its swinging extends her experience by sharing it with her tuned-in caregiver. Taking the time to be in the moment with a child, rather than vaguely responding, "Oh, that's nice," provides the kind of emotional connection that stimulates brain development. These moments recognize Kelly's connection to the natural world and just might plant the seeds for an interest in science.

---

3. Learn each child's unique ways of communicating (cries, movements, gestures, facial expressions, body positions, words) and teach them yours. Don't underestimate children's ability to communicate even though their verbal language skills may be nonexistent or minimal.

Interactions between people take place through communication. It's important to recognize that interactions with infants and toddlers involve many kinds of communication, both verbal and nonverbal. *How* adults communicate with children (their tone of voice, the words they use, their body posture), however, is important in setting the emotional tone of the interaction. Infants and toddlers are so impressionable that the emotional content of an interaction carries great weight—as much as or more than the actual words. Children know when a caregiver is tuned in to them and when a caregiver is not. Caregivers can learn to see the often subtle signs that a child is open to a conversation or curious about something. In infants, these signals may include a glance, bright open eyes, raised eyebrows, verbal utterances, a smile, or bodily gestures. Toddlers' signals may include all of these as well as inquisitive questions. When caregivers pick up on and respond to these signals, they communicate to the child that they are interested in her. As the caregiver responds to the child, either verbally or nonverbally, the infant or toddler responds in turn, or so it goes back and forth like a conversation.

Some of the most commonly occurring "misbehaviors" of toddlers are simply their ways of communicating a need. Young children are actively trying to figure out their place in the world. Usually young children will use their bodies, sometimes in combination with cries or sounds, before they use verbal language to communicate a need. These actions may include aggressive or assertive acts upon their peers. We can respect children's intelligence by realizing they are telling us what they need or are ready to learn. Our attitude can be either supportive ("It looks like you have a lot of energy for kicking. Here's a ball for you to kick. Kicking people is not okay") or punitive ("Stop kicking him").

Consider the following chart:

Child's Action	Child's Need	Respectful Response
Climbing on a table	Practicing climbing skills	Provide a safe place to climb
Hitting, hair pulling	Entering play	Help children understand how to enter play; tell them, "Try saying hi, or wave"
Shoving, kicking	Energy release	Offer an object that can be pushed or hit; offer large-muscle play
Chewing on or mouthing toys, or biting others	Teething relief, experiencing muscle tension	Offer a teether or a washcloth to bite on
Crying	Comfort; assistance	Respond quickly, talking to and physically comforting the child

When caregivers see that these "problems" are really efforts at communication, they are better able to respond to the child's needs. They can give the child alternative actions that meet her needs better. It takes time and effort to understand each child's ways of communicating, but the effort is well invested if, as a result, the program works better for caregivers as well as for the children.

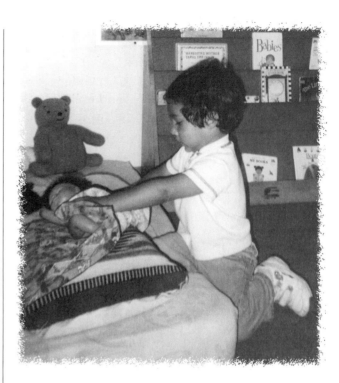

4. Invest in time and energy to build a total person (concentrate on the "whole child"). Don't focus on cognitive development alone or look at it as separate from total development.

There are many opportunities for acknowledging a child's interest and abilities throughout the caregiving day. For example, consider this story:

Sixteen-month-old Molly sits on a floor pillow, legs straight out in front of her body. She cradles a baby doll with her right arm. With her left index finger, Molly touches the doll's nose, saying "Nose." Continuing, Molly points to other parts of the doll and says, "Eye...ear...mouf...hair." The nearby caregiver, Kathy, notices and responds, "I hear you name all those parts of the doll's body, Molly. I am impressed at how much you know." Molly smiles.

Kathy could have launched into a full-scale test of Molly's knowledge (or lack of it) by grilling her with questions: "Where's the belly button? Where's the knee...elbow...shoulder?" Instead, Kathy appreciates all that Molly wants to share at that moment, which is most respectful of Molly's current knowledge. If Kathy's goal is to teach more names of body parts, she could include them in everyday conversation, with comments like "Oh, you've skinned your right *elbow*; let's wash it and put a bandage on it" or "Would you like your socks pulled up to your *calf* or down by your *ankle?*"

As Bev Bos says, "Life is a conversation, not a test!"

5. Respect infants and toddlers as worthy people. Don't treat them as objects or cute little empty-headed dolls to be manipulated.

If caregivers believe that children are unable to understand adult conversation, they may talk about them to other adults in their presence as if they were not there. Making assumptions about children's intelligence and capabilities also tempts adults to have children "perform." This robs the child of freedom of expression and makes the adult rather than the child the one who is in charge of the child's learning.

Consider these two alternate versions of the same scenario:

Fifteen-month-old Julia is being picked up by her mom, and caregiver Monika is sharing an incident that happened that morning. Julia wanders around the room but stops when she hears Monika say her name. Monika says, "Julia did a funny thing this morning. She was holding two pop beads, and one of them fell out of her hand and rolled under the table. She lay on her tummy, trying to reach the pop bead, but she couldn't get it, even when she swiped her hand back and forth. Then she walked around the table, sat down, and saw the pop bead under the table again. She rolled over on her tummy, and from that side she could reach the pop bead." Both Monika and Julia's mom silently look at her. Julia's head drops.

Now imagine if it happened this way:

Monika says, "Julia, I want to tell your mom how you figured out how to get that blue pop bead from under the table. Remember when you dropped one and it rolled under the table?" Julia looks at the table where it happened. She points and smiles as she turns to her smiling mom to be held. Monika continues, "You lay on the floor and stretched your arm but couldn't quite get it. Then you walked around the table, sat down on the floor, and you saw the blue pop bead again. From that side you reached the pop bead easily, and when you finally got it you clutched it proudly with a big smile." Julia smiles broadly and says, "Bead."

It's clear that when Monika includes Julia in the sharing, Julia feels connected and special. She also wants to add something to the conversation.

What is different about the second scenario?

1. The caregiver understood Julia's ability and glee at retrieving the bead herself. She included Julia in the telling.
2. Julia felt connected to the story, and showed this by running to be held as the caregiver was sharing it.
3. Because Julia was included in telling the story, she felt invited to add her own response. She did so by pointing to the table and by saying "bead."

This early experience of being involved in a conversation sets up the likelihood that Julia will share her own experiences later. If you think about it, we would not talk about another adult in the third person as if she weren't present. Why do we think it's okay to do so with children and infants? They deserve the same respect, no matter how young they are.

6. Be honest about your feelings around infants and toddlers. Don't pretend to feel something that you don't or not to feel something that you do.

As evident in the following scenario, young children can be sensitive to the feelings of others, especially adults. When caregivers are honest and express their true feelings, they help children learn to identify their own perceptions and to begin to understand the feelings of others.

*Emily, who loves to climb and is very good at it, lifts her foot onto the bookshelf (for the fourth time) as she glances at Marilyn, who is reading a book to three other toddlers. "**Emily**, I am very frustrated that you have not listened to my words about not climbing on the bookshelf. It's not safe. Please choose to either climb on the couch or keep your feet on the floor."*

One of the best ways for young children to learn about feelings is for adults to respectfully model their own feelings with "I" messages. Emily is hearing about and feeling Marilyn's concern for the situation. All feelings are okay, and it's appropriate for children to hear about adults' feelings, as long as children are not shamed, blamed, or physically or emotionally abused.

What if Emily persists and keeps climbing the bookshelf?

Quite normally, Emily attempts again to climb on the shelf. Marilyn excuses herself from the reading group, saying "I'll be right back," and goes to Emily. Without blaming or threatening, Marilyn firmly holds Emily's shoulders, makes eye contact, and says, "I can tell you really need to climb, but the bookshelf is not a safe place for climbing. I'm going to let you go outside to climb on the slide or up in the A-frame." As Marilyn opens the door and Emily runs out, Marilyn lets the outdoor caregiver know that "Emily really needs to climb something that is safe."

Caregivers who express honest feelings help toddlers learn that words are meaningful.

---

7. Model the behavior you want to teach. Don't preach.

Modeling is one of the strongest teaching tools caregivers have at their disposal. *How we act out what we say has a direct influence upon very young children.* It's basic respect to behave in the same manner that we want the children to learn. Even the simplest actions—for example, not sitting on tables or sitting down when we eat—model the same behavior we ask of the children. The following scenario gives several clear examples of how common responses can actually undermine the lessons caregivers want infants and toddlers to learn.

One toddler, Ryan, sits shoveling sand into several containers. Another toddler, Amy, walks up and stands next to Ryan, observing him for five seconds before grabbing his shovel. Ryan hangs on tightly, saying "Mine!" The caregiver, Mark, says, "No, Amy, that's Ryan's shovel," as he takes the shovel out of both of their hands and gives it back to Ryan. "I'll go get another shovel for you."

How was Mark's response ineffective?

1. Amy's desire to play with a shovel was ignored.

2. Ryan's response ("Mine!") was not acknowledged.

3. Mark's action (grabbing the shovel from both children) models that grabbing is okay, even though he was telling the children that it wasn't.

Let's see how a few small changes in Mark's response allow him to model the behavior he wants the children to learn:

Amy grabs Ryan's shovel, and Ryan holds on tightly, saying "Mine!" Mark says, "I can tell you want a shovel too, Amy, but please listen to Ryan. He's saying 'Mine!'" Mark gently holds Amy's arm just enough to keep her from pulling the shovel out of Ryan's grip. Amy releases her hold on the shovel. Mark says, "Thanks for listening to Ryan. I bet you can find another shovel so you can play with Ryan. Do you want to look around yourself or do you need help?" Amy says, "Hep," and nods. Mark says, "Let's walk around together," and they both stand up. Mark spies another shovel and, without saying anything, heads in that direction, demonstrating the concept of looking around by his head and eye movements. Amy sees the shovel and runs to pick it up, smiling, and then heads back to sit down near Ryan.

How did Mark model for the toddlers?

1. Mark gently held Amy's arm until Amy released her hold of the shovel to give it back to Ryan.

2. Mark used simple language to define and resolve the conflict.

3. Mark modeled actively walking around and searching for another shovel. He allowed Amy to locate the shovel herself, developing autonomy.

This responsive interaction by Mark might have taken an additional minute, but more importantly it involves both toddlers in a conversation-like exchange. The exchange prepares the children to independently handle a similar problem in the future. After repeated interactions like this one, instead of grabbing someone else's shovel, Amy is more likely to look around for another first.

---

8. Recognize problems as learning opportunities, and let infants and toddlers try to solve their own. Don't rescue them, constantly make life easy for them, or try to protect them from all problems.

Adults actually do children a great disservice when rescuing them from frustrating situations that they have put themselves into. Not only does this deny the child the experience of her own real feelings, it robs her of an opportunity to complete or finish a task she has chosen. Note how the caregiver in the following scenario allows a toddler to complete a task from beginning, through frustration, to successful accomplishment.

Michael, who is eighteen months old, has a ball under one arm. He tries unsuccessfully to pick up another ball without dropping the first one. He tries again, maneuvering his body close to the second ball and squatting so he can use both his free hand and the hand of the arm that is already holding a ball. Michael is persistent even as one ball repeatedly rolls away. "Ball!" he yells, stamping his foot. Martina, an attentive caregiver, gently protects his space and the two balls from intrusion. After five full minutes, red-faced and beaming, Michael has a ball under each arm.

Michael has a clear goal in mind: to hold two balls at the same time. By not stepping in and helping Michael with this goal and by keeping other children from interrupting him, Martina allows Michael the space and time to solve his own problems. Michael's perseverance is rewarded when he accomplishes what he set out to do.

---

9. Build security by teaching trust. Don't teach distrust by being undependable or often inconsistent.

Erikson theorizes that young infants learn trust or distrust in the first year of life. Caregivers can teach trust by learning each infant's patterns of behavior and preferences related to meeting routine caregiving needs.

Ten-month-old Aaron is used to having a little something to eat or drink each day upon his arrival at the center. Therefore, the infant caregiver, Jim, has a bottle or a serving of food ready for him after his mom or dad leaves. With Althea, who is eight months old, Jim builds trust by accepting that she has to fuss or cry a bit before settling to sleep. He acknowledges this pattern by remaining calm and gently comforting her.

Jim has learned the specific patterns or routines of each infant. Accepting their personal tendencies, he meets their needs predictably and consistently, which builds trust.

After the first year, it's just as important to maintain the learned trust and consistency by following through and being dependable for toddlers. For example, if a caregiver gets briefly interrupted from reading a book to a toddler, it's important to follow through and return to the book and at least attempt to finish reading it to the child. Here's another example:

Sixteen-month-old Nischal is busy pushing a cart around the cement path, a large poop oozing from his diaper. Nancy, the caregiver, says to him, "We need to go in and change your diaper. I'll hang the cart up here on the fence so you can continue pushing it after I change your diaper." When Nancy and Nischal come back out into the play yard, Nancy returns the pushcart to Nischal to remind him of his play, whether or not he remembers to ask her for it.

Nancy's follow-through after the diaper change is the important step. Nischal learns from it that his play is important enough to "save." He also learns that Nancy is dependable.

Caregivers teach children trust by learning about individual patterns and following through on interrupted interactions or play. Infants and toddlers can proceed through the many processes of their lives more securely when caregivers build such trust.

---

10. Be concerned about the quality of development in each stage. Don't rush infants and toddlers to meet developmental milestones.

Infants and toddlers are developing in many ways at once, and their development follows predictable patterns. For example, just as children's emotional developmental stages follow a predictable and sequential path (described by Erikson as moving from trust to autonomy to initiative), so does infants' physical development, which moves through the stages of rolling, creeping, crawling, sitting, pulling up, cruising, and walking. Normally, infants go through each stage sequentially, and each child has her own pace. They deserve respect, space, and time to practice.

Furthermore, each developmental stage is support for the next, rather than preparation for it. This is a subtle point, but a crucial one. The term *preparation* implies an event that will happen some time in the future, while *support* implies an ongoing process. The idea of preparation does not take into account the ongoing, overlapping nature of human development. If we think of each stage as support for the next, it is clear that the next stage will emerge when the child is ready for it.

Developing faster is not necessarily better. It is more important for a child to experience each stage fully. For example, consider the physical development of infants. For a young infant newly experiencing time away from cradled arms, a cocoonlike space on the floor between soft pillows or a caregiver's extended legs can be a comfortable place. As she gets stronger, she'll push against objects or the floor to roll over. An infant who is adept at rolling over and over can get anywhere on a floor with open space to move in and objects available to push against. As she pushes off the floor to roll over repeatedly, the infant's legs and arms get stronger and stronger. The "push offs" become pushups, and the baby bends her knees to push against the floor for the initial movements towards creeping. Soon she'll start crawling. Strong tummy muscles from lots of practice rolling over help an infant into a sitting position and give her the ability to control getting out of that position as well.

What happens when an infant's process of learning to sit up on her own is short-circuited by being propped into a sitting position before she can attain it on her own? Consider the following scenario:

Five-month-old Susie arrives with her father. He places her on the floor in a sitting position and goes to put away her supplies. Flailing her arms, she soon topples onto a pillow and begins to fuss. The caregiver, Cara, approaches, saying "Hi, Susie. You fell over, huh." Picking her up, she continues, "Dad and I need to talk about your morning." At pickup time,

Cara approaches Susie's dad to discuss what happened. She says something like this: "Hi, Dave. Remember when Susie fell over this morning? I wanted to explain a little more about our philosophy and how it works. We don't put kids into positions that they can't get into by themselves. Susie's a great roller. Those muscles she's developing by rolling will help her get into a sitting position when she's ready, and they'll hold her stable once she gets there. When she's propped up, Susie doesn't know how to get down without falling over. That makes her more dependent on us. Also, we don't want her to think she should be able to sit up, or that rolling over is not okay or not enough."

A child needs experience in negotiating balance and gravity. Susie simply has not yet practiced the movements enough to get into the position herself. Adults do infants a great disservice when they encourage actions that require a developmental level that has yet to be reached, such as sitting up or walking with adult help. Unless babies have been seduced into thinking it's not enough, they love to do what they know how to do at that moment. By providing a prone infant with objects to push against and reach for, adults can help infants practice and learn to move by themselves. In this way, caregivers can respect the child's current level of development as just fine. This gives the child's self-respect a supportive beginning.

An Environment That Fosters Independent Learning

Children will develop to their fullest in an environment that is set up for them to safely explore, experiment, and practice interacting with objects, other children, and adults. To provide an environment in which young children can explore freely, caregivers must "think like a kid" when putting out toys or making changes at levels within a child's reach. For example, anything that looks like a ball probably will be thrown! Anything with horizontal "steps" looks like a climbing structure and probably will be climbed upon. Toddlers who can move independently will want to feel where their bodies fit in spaces, including inside boxes, crates, and toy shelves and under tables, chairs, rugs, and mats.

Knowing that infants and toddlers use their senses to explore the environment and to construct reality, caregivers can provide objects that can be mouthed and washed, as well as open-ended toys that allow for discovery of cause and effect. Simply connected manipulatives, baskets for dumping and filling, hand-held vehicles, and soft things for throwing (like clean, balled-up socks) can always be available indoors.

"Pockets of play" (defined areas for small group interactions) can also be set up to accommodate both side-by-side and interactive play by small groups of children. These might include spaces for sand play, water play, ball play, block building, dramatic play, or reading. For example, four dolls and purses might be set out together to encourage play by several children. Similarly, several buckets and shovels can be set out around a mound of sand, or two slides can be set up side by side. Toddlers can often move independently between indoor and outdoor environments as they practice integrating their many skills, among which are negotiating gravity, balance, and mobility; large- and small-motor tasks; and problem solving.

Other children and caregivers are part of the child care environment as well. When the objects in the environment are safe and enable children to explore independently at their own pace, caregivers have more time to observe individual children and their interactions with one another. Knowing that the social and emotional development of infants and toddlers will occur as they literally bump into one another, caregivers can help turn collisions into connections by responding in ways that respect both children. As toddlers freely explore their effects on one another, caregivers can facilitate conflicts as learning opportunities for *all* involved in the interaction.

Extending Respect to Families

A relationship with parents begins with their first phone call inquiring about care for their child. As parents inquire about openings, fees, hours, ratio, staffing, and the waiting list, they too are learning from this first interaction whether or not a center's staff can be trusted. As parents proceed through the steps of touring the center and actually enrolling their children, there are things caregivers can do at every step of the way to make them feel more comfortable and to ensure that their family is respected at the center.

Touring the Center

Oftentimes, parents' visit to an infant/toddler center is the first and very scary step toward turning over care of their child to someone else. When parents are placing their children in child care that is not provided by a relative, that "someone else" is a stranger or group of strangers. Most of the time parents confess, "I don't know anything about child care" or "This is only the second place I've visited." An attentive caregiver can take some of the pressure off by asking

friendly questions that parents do know the answers to, such as "Did you find us okay?" or "How did you hear about our program?" That question alone usually generates a smile and a relaxed manner, as often parents have heard nice things about a program from a friend or co-worker. It also helps to acknowledge the complicated feelings involved in looking for child care and in turning over care of their child to someone else by saying things like "I can tell this is hard for you, but we are here to support your need to return to work" or inviting parents to "Please ask any questions along the way as we walk through the center. No question is dumb."

It also helps to reassure parents by reminding them that "*You* have to be satisfied with the place you choose for your child, or else it won't work." In this way, a caregiver can demonstrate that the pressure is in fact on the center to live up to the high standards parents expect from someone else who is caring for their children. By respecting the parent's difficult job of finding child care that she can feel comfortable with, caregivers can extend a hand of support and encourage the parent to scrutinize the program.

Being open to all the questions a parent asks and responding to them frankly creates an atmosphere of trust and honesty from the start. The many questions parents ask reflect their needs and concerns. Here are some common ones:

- How many infants/toddlers do you have?
- What is the ratio of staff to children?
- Do I bring diapers or food?
- Can I come to nurse my baby?
- How many staff are there? How long has the staff been here? What is their background?
- Do the infants ever go outside?
- Will you accommodate my son, who is a vegetarian?
- How do parents participate in the program?
- How do you discipline a child?
- What will my child learn here?

During a parent's first tour it also helps to mention the connections that families can establish with the program. At ITC there are many ways for parents and families to participate in the center community—from hanging out to camping out, from fixing a leaky faucet to installing a sprinkler system, from sharing a snack to sharing a family cultural practice. There are usually photographs on display of such events or other daily happenings at the center that can serve as easy icebreakers to conversations and relaxed feelings.

One of the easiest and most natural connections for parents is the kids themselves. If parents have time to linger, they can observe and interact with inquisitive toddlers. If a parent has a baby in her arms, the toddlers are naturally curious and want to see the infant up close. Visiting toddlers usually scramble from their parents' arms to investigate toys, other kids, or the yard.

Enrolling a Child

When a family has made the choice to enroll their child at a particular center, they are almost always asked to fill out a profile that tells the center more about their child. The questions on the profile not only convey information to the center, they also tell the parents what is valued there.

At ITC the profile asks parents to explain their child's home schedule and gives us insight about their child's preferences. An additional page of information requests specific family cultural practices that may be shared at ITC. When English is a second language, parents are asked to provide key native-language words or phrases that the child might use or recognize when spoken by caregivers. Caregivers also request family photographs and products, cans, or bags that are labeled in the child's native language so they can be displayed or used by the children. The goal is to reflect the various cultures within the environment so that the children are both comfortable with and enticed by differences among people.

Janet Gonzalez-Mena discusses the importance of dialogue in exploring cultural differences in her book *Multicultural Issues in Child Care* (Mountain View, CA: Mayfield Press, 1997):

> The goal is for adults to discuss potential conflicts and learn to dialog about them so that children in child care experience fewer harmful conflicts in approach when the teacher or caregiver and parents disagree about what's good or right. It's important for teachers or caregivers to clarify what they believe is good practice, as well as begin to open up to other perspectives—even those that may conflict with their own.

At ITC we see every family as having a unique culture and strive to build a respectful relationship with each. We also recognize that each family comes from a cultural foundation of personal history and tradition. We see these traditions evidenced when families share celebrations and cultural practices with us. With ten of us on the staff, families have the choice and opportunity to interact with those who are most comfortable or compatible regarding a specific issue, such as weekend caregiving, toilet learning, or appropriate parties for two year olds. These ongoing relationships become the basis for the dialogue necessary to discuss specific issues and resolve any future conflict.

The pieces are in place to resolve conflict when a family's concerns are taken seriously, their questions are researched and answered to the best of the caregivers' ability, their children are loved for themselves, their interests are shared, and their participation is welcomed. Even if total resolution is not possible, when caregivers and parents have established caring relationships they can come to consensus about how to handle the differences in their approaches. They can agree to disagree, revisit the issue, work to educate one another, or find a compromise.

One commonly occurring area of differing values is gender roles. This may be an issue among staff members as well as between staff and parents in the program. Understanding gender issues may include expanding one's definition of family or coming to accept all notions of work, interests, and relationships expressed by members of the center community. Female plumbers, stay-at-home dads, and families with two moms or two dads have equal validity and deserve equal respect in a child care center.

It is important for caregivers not to comment (even inadvertently) or make judgments about children based on their personal ideas of gender appropriateness. In play, caregivers can follow the child's lead, allowing any safe behavior. Caregivers need to be especially mindful in the arenas of clothing, activity or energy level, and physical affection and in their expectations around language develop-

ment and toilet learning. When Sarah plays with the trucks, caregivers can say, "It looks like you're having fun!" When Max puts on low heels, caregivers can say, "Look how you can balance in those shoes!" It's important to recognize that expectations of children based on their gender are culturally based, as well as founded on caregivers' and parents' individual experience and convictions.

Communication proves to be the connection. When caregivers explore these issues with parents, they usually find that they want the same things for the children, although they may use different labels. Our goal at ITC is to respect each family's values while being true to ourselves and our program philosophy. When there is a conflict, we begin resolution by trying to explain how and why we do what we do and listening to the parents' response. We don't expect families to change what they do at home, but we do share what we do at the center. For example, at ITC older infants or younger toddlers are encouraged to feed themselves sooner than is practiced in some cultures. We give infants spoons when they show an interest in self-feeding. This explains to the parents why the infant may grab the spoon at home. We invite parents to visit and observe at mealtimes. They can see a continuum of eating skills as older children feed themselves successfully and younger children are assisted as needed. And through observation, they can see that we don't let babies choke or go hungry. What is most important is the respect the children's parents and caregivers have for one another, not that practices are absolutely consistent between home and center.

Making the Commitment to Caring Interactions

Caring for infants and toddlers in groups can be exciting, frustrating, exhilarating, demoralizing, demanding, fun, informative, instructive, _____ (fill in the blank from your own experience), and sometimes all of these at the same time! Doing it well day by day, hour by hour, minute by minute, can be exhausting. If doing it is also to be rewarding, caregivers need an attitude that gets them over the humps. It is this attitude, this mental orientation, that determines how caregivers meet the daily challenges and delights in caring for infants and toddlers.

Just as knowledge of child development changes caregivers' response to young children, attitude sets a tone for interactions with them. Attitude influences the ways caregivers fulfill the goals set out in their philosophy and how long they stay on the job. We at ITC have developed an attitude of *caring* and *commitment* that sustains our interest in doing this important job.

When asked why they chose child care as a profession, many caregivers say they "just love kids." Certainly, caregivers care for and about young children. How this feeling is played out in the everyday interactions in group care with infants and toddlers, however, makes a huge difference in the impact of those feelings on the experience of the children. *Caring* is characterized by responding to children in ways that communicate to them that they are participants in the rhythms of their lives, not just recipients of our attention. Caregivers can set the stage for this kind of caring interaction by remembering that infants and toddlers live in the moment. It is what is happening *now* that has meaning for them. Under this perspective, caring interactions result when caregivers

- pay attention to the children,
- see their attitude reflected by the children,

- recognize the effect they have on children, and
- learn about themselves from the children.

Caregivers Pay Attention to Children

Here are two possible ways the concept of "paying attention" could play out in a child care setting. The differences in the way the caregiver responds may seem minor, but the effect on the child is significant.

Johanna and Cora are the two caregivers in the yard. They are standing together and talking about a movie they had both seen recently. When twenty-six-month-old Emma approaches with a seed pod in her hand, Johanna looks at it, nods, says, "Oh, you found a seed pod," and continues her conversation.

Here is a different possibility:

The caregivers have purposely situated themselves to be observing in different directions—one sitting and one standing a few feet away. They are talking briefly. Emma approaches Johanna, who is sitting. "Just a minute, Emma, we're talking," Johanna says as she places a hand gently on Emma. Less than ten seconds later, Johanna turns her full attention to Emma, and says, "Oh, you found a seed pod. Where do you think it came from?" Emma says, "Kiral dropt!" "Oh, a squirrel probably did drop it. Where did you find it?" Johanna asks, standing up and holding out her hand. Johanna and Emma walk across the yard.

Put yourself in Emma's place. How is her experience in each of these two scenes significantly different? In the second scene, Johanna takes the time not only to acknowledge Emma's discovery, but also to extend it by asking Emma a question. She turns her attention fully from her conversation with the other caregiver to Emma, and this makes room for Emma's response and the beginning of a conversation between them. The message to Emma in the first scenario is that she is not important enough for Johanna to leave her conversation with the other caregiver; in the second scenario, it's exactly the opposite.

Caregivers See Their Attitude Reflected by the Children

Young children look to adults for clues about making their way in the world. Caregivers are demonstrating this to them all the time. Consider the following scene:

After lunch, toddlers are transitioning to story and nap time. Two-and-a-half-year-old Shayla has started to scream gleefully in the main room of the center. There are babies sleeping in a room nearby. Danny, who is eighteen months old, soon joins into the screeching. "Shush! Babies sleeping!" caregiver Larry says loudly. "We need to be quiet inside." Shayla moves away from Larry with downcast eyes. Danny yells again, and Larry turns, but before he says anything, Shayla says, "Shushhh," louder than when Larry said it!

Larry's forceful emphasis on stopping the noise was reflected by the toddlers, who escalated the loudness! Alternatively, Larry could have reacted in a way that would have modeled the behavior he was seeking:

*When the toddlers begin screaming, Larry whispers, "The babies are sleeping. We need to talk softly to let them sleep." Then he quietly draws the toddlers to the door of the adjoining room to show them the sleeping babies. Danny, being younger and having less understanding of the situation, continues to screech. Larry suggests, "**Show** me how strongly you feel—jump up and down or clap your hands!"*

Larry learned a powerful lesson; *how* a caregiver approaches toddlers is reflected in the outcome of the encounter. While caregivers may have to learn to read children's cues, young children are naturally programmed to read and reflect ours.

Caregivers Recognize the Effect They Have on Children

We have talked elsewhere in this chapter about the effect of a caregiver's interactions on the development of infants and toddlers. Most caregivers are of course not uncaring—they just may not understand how important their interactions with children are. This unawareness can also lead to feelings of dissatisfaction. How caregivers interact with children makes a difference in how they feel at the end of the day. Those feelings can often provide clues to how they can change their interactions with children and feel better about their jobs. Asking oneself some of the following questions may be helpful:

- What is the child doing now?
- What difference can I make in this moment?
- How does the child respond to me, the caregiver?
- What might she be learning from this encounter?
- What happened last time?
- What does she need to do to gain my attention?
- How does this experience help her define herself?

Caregivers Learn about Themselves from the Children

Caregivers bring their own child-rearing experience (and their own experience as children) to their current caregiving situations. To ignore these past experiences is to cut themselves off from personal insight and growth. To revisit the child within can be personally instructive and a fun part of caregiving.

Kate is spotting ten-month-old Ken, who is climbing up the slide ladder. She knows he has demonstrated reliable coordination. He is not yet walking, but he cruises and climbs with confidence. Ken loves the slide. He stands "crowing" at the top, and Kate answers, "Oh, you're up high!" from four feet away. A substitute caregiver, Freda, comes dashing across the yard and whisks Ken off the top of the slide. "Oh, you almost fell!" she says, breathing heavily. Ken is crying loudly, looking from the substitute to Kate, who is approaching quickly. "Oh, Ken, that was a shock, huh?" says Kate. She takes Ken into her arms, saying, "I know you love to climb on the slide." As Kate sets Ken by the slide, she says, "It's okay, you can climb back up if you want to."

Turning to the substitute caregiver, Kate says, "I know he looks little, but he's very coordinated and safe on the slide." Freda states matter-of-factly, "We would never let anybody like that climb on the slide." Kate asks, "Where else have you worked?" Freda answers, "I've cared for all my nieces and nephews, and I just decided I may as well get paid for babysitting." Kate says, "I can see you care about the kids. I saw Mayumi make a nice connection playing ball with you." Freda says, "You can't tell to look at me, but I played softball in high school!" Kate adds, "Then you know how much fun it is." She continues, "At this center, we follow the children's leads and let them do what they can on their own. We know Ken well enough to know that climbing on the slide is safe for him. You'll probably get a chance to work at other centers with different approaches."

Resisting tendencies to overprotect, manipulate, and otherwise control infants and toddlers is a challenge for many caregivers. Freda sees infants as needing protection. Her "button was pushed" by a different perspective. If Freda learned about herself and her automatic reactions, next time she could observe the children for signs of distress rather than assume they are unsafe. Freda can begin to see Ken as an individual—a capable climber who happens to be ten months old rather than a ten month old who should not be allowed to do what he is capable of doing on his own.

Caregivers can learn about themselves when they reflect back on frustrating caregiving experiences. The most frustrating experiences are often also the most instructive when viewed through a "rear view mirror." Noting what "pushes your buttons" can help caregivers recognize that priorities are demonstrated by what we *do* rather than what we *say*. What might one learn through the risk of trying it another way?

As we've said, caring interactions result when caregivers pay attention to the children, see their attitude reflected by the children, recognize the effect they have on children, and learn about themselves from the children. Can you identify these four characteristics of a caring interaction in the following scenarios?

Nine-month-old David has arrived with his mom, Heidi, on the second day of his enrollment in the center. He is very active in her arms, swiveling his upper body from side to side and back again. His head is also turning from side to side as well as moving up and down. There is a ceiling fan turning slowly, a banner hanging from the ceiling, and another infant crawling on the floor. "Do you want to play with Laura?" Heidi asks, holding David slightly away from her body. His legs clench her body and he hangs onto her neck. The caregiver, Lee, approaches them and says, "Hi, David. Hi, Heidi. How was your morning?" "He ate a ton for breakfast!" Heidi answers and remembers to write on David's chart when he last slept and ate. Lee is quietly watching David, and he starts to play a bit of peek-a-boo around his mother's shoulder. Heidi smiles wistfully: "I really need to go." Lee responds, "I know. Let's tell David." Heidi says to David, "Mama has to go to work now, but you can stay with Lee." Lee holds out her arms and takes David. He looks back and forth between the two women and screws up his face for a very loud cry. He's wriggling in her arms. Heidi looks paralyzed. On their first day Lee acknowledged how hard it is to leave and suggested that it is best to go after saying good-bye. "Bye-bye, Mom. Have a nice day. She'll be back later," Lee says and waves to Heidi, who gathers herself and bustles out.

David is screaming by now. Lee holds him close, saying, "You don't like to see Mom go, huh. She'll be *back later." David is struggling hard, so Lee sits down with him, near a pop-up box. David squirms off her lap and crawls to the door. "That's where Mom went. She'll be back later," says Lee. After three minutes of intense wailing, Lee notices that her teeth are clenched. She had to leave her own little boy this morning, and although he doesn't cry any more, she wonders if he's okay. David has pulled up on a table and is resting his head on it, still sobbing. Lee moves closer to stroke his back, and she feels herself relax as he does. "Where is that pop-up box you like so much? We played with it yesterday," she says to him. David tips back onto her lap with a sigh.*

Sometimes it is unavoidable that infants begin group care at the stage of development when stranger or separation anxiety is likely to occur. Such timing can be a challenge for all involved, but it can also be an opportunity for the infant to learn trust. By paying attention, Lee has seen the kind of interactions David likes, such as peek-a-boo. She respects his sad feelings and doesn't try to change or deny them. She recognizes her own feelings and can separate from them, adding to her feeling of expertise. Her confidence reassures David and his mother.

How is this next story different?

When Heidi has to leave, Lee jumps at David with the pop-up box. She says to David, "Bye, Mom. Okay, let's sit here and look at this box. You're okay. We're going to have fun. Really. It'll be okay." While she is speaking, David is screaming in her face and pushing away vigorously. She says coaxingly, "Don't you remember this box?" David is looking at her as if he'd never seen her before, and he struggles to get down. Frustrated with David's refusal to be distracted and unaware that her own anxiety about leaving her own son at child care that morning is being triggered by his crying, Lee sets David on the floor and turns her attention to Laura, who is looking anxious as she watches David cry. After five minutes, however, he is still crying, and Lee is attending to Laura. David is sitting on the floor, resisting any consolation or touch.

In this scene, Lee has been with many infants during their first days at the center, and they are always comfortable after a few weeks. She's confident it will be the same for David, even though he does react more intensely than some. While it seems natural to her that kids miss their moms, Lee doesn't fully grasp the developmental factors underlying his reaction. She distracts him in an attempt to speed up his process of adapting to the center. She doesn't recognize that she is reluctant to be drawn into his feelings, and so she misses learning about the joys of connection. She cares and talks to him and would never harm him, but neither does she fully engage him on a level he can connect with. David can only reflect her distant attitude, and it will affect his self-perception and may delay his adjustment to group care.

Developmental factors can present other challenges to a caring interaction. Somewhere between the ages of seventeen and twenty-two months, for instance, toddlers show a new and bold determination in their interactions with others. Up to this stage they have toddled through the environment in a pinball fashion, bouncing from one object or interaction to another. In the following scenario, nineteen-month-old Randy asserts himself physically with his peers. Note how the caregiver responds.

Randy marches across the yard with an intent look in his eye. He stops at a pickup truck in the sand and squats to roll it three feet to his left. Sitting nearby is fourteen-month-old Alice patting sand in a bucket. Randy abruptly leaves the truck, walks to Alice, and gives her a shove so that Alice topples over into the sand with a loud cry. Randy stands over her and watches her face. Jenny, who has been observing, approaches immediately. "Randy, see Alice's face? She is upset. That hurt her to push her over. Did you want to say hi?" She pauses briefly, giving Randy room to respond, then says, "I can't let you hurt her." She pauses briefly again, for emphasis this time, and then adds, "Let's offer her help." Jenny is simultaneously comforting Alice with gentle touches and an offering of open arms to help herself up. "Randy," she continues, patting him gently, "please touch gently. You could wave and say hi. It's not okay to push people—there are the cart and the truck that you can push." Randy runs off to push the cart as Jenny sits down next to Alice. "Next time," Jenny says to Alice, "say no or move your body away. That hurt, didn't it?"

Jenny, the caregiver, was initially paying attention to Randy's movements across the yard. After Randy pushed Alice over, Jenny's first response is to help Randy notice Alice's facial expression and the effect he had on her. Jenny is communicating her caring attitude to Randy and helping him learn to care about the consequences of his actions. Jenny also offers a choice of objects to push so that he has an appro-priate outlet for his energy. Since Alice is also involved in the interaction, Jenny offers some words and actions for her to help herself the next time it might happen. It's just as important to give the victims tools that prevent them from being easy targets or adopting a victim mentality as it is to relate to the aggressor.

Consider a less caring response by Jenny:

Hearing Alice's cry, Jenny turns from talking to another caregiver and approaches. "What happened here, Randy? Did you hurt Alice?" She grabs Randy's arm and says severely, "Pushing is not okay!" As Jenny gets in Randy's face, he begins to cry too. She lets go and stands up with an exasperated sigh. Both Randy and Alice are crying with their eyes shut tight.

Jenny's lack of attention prior to what happened to Alice caused her to approach in an angry and exasperated manner. Hopefully, Jenny could learn from this scene that it's okay to admit to the toddlers, "I did not see what happened, but I can see that Alice is upset. Randy, what happened?" When caregivers are honest, most toddlers will be also. Jenny's exasperated attitude was reflected back to her by both children crying. She failed to take responsibility and model a problem-solving approach.

The time that caregivers take to have caring interactions builds strong connections between caregiver and child. These connections captivate caregivers and form their understanding of the children in their care. As Nancy Weber points out, patience runs out while understanding does not. The resulting joy that caregivers feel transforms their work on a day-to-day basis.

2

Being with Babies: Strategies for Caring for Infants and Toddlers

Having talked about *why* we suggest approaching infants and toddlers in a certain way and defined what we mean by a "caring interaction," we move in this chapter to *how* caregivers can apply the Ten Principles of respectful care to their everyday lives with babies. The seven comprehensive strategies we discuss can be used in every situation caregivers encounter with infants and toddlers. The strategies are the first step in creating a caring interaction, and they further a caregiver's relationship with individual children during routines and play experiences. The strategies also form the basis for the planned experiences in the next chapters. They set the stage for learning by honoring children's curiosity, building emotional connections, and supporting the developing physical coordination of infants and toddlers.

These are the comprehensive strategies we use every day with infants and toddlers:

1. Observe individual children and provide "optimal stress."

2. Model the behavior you wish to see.
3. Acknowledge feelings.
4. Anticipate transitions, unusual events, and changes in routine.
5. Help children articulate their needs and wants.
6. Offer real choices.
7. Set consistent limits.

1. Observation and Optimal Stress

Observation is a powerful tool for caregivers to learn about individual children. Observing is a way for caregivers to see the world through a child's eyes. In a way, it is an initial silent interaction with a child: watching the child for cues to what he is looking at, feeling, or doing. It is an active watching of individual children, rather than a passive scanning or a visual tracking of them in a supervisory way. Without individual observation, infants and toddlers in a group care setting become just that—a *group* of kids to scan and supervise and keep safe. With observation, the group is transformed into a collection of individuals whom caregivers know thoroughly and can easily tell apart.

Individualizing the group helps caregivers to understand the developmental levels of the children in their care. Think of children in your care right now. Who uses a spoon? likes bugs? rolls over? goes up stairs? loves to fingerpaint? gets needs met with little crying? enters play with peers nonaggressively? bites other children? has difficulty at the end of the day? You know the answers to these questions because you have observed the children, and these observations give you information about children's developmental levels.

Knowing a child's stage of development allows caregivers to offer opportunities to practice and take the next step. This is also called *providing optimal stress.* As described by Janet Gonzalez-Mena, optimal stress is like the stress of drought that signals a flower to use energy to bloom. It is just enough of a challenge to be interesting to the child, but not so overwhelming as to be defeating or overly frustrating. For example, introducing a cushion or pillow to a newly crawling infant introduces additional challenges of strength, control, and balance.

As a strategy, observation also helps caregivers promote the three Cs (curiosity, connection, and coordination) in the children with whom they work. Caregivers can observe to find out when a child is *curious* and how the child explores the environment. When they pay attention to a child in a structured, routine way, caregivers acquire the information needed to support the child's experience, follow the child's interest, offer appropriate information, and promote the child's self-awareness (all of which feed curiosity).

Caregivers can use observation to promote *connection* by paying attention to a child's interactions with others, such as children, family members, caregivers, and new people in the environment. The child's preferences in building relationships becomes clear when caregivers observe to answer questions like these: Does the infant engage others with active body movements or with eye contact and facial expressions? How does the child exhibit attachment or connection with family members? How does the toddler interact socially with peers, by physically shoving and pushing or by greeting verbally? How does a child connect with caregivers? Through observation, caregivers can learn and respect a child's expressions of social-emotional needs and strengthen connections with other people.

Observation also helps caregivers support children's physical *coordination.* Caregivers learn how an infant moves by watching him swipe at a mobile with his arm or leg. They can assess a toddler's coordination by focusing on how he wields a paintbrush or attempts a puzzle. Paying attention to this can help caregivers provide the right equipment for practicing physical skills.

When a caregiver observes a child, the goal is to learn specific information. Here are some of the questions we might ask about seventeen-month-old Carl:

- What attracts Carl's attention?
- How does he respond to loud sounds?
- Is he excited or cautious around other children with high energy?
- Does Carl move slowly and purposely or quickly and impulsively?
- How long does Carl focus on something?
- What distracts him?
- How does he respond to another child's touch?
- What makes Carl smile, laugh, or cry?
- When he falls down, does Carl cry out for help or pick himself up?

By actively watching a child move through the environment, a caregiver can learn answers to questions like these, which give helpful clues to how Carl approaches life. When a caregiver has the time, *writing* observations can further focus attention on valuable information about a specific child. There are several kinds of written observations, such as running records, anecdotal records, and charting.

Running Records

A running record is a written description of what a child is doing for a specific time period. Ten to fifteen minutes is long enough, and it's usually possible to find this amount of time in a group setting. To create a running record, a caregiver follows a child around, writing down each movement. For example,

Carl runs through the open door to the play yard. He runs twenty yards straight ahead to the spring horses. He stops at the nearest horse, right hand on the saddle, left hand on the handle. He hears a pushcart approach from his back. He turns to look before climbing onto the horse. With both hands holding tight, Carl rocks back and forth with exuberance. His body moves solidly as one unit, and he looks down to watch his legs and torso. Carl moves his head back and forth and tilts it backward as he smiles and shuts his eyes. Maria approaches the other spring horse,

saying "Horsy." Carl opens his eyes to look at Maria as he slows down his rocking. His smile disappears as she climbs on the other horse. He climbs off his horse and backs away from Maria, who has climbed onto a horse. He puts his head down and runs away. He comes across a pushcart and begins running and pushing the cart with both hands. Rounding a curve in the path, Carl loses his balance and falls to the ground, rolling over once. He looks around, dazed, with eyes wide open. He looks at Nita, the caregiver, and starts to cry, holding both arms up. Nita walks over and says, "I see you fell down, Carl. Do you need help getting up?" She kneels down next to him with her hands extended. Carl touches Nita's fingers, pulls himself to a stand, and retrieves the pushcart for more running and pushing.

From just a few minutes of observation, the caregiver can learn the following about Carl:

- He actively runs from experience to experience.
- He can be distracted by sounds (the first pushcart).
- He enjoys the feeling of his body rocking on the horse.
- He was not comfortable with Maria joining him on the other horse and moved away to something else.
- He was okay when he fell down but cried out when he made eye contact with the caregiver.
- Carl picked himself up and continued his active play when Nita acknowledged his situation and offered help.

Co-workers must be supportive and vigilant with the larger group of children when one caregiver is keeping a running record of a child. When running records can be done every month, all caregivers can gain insightful, specific information and see developmental changes. Next month, Carl might enjoy another toddler's presence nearby. He might make it

running around the curve. Or he might pick himself up without crying for help.

Anecdotal Records

This type of observation provides information about a child based on a very specific interaction or experience. When caregivers take time to notice and record special interactions or events in a child's day, they can appreciate the child's joys and accomplishments. For example, when two toddlers join together to play with a bulldozer and a dump truck in the sand, a caregiver may see evidence of the developmental milestone of interactive play, such as one child filling the scooper with sand and the other child maneuvering the dump truck to accept the load of sand.

Anecdotal records become precious records of a child's development that caregivers can share. For example, the record may be put in a parent mailbox or shared at parent-staff conferences. Parents love to read them and keep them for lifelong memories. And they appreciate knowing what their child does during the day and that a caregiver is paying attention. Keeping a copy of such moments gives the center a record of children's development, as well. It can be placed in a file to track a particular child's development or behavior or shared at staff meeting so other care-givers can learn about specific children.

Here is a sample of an anecdotal record:

Name: Lisa   Date: 2/4/98

After lunch today, one of the toddlers who is new to the center became upset. Lisa, another toddler at the center, had been playing with him earlier, and she responded right away. She brought him a book, holding it out to him as he lay crying. She leaned close to pat his arm and after a minute said, "You play? You play?" A caregiver knelt close, telling her how friendly it was of her to be concerned. The caregiver reassured Lisa that he would probably feel better after a nap, and then they could play.

Charting

Charting is a means of keeping a written pattern of routine caregiving experiences, such as when, what, and how much a child eats, what times diapers are changed, and when and how long a child naps. Charts are almost always used on a regular basis in infant/toddler programs to keep track of these everyday happenings, but they can also be used to track specific issues such as food allergies or toilet learning.

The following page shows an example of a typical infant room chart, which records diaperings, feedings, and naps.

	Monday	Tuesday
Diaper Changes	10:30 dry 3:10 wet 4:15 ✓ 4:50 wet	12:30 dry 12:45 ✓ 2:10 wet 4:15 wet

Nourishment	7 a.m. nursed
	9, 11, 12, 12:30 offered
	12:45 nursed
	1:40 1 oz. rice w/ formula
	    1 oz sweet potatoes
	    1 oz formula in cup
	3:20 2 oz formula
	4:45 1 oz formula
		9:30 oatmeal
		11:30 nursed
		1:00 1 oz rice, formula
		    1 oz sweet potatoes
		    1 oz formula in cup
		2:00 sips of formula = 1 oz
		2:40 1.5 oz formula
		3:50 2 oz formula

Nap Times	10–10:30 (woke at doc's) 12:45–1:20 2:00–3:00	

2. Modeling Behavior

Modeling is one of the Ten Principles, but we think it is so important that it is a strategy in itself. How caregivers behave with children and how children see caregivers behave with others communicate the caregivers' attitude, values, and priorities. Caregivers can be themselves and be honest with children, or they can manipulate children into doing their bidding. Either way, caregivers will see themselves reflected in the children's actions.

Caregivers have numerous opportunities to model behavior for children. In fact, everything a caregiver does within a child's range of vision or hearing is modeling! For example, since caregivers require that children wash their hands before eating and after diaper changes and toileting, caregivers can model for the children by being among the first to wash. Another way for caregivers to model is to take the time to be gentle as they touch and connect with each child throughout the day. Young children can experience "gentle" when they see a caregiver model it. For instance, "Jeremy, Elon didn't like to have his hair pulled—try touching him gently, like this," the caregiver might say as he strokes Jeremy's face or part of his body. A further way for caregivers to model is to "self talk," or talk out loud about their inner thinking process. This connects the child to the moment's experience and models appropriate responses.

Caregivers can model curiosity in a way that teaches respect for a child's own curiosity, even when the caregiver doesn't share the child's interest. Consider the following scene:

Ann, the caregiver, sees a toddler approaching with a snail on a board and says, "Oh, Beth, you found a snail crawling on the board. See the trail behind it? That's the snail's slime trail. If you pick it up you can feel the slime. I did once and didn't like it, but you can feel it if you are gentle with the snail. Just try to put it back in the same place because the snail can tell where it is from its trail."

Even though Ann has an aversion to snails, she can model respect for both Beth's lack of aversion and the snail's existence. If she hadn't been thinking about modeling, she might have responded automatically from her own aversion, said, "Yuck, a snail," and smashed it in front of Beth. Because she was aware of the effect of this kind of behavior, Ann was able to model respectful behavior toward living things while still being honest about her own feelings.

Problem solving is another area in which caregivers can model desired behavior. If children are to respond to problems or frustrations calmly, caregivers must talk out loud about an issue's possible solutions as much as possible. Consider the following two scenes:

Eleven months old and cruising, Anita pushes a toy shopping cart along a sidewalk in a straight line. Her cart stops up against a tire and won't go anymore, even though she keeps pushing. Nearby caregiver Janice says out loud, "Oh, your cart is stuck, Anita. Can you see it against the tire?" as she points to where the tire and cart meet. "Let's turn your cart together so you can go around the tire." With Anita's hands still on the push bar, Janice places her hands on top of Anita's and gently pulls the cart away from and then around the tire. Janice repeats this modeling several more times when Anita continues to get stuck.

Instead of freeing the cart *for* Anita, Janice's hands on Anita's allow Anita to *feel* the movement necessary to do it herself. Anita can both continue pushing the cart and learn an approach to problem solving.

A different problem-solving situation in the everyday life of a center occurs when specifically needed caregiving supplies run out. Consider the following scene and how the caregiver responds to a problem in the presence of a child:

Two-and-a-half-year-old Caleb has finished toileting and has washed his hands at the sink. He reaches for a paper towel at the same time as Brad, the caregiver, who has finished washing his hands at the big sink. The paper towel dispenser is empty! Brad says, "Oh

darn, the towels are all gone. I'll have to get some more." As Brad turns to the cupboard, Caleb says, "What doin'?" Brad explains, "I'm getting some towels for the dispenser." Caleb watches intently as Brad opens the box on the wall and loads the feeder slot. They each finish drying off their hands.

Brad responded calmly to this problem and modeled a relaxed manner in handling the situation. Since the job of keeping such caregiving supplies stocked is someone else's job this week, Brad could have shown more frustration, but didn't. He took a few minutes to carry through and fill the dispenser, much to Caleb's fascination. Young children can learn much from a caregiver's response to frustrations that spontaneously pop up in the course of a normal day.

Modeling makes a caregiver aware of the questions "What is this child going to learn in this moment based on my response?" and "What will he take away from this interaction to use another time?" With these questions in mind, simply modeling desired behavior becomes the most effective way to teach it.

3. Acknowledging Feelings

All feelings are okay. They are simply an emotional response to what is happening to a person at any given moment. It's the *expression* of feelings that troubles many people, and certainly feelings may be expressed inappropriately, by either children or adults. However, some adults become uncomfortable when children express their feelings at all. Not understanding the difference between the feelings themselves and the way a child is expressing them may lead people to label children by the way they behave. For example, they might say to a child, "It's selfish of you not to share!" Certainly these adults mean well, but their approach fails to help the child identify or learn appropriate ways to express feelings.

To express feelings appropriately means to let others know one's feelings without hurting oneself or others. Caregivers can help children learn to identify their feelings by acknowledging the feelings of even the youngest infants in their care. For example, there are physical feelings of comfort or discomfort that can be acknowledged when caregivers feed infants, help them relax to sleep, change their diapers, or help them stay warm or cool off. Recognizing how natural it is to feel hungry, tired, cold, hot, or uncomfortable, caregivers can meet the child's needs while acknowledging the feelings that go with them. Many caregivers do this naturally by saying things like "Oh, your diaper is wet. I bet you're uncomfortable. There, that dry diaper feels better, doesn't it?" Children learn to recognize their own feelings when caregivers label their feelings for them in this way.

It often seems easier to acknowledge physical feelings and needs. However, strong emotions such as sadness, disappointment, and anger are just as natural as hunger, thirst, or cold. The challenge for caregivers is to acknowledge the feeling and help children figure out how to express it appropriately. Just as it is appropriate to offer food when a child is hungry, it's also appropriate to help him channel anger or frustration to safe but expressive words or actions (like punching a pillow, running, or pushing a cart), rather than physical violence against another person. The important first step is to acknowledge the feeling. It is very real for the child, so it's important to acknowledge and identify it.

Consider the following infant/toddler scenarios:

Jeff has just fastened the last buckle of the car seat around Allison, his five-month-old daughter, as they prepare to leave the center to go home. Allison's face wrinkles up, and she begins to whimper. Jeff says, "I know you don't like to be in the car seat, but it'll just be for a short while until we get home." Allison clutches a favorite toy as Jeff carries her out of the center.

Jeff's response is more reassuring and respectful to Allison than "You're fine. Don't cry." Jeff has learned and applied the approach of acknowledging Allison's feelings when she expresses them. The simple validation of Allison's dislike of being in the car seat sends a reassuring message that, over time, Allison will interpret as "I may be upset, but it's okay and it won't last a long time."

As toddlers develop their emotional self-concept and connection with peers, they express their feelings clearly and without question. Consider a toddler's frustration:

As sixteen-month-old Riley tries repeatedly to fit a shovel inside a jar, he wails loudly, head thrown back, banging the shovel on the jar. Caregiver Peter says, "It's frustrating when it doesn't work the way you want, Riley. I'll help if you want." As Peter sits down next to Riley, he stops crying and tries again. This time the shovel slides into the jar, Riley beams, and Peter acknowledges, "You figured it out! Doesn't that feel good?" Riley says, "I did it!"

Peter names Riley's frustrating feeling for him and offers help and support by sitting next to him. That's enough to enable Riley to persevere and succeed after repeated efforts at putting the shovel into the jar.

What if Riley still hadn't been able to get the shovel into the jar? Peter could still acknowledge Riley's frustration and model problem solving. He could acknowledge Riley's feelings by saying something like "Wow, that really is frustrating, isn't it?" Saying "Take your time" and holding Riley's hand with the shovel, he could guide just enough to enable Riley to move past his frustration.

Here's another familiar scenario in which two toddlers exhibit strong feelings when they collide: When two toddlers simultaneously reach for the same toy and both scream, "Mine!" the caregiver says, "I can tell you both want to play with that. Who's going to go get the one over there?" as she gently holds the object between them. One of the toddlers scurries to the other identical toy. The caregiver has offered a way to solve the problem while respecting the feelings of both children. Simply validating the feelings of two toddlers wanting to play with the same toy is often enough to help them calm down and solve the problem. Sure, there was a conflict, but the *first* thing to occur was the toddlers' desire to play with the same toy. By building on that mutual feeling and offering another approach for the toddlers, the caregiver can help the toddlers bypass the potential conflict. The toddlers can then build on their connection by playing with identical toys!

Acknowledging children's feelings can support their development on all levels. As infants and toddlers explore, discover cause and effect, and assimilate knowledge, their curiosity brings feelings with it. The caregiver can acknowledge these feelings, using phrases like "You've been working very hard," "It's hard to stop," and "You're really enjoying that."

Go beyond simple descriptions (such as mad, sad, or glad) when describing children's feelings. Toddlers are able to understand new descriptions, such as disappointed, frustrated, gleeful, excited, content, thoughtful, and satisfied.

One way caregivers can label and acknowledge children's feelings is to observe children's movements and facial expressions. As children try on different responses to their feelings, their expertise in what is appropriate grows. They learn that once they have identified what they are feeling as frustration, for example, asking for help works to achieve their goal. If they misidentify it as anger, it might lead to hitting, which is less likely to achieve the goal.

Here is a sample list of phrases to name and acknowledge feelings:

- "I can see by the smile on your face how much you love the bear."
- "It was thoughtful of you to bring her that blanket."
- "I can tell you are very angry that she won't leave you alone."
- "I know you hoped Auntie Mina would pick you up. You are disappointed she couldn't come today."
- "We're delighted to be outdoors after all that rain."

It also makes sense for caregivers to acknowledge their own feelings in the presence of children, which is the sixth principle. Kids are keen observers, and they know when caregivers feel strongly about something. It's confusing to children when their observations contradict what caregivers say about themselves. Perhaps you've had a toddler ask you if you are sad, simply because you are relatively quiet that day. Of course, these expressions are not limited to negative feelings. What if you received a phone call at work notifying you that your program had won a grant to improve the premises? The children would be able to see your excitement. With a little explanation, they could understand why you are excited and add the experience to their growing understanding of feelings and how they are expressed.

Caregivers who are uncomfortable around children's feelings may also have difficulty identifying their own feelings and separating them from those of the children. It's confusing for children to be assigned emotions they are not feeling. The children know when an adult projects feelings onto children or makes assumptions about what the children are feeling. A caregiver who knows that it's too rainy for children to go outside and is afraid of the children's disappointment might say something like "You don't really want to go outside, do you?" This negates the children's feelings. A more honest response that acknowledges the children's feelings would be something like "I can tell you really want to go outside. It's too rainy right now, but maybe we can go outdoors tomorrow." In another example, a caregiver who knows that a child's blanket was accidentally left at home that morning and who is afraid of the child's distress might say, "You didn't care about that old blanket, did you?" in an attempt to distract the child, whereas "You want your blanket right now, don't you?" acknowledges that the child cares about the blanket. Acknowledging children's real feelings often helps them move on more quickly and completely than denying that the feelings exist.

Finally, toddlers' happy feelings are often expressed physically. If this active energy is squelched, the feelings of exuberance are denied as well. Children can't separate the two. Sometimes, however, exuberant toddlers get in one another's way. Caregivers can offer appropriate alternatives so all feelings can be expressed by saying something like "There's lots of room at the end of the grass to twirl, Jing. Luke can twirl at this end."

4. Anticipating Transitions, Unusual Events, and Changes in Routine

Caregivers can help children transition from one place, experience, or idea to another by letting them know what's going to happen next. This is called *anticipation*. Imagine when random unplanned things happen to you and how you respond or react. Think too of how comforting it is when you know ahead of time about an impending change and can mentally prepare for it. Young children deserve the same opportunity to be prepared for what is going to happen to them. Think of them as little scientists doing work that is as important as Einstein's. If Einstein was working in his study, you wouldn't rush in and say, "Time for lunch!" Maybe he just had the unified field theory composed, and you knocked it right out of his head! Children's experiences, investigations, explorations, and discoveries about their world deserve the same respect. Even the youngest infants deserve this respect. Infants live in the present because they are so tuned in to the sensory information they are receiving at that moment—resting on a hard or soft surface, feeling a wet or dry diaper, seeing pictures, hearing sounds, or chewing on a teether. To help a child begin to anticipate an upcoming caregiving experience, the caregiver can make eye contact and then say something like "I'm going to check your diaper after Eleni falls asleep." In this way the caregiver can help a baby begin to recognize when a change is coming.

Toddlers live so much in the moment that they have difficulty keeping track of long periods of time. A regular schedule provides security to children, and when caregivers help them anticipate upcoming changes, the children become aware of and involved in what is happening in their daily lives. Children also need time to absorb the new information and make the connections between where they are, where they are going, and what is going to happen. In order for children to be able to relax and continue exploring, they need to know what will happen next.

Furthermore, as children's autonomy develops, they are more tuned in to their own thoughts and ideas. They are still pretty egocentric and so schedules that do not match their own senses may not seem relevant to them. Why come to lunch if they don't feel hungry? So helping children anticipate upcoming events also helps to bridge the gap between their individual rhythms and the routine necessary in caring for children in a group.

Of course, the manner in which caregivers help children anticipate is crucial. Rather than "warn" children, with the expectation of difficulty that a warning implies, caregivers can casually announce a transition a few minutes before it happens. Here, the attitude is one of simply sharing information, and the attitude speaks louder than the words. One example of the need to anticipate a transition is when moving between experiences. Try using words like these:

> Begin by acknowledging feelings: "I can tell you're enjoying those blocks." Then tell the children what's coming next: "In five minutes it will be time…
> > to get your coat on to go home;
> > to take off your clothes for a nap;
> > to put away the playdough;
> > to get ready for story time;
> > for lunch."

For example, a caregiver might say, "Cecilia, I see you've been digging that hole. You're working hard. I wanted to let you know that in five minutes it'll be time for lunch." In the same way, let children know when the usual routine will be different, using phrases like the following:

- "Remember, Mommy said Aunt Martha will pick you up today."
- "Today we will have a special snack outside."
- "You get to come back after seeing the doctor."

Anticipation allows a caregiver to promote a child's exploration, trust, and connection with people, and it allows children to integrate their skills in their own time, at their own speed.

5. Helping Children Articulate Their Needs and Wants

As young children become involved with and cooperate in transitions, they can benefit from a caregiver suggesting words they can use to express their needs and wants. These "scripts" begin very simply and grow in length and complexity as the child's language skills grow. Building on the language babies understand even when they are not yet talking, caregivers can help children expand their vocabularies to make themselves more clear. For example, many caregivers naturally respond to an infant who gestures towards a bowl of cereal by saying, "More? Are you ready for *more?*" This is an example of a simple beginning script, which gives the child words she doesn't have yet to express her wants.

Through this process the children learn to connect language to their actions, needs, or wants. The infant who has heard the word *more* when he gestures for food will begin to say "mmmm" and eventually use the word himself. A caregiver who serves lunch to toddlers around a table can script requests by rephrasing the children's words while serving. As toddlers say, "More," she serves them, saying "More rice please" or "More milk please." Toddlers learn to be more specific about their needs from the scripts the caregiver gives them.

As toddlers connect with each other and objects, they will also express frustration as a need for help. Consider the following scene:

Twenty-five-month-old Andy, two-year-old Juan, and thirty-month-old Erik run toward the two unoccupied swings. Andy and Juan plop into the seats. Erik sits in the sand next to one of the swings and cries loudly. Having observed this race for the swings, Margo empathizes, "Oh, Erik, you really want to swing too." She pauses and speaks between his cries. "Let Andy and Juan know you would like a turn next," she says. Erik says, "My turn next." Margo also suggests to Andy and Juan that they say "Your turn next" to Erik.

Note how Margo helps Erik put his desire to swing into words. These toddlers can practice the scripts the next time a missed connection or frustration occurs. Eventually they will become proficient in expressing their own needs and wants.

Another common script young children can learn to articulate is "need help." Younger toddlers with few words can learn this easy phrase—or even the shorter version, "hep"—in order to get others to help tie a shoe, wrap up a doll, carry a heavy object, or make objects fit together. Here are some scripts to use every day:

- Mo'; More; More cracker; More cracker please.
- No, me; Me do; Do it myself.
- Eh, eh; Hep; Help; Need help please.
- Mine!; My turn; My turn next please; Your turn next.
- No do that!; I don't like that; Don't do that to me.
- Touch gently; Please be gentle.
- Der [gesture at cabinet]; Pupple; I want to do puzzles.

To the reader, the scripts may sound artificial and stilted on first hearing. After using them and seeing how they work, they can be rephrased in your own style to feel more natural. One advantage of caregivers using scripts like these is that they help children discover what *to* do, rather than what *not* to do. This experience adds to the child's repertoire of "okay" actions and expressions of preference. For example, "Use your words" is an often-heard phrase around child care centers. It's a kind of shorthand many caregivers have fallen into using. In order to grasp the full meaning of this phrase, children need caregivers to help them with the next step. They need caregivers to help them figure out what the "words" are and how to "use" them. Scripting is a natural way to do this, and children need lots of practice. They need to hear the scripts and then use them over and over. As children discover that words help them get what they want or need more effectively, they use them more and more.

6. Offering Real Choices

The value of providing choice to infants and toddlers lies in its lifelong implications. It is not only the practice of making choices that caregivers want them to experience but the understanding that there are *always* choices in life. People can decide to do or not to do something, to find an alternative, to do it with grace, or to go kicking and screaming. When caregivers forget or don't know how to give children choices, they give up the opportunity of joining forces with the children to get caregiving tasks done. They are also ignoring the fundamental human quality of seeing possibility, a quality that nurtures the human creative ability. When caregivers ignore choice, they limit children's investigations of the environment, their self-concepts, and their opportunities to practice skills. People often don't have a say in what decisions confront them every day, but they always have choices. Caregivers can help children begin to be aware of that reality.

Choices really are expressions of individual preferences that are revealed and can be respected as early as infancy. For example, caregivers may experience a baby turning away from or pushing away the bottle during feeding. The infant is deciding that he is satisfied and communicating this choice to the caregiver. The caregiver can confirm the infant's knowing when he is full by recognizing the communication and ending the feeding. In the same way, when grabbing for the caregiver's spoon during feeding, the infant is communicating a preference about feeding himself. When the caregiver gives him his own spoon to practice self-feeding, the caregiver is responding to his communication and respecting his choices.

As caregivers continue to observe a child's responses, they come to see infants and toddlers making choices or decisions all the time in their play explorations and caregiving experiences. In the beginning, these choices involve response to specific senses. For example, Sonja often chooses red toys, Albert is fascinated by the hinge action of books, and Lanie loves the rustle of paper. Recognizing these preferences reminds us of the Ten Principles of respectful care, and in particular principle five: *Respect infants and toddlers as worthy people. Don't treat them as objects or cute little empty-headed dolls to be manipulated.* It's good to be reminded that even the youngest people have preferences and can make choices.

Providing Choices in the Environment

One example of choice in the environment involves toys. Providing multiples of the same toy allows children to choose a preferred object. It also entices two children to play side by side or together with identical toys. Toys available in the infant room at any given time might include two toy telephones, three cloth books, five balls, half a dozen rubber animals, four lightweight scarves, and two shape-sorters. This kind of variety affords each infant the opportunity to express his interest in the objects and investigate those that he finds especially appealing.

In addition to providing several identical toys, caregivers can provide a variety of toys suited to a range of developmental tasks. Children are then free to choose what they want to play with based on their developmental interest. This also helps develop autonomy. In both indoor and outdoor environments, toddlers should be able to choose from a variety of activities (pulling, pushing, sitting, climbing, filling, dumping, wandering, running, carrying, cooking, digging, dressing up, riding, grasping, pouring, squeezing, lifting, jumping). Children's experience is expanded by the number of different alternatives caregivers provide.

Making Decisions

Decision making is a part of life, and young children learn to make decisions by experiencing choices. In addition, it is best if they experience true choices. For example, "Do you want to take a nap?" is not a real choice if it really is time to take a nap. Adults may be used to this type of phrasing statements as polite questions. This works between adults because adults can differentiate between real choices and politely phrased requirements. Toddlers cannot. Let toddlers know what *has* to happen by using a direct statement, and then offer a choice. For example, say, "It's cold outside today; you need to wear something to keep you warm," and then offer a choice of what to wear: "Do you want to put on this sweatshirt or that jacket?" Two things to choose from at a time is as many as a toddler can handle.

The strategy of offering real choices to children curtails possible sources of conflict between them and the adults caring for them. By offering choices, caregivers are both being honest about what *has* to happen and allowing children to have some control over *how* it happens. Providing opportunities for choice honors children's drive for autonomy and involves them in their life processes. For example, caregivers know when a child's diaper needs to be checked based on the time elapsed since the previous change. Often, when presented with such a routine, the toddler will run away. Recognizing children's enjoyment in their separateness, caregivers can offer a choice ("Maria, would you like to have Elane or Juanita change your diaper?"). Because Maria is being given some control and her autonomy is being acknowledged, she is involved in the routine and often returns to make the choice. When caregivers present real choices confidently and clearly, young children learn that they participate in their own lives. As toddlers are given the opportunity to make choices in their life processes, caregivers and adults gain their cooperation and involvement in caregiving tasks.

7. Setting Consistent Limits

Giving choices is also helpful when caregivers need to set limits by redirecting or guiding a child's behavior. When caregivers don't present alternatives (for example, when they say simply, "No, don't do that"), it's as if the child hit a wall—there is no way for him to know what *to do* next or what is *okay*. The child fills with anxiety and may act out or become defiant. Consistent limits reduce the need to test rules. The choices we give toddlers can provide the framework of freedom within which young children may explore securely.

For Every No, Give Two Yeses
One way of thinking about choices in connection with limit setting is to act upon the phrase "for every no, give two yeses." This useful approach was introduced to us by Janet Gonzalez-Mena at a workshop twenty years ago. It is meant to be used at specific times when a child's behavior needs to be redirected from what is *not* okay, safe, or appropriate behavior to

a choice of what *is*. Caregivers can be very creative in offering the "yeses"; numerous opportunities occur in a group care setting. Here are some examples:

- "I can't let you throw the sand; you can throw the tennis ball or the red rubber ball."
- "Tables are not for climbing; you can climb on the stairs or up onto the couch."
- "It's not safe to throw the hard blocks; you can throw the soft pillow or balled-up socks."
- "Please don't rip the book. You can tear the paper off these crayons or pull the stickers off the paper."

After reflection, caregivers present choices confidently and give the child sufficient time to make them. If the child is unable to choose after thirty seconds or so, the caregiver chooses for him and sticks to the decision. In this way toddlers learn that words have consistent meanings and that their actions have consequences. This single technique

- acknowledges the child's developmental need to do certain actions,
- focuses on the behavior, rather than labeling the child,
- gives appropriate alternatives to inappropriate actions,
- involves the child in learning appropriate behavior, and
- initiates a problem-solving approach.

It's a particularly useful strategy for caregivers because it allows them the opportunity to say *yes*, rather than a blanket *no*, to the child's actions. Meanwhile, the child learns not only about the inappropriate or unsafe nature of his action, but also about what *is* okay, safe, or appropriate to do. Caregivers have to remember that an infant or toddler's experience is very limited—he doesn't have all the possibilities accessible in his brain yet. Indeed, the connections are being made during interactions such as these. By using this strategy caregivers are helping infants and toddlers broaden the possibilities and learn how to control their impulses.

The House with Invisible Walls

A metaphor that has helped us at ITC to understand the need for consistency in limit setting with infants and toddlers is that of the house with invisible walls, which we first heard in a workshop fifteen years ago. Pretend you live in a house with invisible walls. These are like the limits we set for children. Surely limits must seem invisible and arbitrary to the children. By testing the walls, you would be able to figure out that the kitchen was inside the front door and two steps to the left and that the bedroom was eight steps down the hall. Then if you weren't very hungry or tired, you could move around the house without bumping into the walls. But what if someone came in while you were sleeping and moved the walls? Perhaps you would get out of bed in the morning and bang into the kitchen door. Or maybe you wouldn't be able to find it. What would you do? Probably, you'd start over, bouncing off the walls to figure out where they were. Some people would give up testing after a time and withdraw. In any event, whatever you had intended to do for the day would be postponed or impossible.

When caregivers set limits consistently, children begin to learn where those walls are. They learn to control their own actions before they run into the limits set for them. Setting consistent limits helps infants and toddlers to learn this inner control. And ultimately, setting consistent limits makes the caregiver's job easier.

One good way to establish limits is through humor. Humor allows a child to say no, explore possibilities, and probably end up at the same place. Consider the possibilities presented in the following scene:

Two-year-old Mickey puts a car on the snack table and pushes it along. The caregiver, Hoa, says, "Please run the car on the floor; Caitlin is eating." Mickey says, "On the table!" At this point the caregiver has a choice. She can insist that the car be placed on the floor, or, knowing Mickey, she can engage him in solving the problem. "On the window!" she says. Without missing a beat, Mickey counters, "On the wall!" "On the ceiling!" she says. "On the door!" he says. "On the rug!" she says. "On the floor!" Mickey says, laughing. He puts the car down on the floor.

Note that Hoa had a split second in which to choose to be an authoritarian over or a partner in Mickey's development. Presenting the choices available to him in the way she did allowed him to participate in solving the problem of deciding where it was appropriate to play with the car.

Toddlers are learning how to learn. They are discovering whether knowledge comes from their direct experiences or from adult control. They base this discovery on the experiences we provide for them. We have found it not only good for children but more satisfying for caregivers to allow children to construct their own experience and learn from it. Just think: Would you rather engage Mickey in a power struggle about where to play with the car, or have a lighthearted exchange with him that brings him where you want him to be? Which would make your day better?

The following chart summarizes the strategies we have discussed so far. These strategies are so inclusive that we have depicted them like the legend on a map. Communication is the medium of interaction, the comprehensive strategy that underlies the developmental and curriculum components. We will add to the chart after chapters 3, 5, and 7.

Communication

(relates to Language Development)

Honor both nonverbal and verbal communication, and respond with respect to child-initiated interactions.

The attitude we communicate determines the quality of each interaction.

Curiosity	Connection	Coordination
(relates to cognitive development)	(relates to social-emotional development)	(relates to physical development and integration of skills)

Comprehensive Strategies That Support Caring Interactions

- Observe individual children; provide for Optimal Stress
- Model the behavior you wish to see
- Acknowledge Feelings
- Anticipate transitions, unusual events, and changes in routine

- Help Children Articulate their Needs and Wants
- Offer Real Choices
- Set Consistent Limits

This chart summarizes the behavior caregivers see expressed by young children in routine and play experiences and presents coinciding approaches for caring interactions. Please note that development of the whole child is a continuing and an overlapping process.

3

Supporting Curiosity

In this chapter we discuss cognitive development under the guise of curiosity. When viewed this way, it is easy to see how cognitive development relates to and overlaps with the other areas of development. Drawn by the sound of a lid landing in a bucket, the infant repeatedly drops the lid in. During this exploration, which is sparked by curiosity, the infant is developing theories about how the world works and practicing her physical coordination.

Gauging the impact they have on objects and people, infants seem to ask themselves questions like "Where is that sound coming from?" and "How can I reach that ball?" "What will happen when I drop this lid into the bucket?" and "Will it happen again?" Infants look to see where a tinkling originated, then bat at the chime ball again and again. Toddlers scoop sand and fill a cup to overflowing repeatedly before moving on to build and knock down endless towers of blocks. The human brain is wired to learn from experience. Curiosity is the beginning point that leads to other development. Curiosity drives a child to investigate her environment and learn from her experience. Really, curiosity is such an inborn human trait, caregivers need only avoid stifling it.

In thinking of infants and toddlers, caregivers can understand curiosity as the expression of a child's desire to make sense of her surroundings by following the trail of information gathered through her senses. Information about their environments reaches children through their senses. Children rely upon their eyes, skin, noses, ears and mouths to gain information about the environment in order to explore, construct reality, discover cause and effect, and put together knowledge about objects, themselves, and other people.

Helping Children Feel Comfortable

Like adults, infants who are anxious or tense are unable to relax enough to be curious. The first step towards supporting infants' curiosity is to

43

help them be comfortable. Many centers ask parents to bring in favorite music, blankets, and photographs of family members. Caregivers can also ask for an infant's home schedule so they can duplicate it as much as possible. For example, when six-month-old Sachiko came to child care within twenty-four hours of arriving from Japan, we were happy to accommodate her family's practice of eating rice at each meal.

Transitional objects that the child can take home from the center and return again are another way to increase children's familiarity and comfort with the center. This practice connects home and center and gives a child extra time to play with a small item of special interest such as a stuffed animal, book, or small toy. Language is a special link as well. Caregivers can learn a few important words in the home language, such as *mama, daddy, car, home, pet, bottle,* and the name a child uses for her lovey. In addition, caregivers can honor a child's spontaneous attachment to a particular caregiver, allowing them to be together as much as possible as the child becomes familiar with the people and routine of the program.

The more physically comfortable an infant is, the more able she is to be open to new interests. Her curiosity is a result of her feeling comfortable in a familiar environment. When caregivers first make eye contact with an infant, most smile in hopes of presenting a pleasant picture. If the caregiver is too close, too loud, or too abrupt, however, the infant may cry or break eye contact. Caregivers can then move back slightly or look away to give the infant a little more space. When a caregiver approaches an infant in a way that is comfortable for the infant, she will respond accordingly by holding the caregiver's gaze, looking relaxed and alert, or smiling with wide open eyes. By providing for and responding to their comfort level, a caregiver can set the stage for infants to be relaxed in their environment.

An infant with a physical or an emotional need (hunger, tiredness, soiled diaper, teething pain, separation anxiety) will be less comfortable and less likely to show any interest or curiosity in something or someone new. First the infant will direct energy to experiencing and then communicating and relieving the current need. Similarly, toddlers may be distracted from exploration by discomfort such as a wet diaper, a loud siren, a clap of thunder, or an unfamiliar person in the environment. A caregiver can reassure toddlers by acknowledging their feelings and meeting any needs they express.

Strategies for Promoting Curiosity

Once children are comfortable, they begin to express their interest in the things and people around them. As curious children respond to their environment, how can caregivers build on that interest? We use these strategies to help us support children's curiosity:

- Provide choices of materials and time to manipulate them.
- Validate the child's experience ("Say what you see").
- Plan to extend the exploration using the child's interests as a guide.
- Offer information ("Say what you know").
- Promote self-awareness.
- Share the caregiver's interests ("Say who you are").

Provide Choices of Materials and Time to Manipulate Them

As curiosity drives young children to investigate their environment, they discover cause and effect by manipulating a variety of materials. For example, a young infant extends an arm and knocks a suspended toy, then watches it swing for several long moments. A mobile infant crawls to a cylinder, knocks it over, and watches it roll away. A toddler finds a basket of Lego building blocks on the shelf, dumps it on the floor, and sits to clunk a red and a blue block together.

As well as providing ample materials for children to play with, it's important to provide multiples of toys, such as several baskets of Legos, three telephones, two barns, and several baskets of toy farm animals. This minimizes conflicts between children and the waiting time for a favored or new piece of equipment. The fewer the interruptions, the longer each child has to investigate the materials. Furthermore, children can use open-ended materials at different developmental levels—an eleven month old will enjoy the rolling action of a small car, while a two year old might use the same car in a play scenario, making motor sounds and rolling it along the table, down the table leg, and onto the floor.

The following are guidelines for choosing materials for infants and toddlers in group care. A selection of materials should be made accessible to the children as they might be in a home (for example, on low shelves, on tables, in storage tubs, and so on). This list is adapted from the guidelines used for accreditation of centers by the National Association for the Education of Young Children.

Infants	Toddlers	Multicultural

• Simple, lightweight open-ended toys that can be mouthed	• Baskets of manipulatives
	  - interlocking toys
	  - wheeled vehicles
	  - stacking toys
	  - large wooden spools
	  - beads/cubes
	  - sand and water toys
		• Multiracial, nonsexist, nonstereotyping toys, photos, pictures, dolls, books, and materials
		  - cooking implements

• Easily washable toys
  - containers
  - balls
  - pop beads
  - nesting cups
  - teethers
  - rings
	• Push and pull toys	• Items that depict people with disabilities being active
		  - photos, pictures, dolls, and books

• Action/reaction toys
  - rattles
  - squeak toys
	• Sturdy picture books	

	• Musical instruments	
• Soft, cuddly toys	• Pounding bench, puzzles	

• Photos and pictures of real and familiar objects and people	• Dramatic play materials
	  - simple dress-up clothes (hats, shoes, vests) and purses
	  - play telephones
	  - dolls, with clothes
	  - pretend toys, kitchen dishes	

• Crawling area with sturdy, stable furniture to pull up oneself	• Sturdy furniture to hold on to while walking	
	• Various sizes of balls	
	• Child-size furniture	
	• Active play equipment for climbing and balancing - slides, tunnels, boards, mats, hoops, cones, laundry baskets	

This list may be used as a starting point to brainstorm appropriate materials for infants and toddlers. A choice of materials from each developmental level for each separate room and outdoors would be most appropriate to promote infants' and toddlers' curiosity.

Whatever materials you offer, time to manipulate them is required for a child to further investigate cause and effect. Time between eating and napping times allows infants plenty of opportunity for free sensory exploration. Allowing for large blocks of play time (at least an hour between scheduled routines) lets toddlers freely choose what they're interested in and gives ample time to play with and explore the materials. Such time for self-directed play allows children to follow their own developmental interests and imagination.

Validate the Child's Experience ("Say What You See")

Validating a child's experience is one of the most important ways of supporting curiosity. There are many ways to do this in the course of a normal caregiving day. One of the most important ways is to talk aloud about what you see a child doing or experiencing. When caregivers notice what a child is interested in, they can bring it to life with descriptive language. In this way, children know they are important enough to pay attention to, and they internalize that importance and feel good about themselves. Caregivers can communicate this importance without interrupting the child's experience by requiring a response. The phrase "say what you see" is a quick way to remember how to recognize and validate a child's experience, and a typical scene involving infants might look like this:

"Oh, Vanessa, you have the blue ball. Here comes Bryan. He wants the ball too. There it goes rolling. Now Bryan has the ball." When Bryan initiates ball play, Vanessa joins in by intercepting his rolling ball and batting it across the floor.

Validating infants' experience is not just a running description of what they are doing. It is putting into words a specific action on the baby's part. For example, when a baby makes eye contact, the caregiver can respond by describing her experience in the moment. For example, the caregiver might say, "I see you chewing on that cold teether," or while cradling an infant during feeding, "I feel you holding my fingers while you drink your bottle" or "Your eyes look very sleepy right now." Of course, every single action does not require a caregiver response, but the more infants' interests "come to life" through a caregiver's verbal description, the more likely children will be able to affirm or validate their own experiences as they get older.

Validating not only reflects a child's actions but also offers the child language. The words a child hears give definition to what she is doing or feeling. She learns to recognize the words consistently used to describe her actions. This is the beginning of receptive language. Based on careful observation, caregivers can use precise and detailed language to describe a child's actions, saying, for example, "You made that ball roll" or "You are stretching your arm to reach it" or "Look how you can balance to sit on the ball." Young children look to trusted adults for responses to their investigations. This kind of verbal description of a child's actions affirms her curiosity, provides new language, and adds to her store of knowledge about her world.

Plan to Extend the Exploration Using the Child's Interests as a Guide

Once the environment has been set up with a good variety of toys, and caregivers have spent time observing children's play and reflecting their experience back to them, then what? As caregivers think about rotating the toys in the room and adding new materials, the attention they've paid to children's interests makes a huge difference. Caregivers can add materials that help the children take the next step in their understanding. For example, infants who shake rattles may be provided with many items that make a variety of sounds, allowing them to have wider experience with things that make noise when shaken and thus deepen their understanding.

Verbal reflection can suggest ways the caregiver could make specific changes or additions in the environment based on children's expressed interests. For example, after noting the fun Vanessa and Bryan had with balls, a responsive caregiver could introduce a basket of balls differing in size and texture, as well as other things that roll, to extend their experience with balls. She could use words like *chime*, *bumpy*, *heavy*, and *light* to describe the new choices of balls. Vanessa might finger the bumpy ball and watch it click across the floor. Bryan might laugh as he tosses the lightweight stocking ball across the room. By enabling them to follow their own curiosity, the caregiver facilitates their drive for understanding the effects they have on objects.

Extending the child's exploration with repeated experiences reinforces the connections made in the brain. When a child's play interest is extended, the neural connections in the child's brain expand as well. The child has *more* to think about a favorite object she enjoys focusing on. When Bryan and Vanessa are given additional balls that act similarly by rolling, yet look different and maybe even make sounds, their experience and knowledge about balls has been enriched. For example, let's follow Bryan, now a toddler, outdoors as he discovers a clear Plexiglas tube mounted on a fence:

Bryan, now nineteen months old, discovers a single tennis ball near the fence. Picking it up, he turns to the Plexiglas tube and drops it in at the high end. The caregiver, Keith, watches Bryan looking intently as the ball rolls out the end of the tube. Stepping to the end, Bryan scoops up the ball and repeats rolling the ball down through the tube. As Bryan rolls the ball a third time, Keith brings him a basket of smaller and larger balls, and a few wheeled toys. "That ball goes down that tube pretty fast," Keith says. Bryan smiles and chooses a truck. "You put the truck down the tube," Keith comments. Bryan chooses a ball that is too large to fit in the tube. "Push," Bryan says. "You're pushing hard to make that ball fit inside the tube," Keith says.

Offer Information ("Say What You Know")

As children show repeated interest in something, caregivers can offer additional information about the object of their curiosity. For example, ten-month-old Evan has learned to identify that he had a toy cow in his hand when his caregiver said, "You have a cow." As Evan grows, his interest in cows continues. He discovers them in books in various rooms. At seventeen months, Evan points to the different colors on a cow. An observant caregiver can offer him additional information, saying "That cow is white with black spots and provides milk for us." When Evan is two and looking at a book with a caregiver and a group of other toddlers, a cow appears on one of the pages. Evan goes to the toy shelf, picks up a black-and-white toy cow, and proclaims, "This is a milk cow!" Evan's cognitive understanding of what a cow looks like has been extended because of his initial early interest and curiosity. Caregivers have provided additional information to match his interest and development. Two-year-old Evan now knows that a cow with black-and-white spots is a milk cow!

Language development is also supported when caregivers offer information about children's play interests. Remember infants Vanessa and Bryan and their interest in balls? As a toddler, Bryan is drawn to the soft socks in the other rooms to throw and roll on the floor. He narrates his own play with phrases like "throw the ball" and "the balls roll fast." The more information adults can share with toddlers and the more detailed the language they use, the further the children's knowledge and curiosity are extended because of the increased neural connections in the brain. These caring interactions become more like conversations as children assimilate the additional information: At twenty-six months, Bryan initiates a conversation with a caregiver, saying "Do you know about balls?" "What about balls?" Yvonne responds. "They're filled with air!" Bryan says, gleefully.

Caregivers can also use the "say what you know" strategy when toddlers are curious about odd or spontaneous happenings. For example, toddlers may be fascinated by the sound of a siren or leaf blower or chain saw emanating from the neighborhood. As they turn their heads toward the sound or ask "What's that?" a caregiver can explain: "That's a siren. It could be from a police car, a fire truck, or an ambulance going to help someone" or "That's a leaf blower for clearing a driveway." Toddlers will continue their curiosity: "*Where* is it?" The caregiver explains, "It's coming from that direction, but we can't see it over the fence or through the trees—we can only hear it."

Using books, books, and more books to further stimulate curiosity can begin in the infant/toddler years. Nine-month-old Derrick is pointing at the picture of a cat on the wall in the infant room. "Caa," he says. Caregiver Lyle says, "Oh, that's like your cat at home. Here is a book with lots of kitties in it." Twenty-nine-month-old Lexy loves trains. After he asks for three train books in a row, a sensitive caregiver amasses all the other train books she can find for him. Lexy is ecstatic!

As toddlers get older, they assimilate knowledge from their experiences. Their cognitive development stretches to include "is not" as well as "is" in naming. The evidence of "is not" in toddlers' language demonstrates their readiness for more sophisticated humor, as in twenty-six-month-old Katie saying, "That's not a cat—it's a raccoon!"

The recognition of odd juxtapositions—one definition of humor—can delight both caregiver and toddler while expanding the toddler's understanding. For example, a caregiver's conversation with a child while playing the game of peek-a-boo runs a continuum from a simple "Where's Marile? There she is!" to "Where's Marile? Did she go for a boat ride? Is she up in a tree?"

This humor is different from teasing a child who doesn't fully understand. To young toddlers, teasing when they don't really know what's going on must feel like a game of keep-away that isn't evenly matched and undermines their confidence in their own perceptions. They know when they don't "get it." Sensitive caregivers do not act in any way that leads young children to believe that something is wrong with them when, in fact, their brains simply haven't made the connections yet.

Promote Self-Awareness

How do children learn or come to know about themselves, their feelings, needs, abilities, preferences, and places in the world? Caregivers act as their mirrors—what children see reflected in them forms their self-image.

Caregivers understand that an individual's basic approach to the world is inborn. Mary Sheedy Kurcinka, in *Raising Your Spirited Child,* describes the traits through which individuals express their basic temperament as mood, energy, first reaction, adaptability, intensity, sensitivity, perspective, regularity, and persistence. There are a wide range of variations in each of these traits and many different ways that they all combine with one another. This knowledge allows caregivers to understand differing responses among children in their care. When caregivers understand these differences in temperament, they can help infants and toddlers learn to identify their own needs and get them met. Through observation, caregivers can note individual responses and preferences.

A responsive caregiver can promote the infant's awareness by reflecting back to the child what might be causing the reaction. As infants begin to wake up from a nap, their senses make them aware of comfort or discomfort. They may wake up feeling hungry or feeling a wet diaper against their skin or feeling cold if the blanket is no longer covering them. Or they may bounce up gleeful and happy after fully resting. A caregiver can promote the infant's awareness by using phrases such as "Looks like you had a good rest" or "Your diaper is a super-soaker after you slept so long" or "I bet you're feeling hungry after your nap. I have some cereal ready for you to eat after I change your diaper." The infant's cry is understood as a communication about her needs, and in return, the caregiver communicates information about the sensations the infant may be experiencing.

In play situations infants communicate with the same intensity, and responsive caregivers can also mirror their experience back to them with words. For example, as a crawling infant explores her environment and discovers steps or ramps up to a loft, she screeches with glee from her high perch. A caregiver can point out her new perspective: "Look how high you are. Isn't that fun to look down?"

Toddlers may also communicate physically or through their moods when they are uncomfort-able. A tired or hungry toddler may get actively irritable and strike out at others or melt into a quiet puddle. A caregiver can promote self-awareness by offering a hug and a lap and saying "I can tell you are upset. Are you tired or hungry? It'll soon be time to eat lunch and then take a nap. Would you like to cuddle and relax a bit?"

The older children become, the more overt are their expressions of preferences. As young children are able to eat a variety of foods, for instance, caregivers can note favored foods and acknowledge them: "Easan, I can tell you really love apples. You can eat many slices." In another expression of preference, a toddler often seeks a private place to have a bowel movement in her diaper. A responsive caregiver can promote this self-awareness by saying, "I can tell you want to be by yourself to poop in your diaper; let me know when you're finished so one of us can change it."

Children's comfort levels with different kinds of play can be seen in the level of their involvement. Some toddlers really like to get wet all over in water play, be barefoot, or dip their fingers into glue or paint. When caregivers note this level of curiosity, they can add to the child's self-awareness by validating it as new knowledge—by saying, for example, "Angelina, I can tell you really enjoy squishing the finger paint through your fingers."

Share the Caregiver's Interests ("Say Who You Are")

Caregivers are part of the infant/toddler child care environment too! A particular way of modeling is to share your interests with the children. Caregivers do this informally simply by the experiences they choose, the clothes they wear, the books they read, or the music they listen to. You want to be mindful that you are always doing this modeling. It is also important for caregivers to respond to children's expression of interest in them as they would respond to a newfound friend with similar interests. Of course, not all children will be interested in the same things caregivers are. But among several caregivers all children can find someone with whom to share their curiosity.

When caregivers share a personal interest, connections with each child deepen. Caregivers who explore these connections to find mutual interests with children model curiosity as a way to learn about and experience the world. For example, consider these scenarios:

John is a caregiver who likes bird watching. He identifies specific birds as they fly through the yard. After he has done this for a while, a toddler shows him a "hummer," a tiny bird sitting on the wire or drinking from the feeder. "Can you see how the hummingbird hovers in the air? Look at her drink from the feeder while still flying," John comments. The toddler listens and then asks, "What's that?" John responds, "That's the song she sings. It's different than the scrub jay's squawk or the mockingbird's many different songs."

Christa wears different barrettes in her hair each day that she works at the center, and several toddlers look to see which barrette is in her hair upon her arrival. Beng greets Christa as she kneels down to say hi. Beng gently takes Christa's face in his hands, turning her head from side to side. "Today?" he asks. "I have two barrettes today," Christa answers. Beng says, "Stars." "Yes, they are purple stars. A pair of purple stars," Christa says.

Caregiver Skip polishes rocks as a hobby. One day he brings some large polished rocks and seeds the sand with them for the children to discover. Meggie discovers one and carries it to show Skip. "Rock," Meggie says. "You found a rock," Skip answers. He adds, "Look how shiny it is. How does it feel?" "It has lines," Meggie answers.

Supporting Curiosity during Routines

Now let's investigate how caregivers can apply these strategies to routine caregiving experiences in an infant/toddler program. In infant/toddler programs, caregivers can spend 65 to 70 percent of their day in routine experiences such as mealtimes, personal care, napping, and transitions. Just the word *routine* may suggest repetitious or mechanical actions. Instead of hustling through these times to get to the next activity, caregivers can think of these routines as special opportunities to relieve any frustration caused by "herding" groups of toddlers or any sadness felt by infants or toddlers when they are rushed or treated like objects. Think of these experiences as the difference between a focused chat with one person over coffee or tea and a raucous party in which attention is easily distracted from individuals. Certainly, adults would experience the difference in comfort and intimacy between the two. Young children feel the same way.

In a center with a curriculum of caregiving and play, all experiences carry equal weight. Procedures for carrying out routine experiences are planned in order to recognize the experience the child will have at such times. It makes sense: Connections in the young child's brain are being made continuously with experience, during routine as well as during planned experiences. When caregivers apply the strategies (see page 44) to routine experiences, a child's curiosity can only be further enriched.

The following scenarios demonstrate how the six strategies for supporting curiosity play out during the routines of child care. Routine provides a reliable framework within which everything else happens. We've gathered routines into four categories: mealtimes; personal care (diapering, dressing, cleaning up); naptime; and transitions to and from the center, and between routines or play experiences.

Mealtimes

Through observation, Consuela has determined that eight-month-old Emily may be ready to sit at the table to eat finger foods. Emily can get into a sitting position by herself, she has two teeth, and she can touch her feet to the floor in order to let herself safely down from the chair. Emily is having her first banana at the table. Mom told Consuela this morning that they tried finger foods with Emily this weekend. They started with bananas, so Consuela offers some to Emily today. Consuela cuts a quarter-inch slice of banana into four pieces and places them on the table in front of Emily. Emily's right hand darts out, her fist shoving the banana along the table. She looks at Consuela, eyebrows up. Consuela responds to Emily's curiosity by saying "It's a banana—you can eat it." Emily's hand moves over the table, falling on top of the banana pieces. She puts her hand to her mouth. Consuela narrates for her: "You squished it. Can you taste the banana? It's sweet." Placing her left hand flat on top of the table, Emily reaches and palms a single piece of banana, closing her fist enough to carry it to her mouth. Consuela notes her success by saying "There you go; you got the banana on your hand and into your mouth." Emily eats the next pieces rapidly, so Consuela cuts up a few more slices. "You really like banana, huh, Emily. I see you smacking your lips."

Consuela is responsive and allows Emily her own experience. She uses words to reflect it back to Emily by observing and then commenting on her observations, using detailed, specific language like "sticky, squishy, sweet, smacking." Because Emily is not talking yet, the questions are rhetorical. They serve to support rather than interrupt the flow of Emily's experience. There is no need to rush her process, and there is time for her to manipulate the banana. Some infants will spit food out, depending on their sensitivity to texture. Some will want to see the banana a few times before trying it. By observing and validating a child's experience, caregivers can honor these sensory explorations.

The strategy of offering information provides a valuable opportunity for toddlers to gain new knowledge. When caregivers sit down with toddlers at mealtimes, simple facts about the food that is being served can be shared. For example, consider this scene:

As Jodie finishes cleaning the hands of eight toddlers sitting at the table with her, another caregiver sets down a tray with a ready-to-serve snack. "Oh, look!" Jodie exclaims. "Fresh pears, some all sliced for us and ready to eat." As she serves each child a slice, she shares further information: "Did you know pears grow on trees? Here is a whole pear, with the stem on it. The stem is the part that attaches the pear to the tree." She holds the pear by the stem, as the toddlers watch and listen. Twenty-six-month-old William says, "Tree!" as he looks and points out the window, then returns to munching a pear slice. After all the sliced fruit is passed out and eaten, Jodie says, "Now I'll slice this whole pear and you can see the seeds inside. Each seed can grow into a pear tree."

Sharing very simple information about the foods caregivers serve to toddlers enables the routine of snack time to be an enjoyable way to gain knowledge. The time of eating together becomes an opportunity to offer information or "say what you know" rather than simply deal out food. Caregivers can show any whole fruit or vegetable that is served in slices. Several bananas in a bunch are special to show as are red and green apples with a stem and leaf, cucumbers with their large seeds, and oranges with their sections.

Personal Care: Cleaning Up

To involve infants in routines like cleaning up, caregivers can talk about what's happening to them and interpret what the infants see and do. In this way the caregiver helps the infant connect to what is going on, and the infant becomes a participant in the experience of cleaning up. For example, consider this scene:

After Emily finishes eating the banana, Consuela continues to tell her what is happening. "I'm going to wipe off the table, and then we'll get you cleaned up. This sponge is for the table. I see you enjoyed that banana. This cloth is for you! It's going to be warm. We'll clean the banana off your hands and face. Let's check your diaper so you can be ready to play."

Consuela offers information to Emily and carries out the actions at an easy pace so that Emily can assimilate texture, temperature, and other information conveyed by her senses. The unhurried pace of the conversation also allows Consuela to observe and respond to Emily's communication through eye contact and motion. The words caregivers like Consuela use enrich a baby's receptive language and add to the pool of experience that will be drawn upon when the child begins to talk.

With toddlers, personal care routines include not only cleaning up and diapering but also toileting. By paying attention to a toddler's gestures or facial expressions, caregivers can have an idea of what the child is thinking or feeling at any given moment. A caregiver can reflect these hints to promote self-awareness. In a way, the gestures or responses act as a conversation opener for the caregiver to offer more information. For example, consider this scene:

Fifteen-month-old Kalena is having her poopy diaper changed. As she lies on the table, the caregiver, Brenda, notices her wrinkling up her nose. Brenda says, "Yes, your poop has a strong smell today. Would you like to see it?" Kalena's eyes open wide as she lifts her head to look down. Brenda shows her the poop in her diaper, saying "Your body made this. Now I'll put it in the pail and wipe your skin clean." Kalena smiles as she makes eye contact with Brenda.

Kalena communicates that she is smelling her bowel movement by wrinkling her nose. Brenda notices this and puts into words what Kalena is experiencing. What is important is the caregiver's simple nonjudgmental reflection of Kalena's sensory experience (the smell is a strong one, not "bad" or "icky"). Brenda also mentions that Kalena's body made the bowel movement, which helps her connect to the process, increasing her self-awareness.

If a caregiver looks at or approaches the task of changing a diaper as an icky or stinky affair, the child will pick up this attitude and feel the same way. By talking about it as a simple sensory experience, caregivers can give the child an understanding of a completely natural act that everyone experiences. A nonjudgmental, easygoing response to changing a diaper could possibly ease stresses related to future toilet learning. Because young children have difficulty separating themselves from their bodily products, it's important to maintain an attitude respectful of this natural process in order to preserve a child's positive self-image.

In the following example, a toddler notices differences between her body and another toddler's. Note how naturally or matter-of-factly the caregiver responds to simple differences in male and female anatomy. This is a classic example of the impact of caregiver modeling and the effect it can have on children. The same approach would be equally effective with any other physical difference—for example, when children notice differences in skin color or physical abilities.

Thirty-two-month-old Thomas, underwear at his ankles, is standing at a potty-chair, peeing into the bowl. Twenty-six-month-old Mariko stands nearby peering at Thomas. She leans over and points, saying "peanut." The caregiver, Audrey, responds, "You see his penis, Mariko." Patting her midsection, Mariko says, "I have a penis." Audrey answers, "You have a vagina, Mariko. Boys have penises and girls have vaginas." Mariko says reflectively, "Oh, 'gina," as she pats herself and saunters off.

Audrey's strategy during this experience is to "say what you know." By offering information to the toddlers, she expands their knowledge while supporting their interest. Her easygoing, comfortable, and calm response to what Mariko sees (Thomas's penis) allows Mariko to learn a new name for a body part. She also learns what her corresponding body part is called. Audrey helps Mariko develop a healthy sense of gender differences. When a caregiver responds naturally, without embarrassment, to such curiosities, children can ask questions, openly and free from discomfort.

Naptimes

Falling asleep is one of the great competencies of life. Newborns seem to do it easily. As infants grow and interact more actively with their environment, they may have to relearn how to fall asleep easily. The following infant room scenario shows how a caregiver can help an infant recognize her signs of sleepiness and communicate them to her. Note, too, how the caregiver is physically in touch with the older infant while verbally acknowledging the younger infant's experience of tiredness.

Six-month-old Raphael has been rolling over, back and forth, reaching for toys and occasionally cooing or gurgling for fifteen minutes. The caregiver, Ruth, is a short distance away, sitting on the floor near a cruising eleven month old. When Raphael rolls toward Ruth, they make eye contact and she says, "Hi" or "You like that soft blanket" or "I see you in the mirror." Then one time when he rolls toward her, Raphael's cooing is higher pitched, he doesn't roll back the other way, and his feet are pedaling. Ruth responds to this change in his actions by saying "Oh, Raphael, are you finished playing? Bet you'd like a nap." Ruth gently lets the cruising baby down onto the floor and moves slowly and deliberately to talk to Raphael and pick him up. He grabs her hair, still moaning loudly. "Oh, you think that barrette is interesting," she says. "Bunnies, it's shaped like bunnies. Let's see about a nap. Here's your blanky."

Notice how Ruth allows both infants to follow their own interests: one rolling over and over to reach toys, the other cruising with her support. Ruth knows Raphael well enough to notice a change from play-type movements (rolling and reaching) to "I'm tired, done playing"–type actions (change in voice pitch and from smooth to jerky leg movements). Ruth calmly reflects Raphael's self-awareness of tiredness. This pattern of back-and-forth responses between the caregiver and child is like a beginning conversation, reinforcing children's self-awareness.

With older toddlers, the signs that they are ready for a nap may be more obvious to caregivers than those shown by infants. Tired toddlers are also apt to cause more conflict when they are irritable and aggressive. However, it is just as helpful to toddlers as to infants for a caregiver to comment gently and compassionately about what she observes and thus promote a child's self-awareness.

Twenty-seven-month-old Sam has just finished wiping his face and hands after eating lunch. He walks over to the couch and flops his torso onto the cushion. Dejon is close behind and jumps up on the couch, jostling Sam's arm. Sam lets out a scream: "No…mine!" A nearby caregiver, Karen, says, "I can tell you are real tired, Sam. Let's get you ready for your nap." Sam screams, "No!" Karen sits next to Sam and holds her arms open. "Would you like to snuggle a bit? You're so tired." Sam crawls into her arms for a hug as she begins to get him ready for his nap. Karen offers, "I get real grumpy and irritable too when I'm tired. I always feel better after I sleep. I bet you'll feel better after your nap too."

As Karen acknowledges Sam's feelings of tiredness, she also shares her own feelings about needing rest, using the "say who you are" strategy. When caregivers can broaden a toddler's experience with adult understanding, they build on the child's natural curiosity about self and others.

Transitions

The strategy of observation does well to help caregivers initiate and guide the many transitions that take place throughout the day in an infant/toddler program. From experience to experience, mealtimes to outdoors, snack to rest, arriving to going home, caregivers can learn the rhythms of each child and the ways the children express their needs. Each infant has distinctive cries and body language, and the ways these change when she is ready to transition is a powerful tool for communicating with care-givers. Following an infant's interests through a transition keeps her comfortable and calm, allowing her to continue to be curious about her surroundings.

The babies are visiting outdoors: a four month old lying on a blanket under a tree; an eight month old scooting and reaching up on top of milk crates for toys placed there; and an eleven month old pushing a small cart. After twenty-five minutes, the eleven month old doesn't get back up after the fifth time he plops down, and the four month old begins to suck her thumb. Either of these actions could signal the caregiver, Bob, that it's time for a change. Bob says to the babies, "We've had a lot of fun being outside. I can tell you're running out of energy. Let's go back inside. Terry will help us all go in together so we can eat."

By allowing infants their own experience, caregivers can validate their curiosity in play and offer information by letting them know their needs will be met. Note how Bob observes the infants for specific changes in expression, validates their experience of fun being outside, and verbally anticipates a transition to go inside to eat. Finally, knowing that trust is always an important message to convey to a young child, and since one adult cannot carry three infants, Bob assures them that all will go together with the help of a another familiar caregiver.

Bob has learned these infants' ways of communicating. He consistently responds to their cues and matches his response to the need they express. He promotes their self-awareness by identifying and responding to the changes in their behaviors.

With toddlers, transitions are usually initiated by caregivers and are most easily completed with the toddlers' involvement. Like any of us, toddlers prefer to know what's coming, and they will participate if they can anticipate what happens next. Once this information is offered, it is critical to follow through so that children develop the sense that their world is orderly and predictable and that what we say is meaningful.

In the following scenario, a toddler's play experience is validated and respected as the caregiver announces an approaching transition to mealtime. The toddler becomes involved in the transition rather than being herded or carried through it.

Nico is playing outside in the yard with a favorite truck. The caregiver, Clare, is aware of the daily schedule and that lunchtime is approaching and says, "Nico, I can tell you've having fun with that truck. In two minutes it'll be time to go in for lunch." Two minutes later, she is mindful to follow through by saying "It's been two minutes, Nico. It's time to go in for lunch. You can play with the truck later. Shall I save it for you on the fence or in your cubby?" Nico points and says, "Fence" as Clare lifts the truck to the high resting place.

To respect his play process as important enough to preserve, Clare engages Nico's involvement in the necessary transition to a caregiving need. Clare is using several strategies here: providing choices of materials and the time to manipulate them, validating Nico's experience, and planning to extend his exploration later. By honoring that exploration, the caregiver gains the toddler's cooperation, becoming a partner in his transition.

In group care the needs of the group often necessitate transitions to scheduled meals. Nico has been assured that his play interests are seen as important by having time to get ready. Caregivers need to know individual children to present effective anticipation of and choices for a smooth transition.

These approaches to interactions with infants and toddlers during routine experiences promote a child's curiosity. Caregivers have this precious time to reassure young children that they will be cared for and are cared about as individuals. When caregivers validate a child's experience, extending her play with choice and additional information, she can be a participant in life's routines, all in the context of helping young children lay a foundation of emotional stability within cognitive development.

On the following page is a chart summarizing the child tasks and correlating caregiver responses we have discussed in this chapter. As you can see, we have added this material to the map located at the end of chapter 2.

Communication
(relates to Language Development)

Honor both nonverbal and verbal communication, and respond with respect to child-initiated interactions.

The attitude we communicate determines the quality of each interaction.

Curiosity (relates to cognitive development)		Connection (relates to social-emotional development)	Coordination (relates to physical development and integration of skills)
Child Tasks	**Caregiver Strategies**		
Use senses to explore environment to construct own reality	Provide choices of materials and time to manipulate them.		
	Validate the child's experience ("say what you see").		
Discover cause and effect	Plan to extend the exploration using the child's interests as a guide.		
Assimilate knowledge	Offer information ("say what you know").		
	Promote self-awareness.		
	Share the caregiver's interests ("say who you are").		

Comprehensive Strategies That Support Caring Interactions

- **Observe individual children; provide for Optimal Stress**
- **Model the behavior you wish to see**
- **Acknowledge Feelings**
- **Anticipate transitions, unusual events, and changes in routine**
- **Help Children Articulate their Needs and Wants**
- **Offer Real Choices**
- **Set Consistent Limits**

This chart summarizes the behavior caregivers see expressed by young children in routine and play experiences and presents coinciding approaches for caring interactions. Please note that development of the whole child is a continuing and an overlapping process.

Playing with
Curiosity

Seven-month-old Nicholas crawls ten "steps" across the floor to a toy shelf. He rakes the tissue box off the shelf with his right forearm, sitting back on his bottom. Pulling at the scarf poking out of the box, he begins to crawl toward another infant. The scarf is tied to another, and another. After four "crawl-steps," still holding the scarf, Nicholas stops, sits, and turns to look behind him. With a huge grin, he retraces his steps and pulls out all the scarves. The caregiver places a few more stuffed containers around the room.

"More cows, more cows," twenty-eight-month-old Gavin insists. "You want more cows?" the caregiver responds. A vigorous nod of the head accompanies a reach across the table to another "farm." The caregiver says, "Maybe Yukiko will trade with you; why don't you ask her?" Gavin quickly holds out a horse to thirty-two-month-old Yukiko and says, "Horse. More cows?" The caregiver repeats, "Gavin would like to trade a horse for a cow." Yukiko takes the horse before carefully choosing a cow to give to Gavin.

Two-year-old Tom stands by the table clutching a round bead in his hand. He pokes the stiff end of a string through and grabs it with the other hand. Still holding the bead, he watches it for twenty seconds before dropping it so it travels down the string. Last time he missed the hole and the bead dropped to the floor. Sitting nearby, seventeen-month-old Carmen places some beads on the nails in a nail board. Today she continues to fill the whole board by placing beads wherever they will fit. A caregiver sits nearby, making eye contact with the children and reflecting evident satisfaction.

In these scenes infants and toddlers are participating in planned experiences. Planned experiences are one way to set up the environment in order for caregivers to facilitate hands-on discovery. Facilitating implies a back-and-forth exchange to support children's development. When our attitude is open and facilitating, rather than literally teaching, we invite a response, thereby involving the child.

What Is a Planned Experience?

We think of an "experience" as something a caregiver sets up to support children's *learning* through repeated exploration of the environment, materials, or equipment. We use the word *experience* instead of *activity* to focus on the process rather than the end product. We see experiences as more child-directed and open-ended than activities, though some activities may also fit this definition. During an experience, materials are provided for free exploration and manipulation by a small group of children, usually no more than four.

Just as meals are planned to meet nutritional needs, we can provide planned experiences to promote children's needs for exploration. Our goal is to provide an opportunity for children to interact with materials. In a small group setting, there is less chance for distraction and more opportunity for interaction.

Why Use Planned Experiences?

Planned experiences offer valuable one-on-one or small-group interactions for infants, toddlers, and their caregivers. These experiences are intended for small groups in which observation, response, language, and facilitation by the caregiver can be more intimate or personal than when several caregivers are working with a larger group of children.

By planning specific experiences caregivers can

- observe individuals to get to know them
- respond to individual interests and skill levels
- provide for different developmental levels within the group
- expand their own skills and broaden their own awareness of everyday materials
- recognize and value how young children learn

Planned experiences include these common characteristics:

- Children's play is self-directed in a small group
- Children are involved in making choices and decisions
- Children discover spontaneously how things work
- Children learn the consequences of their own actions through their experience and through guidance by caring facilitators
- Children of different developmental stages and abilities can participate in the same experience

Guide to Using the Planned Experiences

Chapters 4, 6, and 8 of this book contain planned experiences that support the three Cs of infant/toddler development: curiosity, connection, and coordination. Of course, the three Cs overlap one another, and each experience supports more than one of these attributes.

For each planned experience there is a description, a list of materials, and a procedure that is laid out in a straightforward manner. There are also tips to help caregivers anticipate how infants and toddlers may respond to the materials. In addition, we've included a list of the limits we most commonly set around these experiences and common choices we offer the children in response to those limits.

The experiences are essentially flexible and may be adapted to a range of skills and development. Although we have designated some experiences as most appropriate for infants and some as best for toddlers, they can often be adapted for either age range. Look for adaptations in the "Other Things to Think About" section. Don't forget to consider the time and effort necessary to clean up each experience and transition to the next part of the day. At the end of each experience, we've included a scene to illustrate how caregivers might employ one or more of the strategies discussed in chapter 3 to support the children's play and extend their learning from the experience.

Floor Pictures

Crawling, creeping, or scooting infants love to find new things on the floor. Attach plastic mirrors and pictures or photographs to the floor with clear contact paper to engage the infants' curiosity. Mirrors promote their self-awareness, and pictures or photos offer brain-stimulating information!

What You'll Need

- Plastic or acrylic mirrors 6 by 6 to 12 by 18 inches.
- Pictures or photos of real objects, animals, or people.
- Clear contact adhesive paper.

What to Do

- Choose mirrors and/or pictures to display. You may want to start with just a few and add more over time.
- Cut clear adhesive paper into pieces a few inches larger on all sides than the chosen pictures or mirrors.
- Thoroughly clean and dry the spots on the floor where the pictures will be placed.
- Place the contact paper on a work table or counter with the sticky side up. Put the picture or mirror face down in the middle of the contact paper, so it will be face up on the floor.
- Stick the contact paper with the image or mirror attached down on the floor and smooth out any wrinkles. Press hard with a stiff object like the bowl of a spoon to make sure the contact paper is firmly attached all the way around, right out to the edges.
- Observe the infants as they discover the new pictures, and narrate their discoveries, using phrases like "You're sitting on the elephant" or "I saw you crawl to the picture of the wolf."

Limits

These are infants, remember. Limits provide redirection and intervention for safety.

- Offer alternative mirrors or photos for infants to carry around if they try to pick at the items stuck to the floor: small 4-inch plastic mirrors and laminated pictures to carry around, teethers to chew on.

- Use phrases like these too:

    "Let's leave them on the floor."

    "You can use your eyes to look at them."

    "Here's a mirror you can hold and carry around."

Other Things to Think About

- Test to make sure the pieces of contact paper stick fast during routine mopping of the floor. You may need to hand scrub them or be prepared to replace them frequently. (Our experience is that they last for months.)

- Note the individual preferences of the infants in your program: observe which pictures the babies respond to and provide others that are similar to extend their exploration.

- It might be necessary to tape down the edges as a "frame" to discourage picking at the contact paper.

- If mirrors do not reflect through the clear contact paper, use frames of tape to stick the mirrors to the floor.

- Photos, mirrors, and pictures may be similarly placed within infants' sight level in other parts of the environment: low down on walls, on the backs of toy shelves, or behind acrylic frames on the wall.

Supporting Play

Use these strategies to support the babies' experience, as Kim does in the following example:

- Validate the child's experience; "say what you see"

- Plan to extend the exploration, using the child's interests as a guide

- Offer information; "say what you know"
- Promote self-awareness

> *Kim is sitting on the floor with three babies. When an infant stops to trace with a finger or look more closely at a picture, Kim offers information: "Sally, you're pointing at the dog....The dog says, 'woof-woof.' I know you have a doggy at home." Sally looks intently at Kim, who continues, "Your dog is named Rags!" Sally immediately grins, looking back to the picture of the dog. Sally's family has included Rags in the family photos from home, so Kim points out that photo too. Kim can also make sure that there are books featuring dogs in the infant room and offer them to Sally later. Now Sally has moved to the mirror and leans over to kiss the image. "That's Sally in the mirror," Kim comments. She moves to include herself in the mirror. Sally looks intently from the image to the real person.*

Note how the caregiver responds to Sally's interest in the picture of a dog by offering more information and planning to extend that interest later through books. Sally's self-awareness is strengthened by having the caregiver name her image in the mirror.

Scarf Box

Stuff a box with scarves, so infants can pull them out like tissues. Many scarves (at least three) may be tied together so as the infant pulls, more and more come out.

What You'll Need

- An empty cardboard tissue box or a plastic box with a hinged lid (from diaper wipes), or any similar small box with a small opening.

- Colorful scarves, such as bandanas, or lengths of lightweight, washable fabric, such as nylon, silky polyester, or cotton.

What to Do

- Stuff scarves into an empty tissue or plastic box. They may be tied together, or not. Stuff the scarves through the opening carefully or, with a cardboard box, open from the bottom and reseal.

- Leave one corner of a scarf sticking out of the box and place on a shelf or the floor for the infants to discover.

- Watch the infants discover the scarf box, and use words like these to reflect their experience:

     "You noticed that box on the shelf."

     "I saw you pull the scarf out."

     "I see how much fun you are having with those scarves in the box."

Limits

- Offer teethers or cold washcloths for infants to chew on if they chew on the scarves.

- Use phrases like "Boxes or scarves are not for chewing."

Other Things to Think About

- Clean-up: Replace used scarves with clean ones daily. Gather smashed cardboard tissue boxes and replace them with new ones as needed.

- Infants' reactions will vary. Caregivers may see overt surprise at the new toy or pure glee when the scarves continue to come out of the box, or an infant may simply look at the box and move on. Some babies will stuff the scarves back in; some will initiate a game of peek-a-boo.

- Infants have probably seen scarves before and perhaps played peek-a-boo with them. If the scarves are tied together, the infants often are surprised to see more coming out of the box.

- Older infants may stuff the scarves back in to do it again. This is an example of an infant's using a primitive scientific method to explore cause and effect by acting on an object, noting the results, then repeating the action. Through experimentation he is trying to answer questions like these: Does this one work the same way as the other one? Does it work the same way every time I do it? Does it work the same today as it did yesterday?

- Plastic boxes with small openings will last longer; cardboard tissue boxes will get smashed.

- Experiment with different colors or patterns of scarves, perhaps incorporating some from infants' homes or choosing representative ethnic designs.

- Provide at least one box for every two infants.

Supporting Play

Use these strategies to support children's play with the scarf boxes, as shown in the following story:

- Validate the child's experience; "say what you see"

- Plan to extend the exploration using the child's interests as a guide

As two crawling infants move past the box on the floor, the tail of a scarf catches Rose's eye, and she rocks back on her bottom to investigate. She begins pulling on the scarf. The caregiver, Susan, says, "I see you pulling the scarf out of the box." As Rose discovers that the scarf is attached to another, Susan responds to her look of surprise by saying "Oh, now what's happening?" Then, as Rose pulls scarf after scarf out of the box, Susan says, "I see you pulling and pulling those scarves, Rose." When the last scarf comes free of the opening, Susan says, "The box is empty. You have all the scarves." Using both hands, Rose pulls up the last scarf in front of her face. Susan says, "Oh, you want to play peek-a-boo. Okay, Rose. Where's Rose? Where's Rose? There she is! Peek-a-boo!"

Notice how Susan observed closely and tailored her comments to Rose's exploration. She could easily be doing this while feeding or rocking another infant or while supporting another child's play with the same kind of comments.

Wind Chimes and Windsocks

The experience of watching a windsock or hearing a wind chime ignites a child's senses of sight and hearing. This experience may take place indoors or out.

What You'll Need

- Wind chime or bell.
- Banner, windsock, or streamer.

What to Do

- Indoors: hang the wind chime or windsock securely by a window or fan.
- Outdoors: hang the wind chime or windsock securely from a tree or wherever it is easily visible and moved by a breeze.
- Hang either one outside a window for children to see or hear from indoors.
- Let children discover the motion or sound on their own.

Limits

None needed

Other Things to Think About

- Hang the chimes or streamers high enough that children cannot reach them.
- Periodically check to make sure they are attached safely and securely.
- Move them from place to place every so often to keep the children interested in them.

- Offer open-ended questions to expand children's observations, using phrases like these:

    "What do you see?"

    "What's happening?"

Supporting Play

This story of a quiet moment in the infant room shows the caregiver using these strategies:

- Validate the child's experience; "say what you see"

- Offer information; "say what you know"

> *Five-month-old Hannah lies on her back, chewing on her fingers. Twenty-two-month-old Yotam sits nearby looking at a book. A breeze comes up and a tinkling sounds out. Hannah startles a bit as she looks up. Yotam looks at Aira, the caregiver, who is nearby, feeding Dick. Aira says, "Can you find what made that sound?" She lays a calming hand on Hannah's shoulder as Hannah sights the moving wind chime and reaches her hands toward it. Yotam watches the windsock blow, then looks at the chime. Aira says, "See how the wind makes them move? What's happening?"*

Note how Aira allows the children to discover the wind chime and windsock on their own. She does not respond until Hannah and Yotam react to the sound. Then Aira validates what they heard and saw and offers additional information about how wind makes some objects move.

Bubbles

Infants and toddlers all enjoy the ethereal nature of bubbles floating through the air. Watching the transformation of liquid to apparent solid seems magical and is especially delightful when toddlers can take part.

What You'll Need

- Liquid dish detergent (Dawn works well).
- Water.
- Bubble wands of various sizes and types.
- Containers to accommodate them, such as a flat dish for large wands, or cups for small ones. A 9- or 10-inch Frisbee flying disc works well to hold the liquid for a 6- or 7-inch circular wand.

What to Do

- Make bubble liquid by adding one part detergent to three parts water. You may want to make a quantity in advance, keeping a gallon or so on hand. If the bubbles pop too easily, add more detergent.
- Pour the liquid into wide shallow containers (for big wands) or small deep containers (for small wands).
- Dip the wands into the liquid and blow gently, allow the wind to "blow" the bubbles, or move your whole body in a circle, holding your arm rigid with the wand at the end of it (this works well with large wands).
- Toddlers will want to blow the bubbles themselves. Hold the wands near their mouths and let them blow.
- Small groups may hold their cups and small wands to dip and blow on their own.

Limits

- The soapy liquid is not really dangerous but could cause illness if swallowed.

- Use phrases like these to remind children:

    "Just blow through."

    "Not for your mouth."

Other Things to Think About

- Small groups with their own cups and wands need supervision.

- Avoid waving the wand near upturned faces and eyes. Flush with running water if liquid gets into a child's eyes.

- Observe the toddlers experiment with blowing hard, soft, fast, slow; reflect what you see and make suggestions for success if they want it.

- See how this experience in curiosity can move to practice in coordination as children chase, reach, bat, clap, and stomp the bubbles.

- After a while of dipping, the bubbles get "fuzzy," or "tired"; notice this as it happens, and it becomes a natural endpoint to the experience.

- Toddlers may need help to figure out how to hold the cup steadily in one hand while blowing through the wand in the other. Or use a table to hold the cups.

- Tiny bottles of bubbles are available in party and craft stores. These could be refilled over and over, and the amount of liquid they hold works as a natural endpoint to the experience. These work well with older toddlers; careful supervision is needed with younger toddlers, because some brands of tiny wands will come apart into small pieces if children bend them.

Supporting Play

Use these strategies to support children's play, as shown in the following scene:

- Validate the child's experience; "say what you see"

- Offer information; "say what you know"

- Share the caregiver's interests; "say who you are"

Toddlers of a wide age range are wandering on the grass and trotting through spaces filled with floating bubbles. Fourteen-month-old Diane stands still and pokes at a bubble that floats by her. It pops and she giggles. "You popped that bubble, Diane. Was it fun?" says Chris, the caregiver. "Who can see the vivid colors?" Two-year-old Mechee shouts, "I see blue!" as she claps a large bubble between her hands. Chris says, "I like to watch one float way up high—there goes one. Let's see how high it goes before it pops." Many of the children stop to watch with Chris.

Rather than simply entertaining or distracting, Chris makes the bubble experience into an exchange of information.

Clear Tubes

Clear tubes offer infants and toddlers direct experience of cause and effect. When they are mounted on the wall at an angle, an object inserted at the top will travel to the bottom.

What You'll Need

- Clear plastic or acrylic tubes 2 to 3 feet long, 4 to 5 inches in diameter.
- Objects of varying diameters, such as balls and toy cars.
- Mounting materials, such as Velcro or rubber straps.

What to Do

- Mount the tubes on walls or fences indoors or out. They may be attached securely, for instance, to a stair railing. Be sure to leave room for the objects to roll out from the bottom.
- Place a basket of toys nearby. Make sure most of them (not necessarily all) will fit in the tubes.

Limits

None needed if the tubes are installed properly

Other Things to Think About

- It's fun to mount the tubes in pairs. Two tubes can be mounted about 18 inches apart. Setting them up as mirror images allows children to watch each other.
- Try tubes of differing diameters and lengths.

- Try mounting the tubes at various angles so children can compare how objects move faster or slower in the different tubes.

- Watch for edges that become sharp or brittle over time.

- Let children discover the possibilities rather than showing them.

- "Say what you see" as you watch infants and toddlers experiment.

- Outdoors, children often first use sand or whatever ground cover is available.

- Caregivers may need to help toddlers with taking turns and trading skills when they play at the paired tubes.

Supporting Play

The caregivers in these stories use the following strategies to support children's play with the tubes:

- Validate the child's interests; "say what you see"

- Offer information; "say what you know"

- Promote self-awareness

There is a newly mounted tube on a railing in a room infants use for play. Eleven-month-old Chantelle is cruising past the familiar railing. She stops, and looks briefly before fitting her hand down into the top of the tube. Josef, the caregiver, says, "Oh, you see our new tube, Chantelle? I hope you will have fun with it." He watches to see what Chantelle will do next. She stoops to get a pop bead and drops it in the top of the tube. She follows it with her eyes all the way down. Then she crawls quickly to retrieve her toy from the bottom of the tube. Chantelle crawls back to the top of the tube, pulls up, and drops the bead down. This time she clearly knows where it will end up; she's crawling toward the other end of the tube as soon as she lets go of it. Josef says, "I see you think that's fun, to drop the bead and have it travel down the tube instead of fall to the floor." Chantelle looks intently at Josef for ten seconds before continuing her game.

Two-year-old Mike chooses a shovel from the crate of toys between two tubes mounted on the fence. Mike scoops up a shovel of sand and puts it into the top of the tube. He repeats this, then goes quickly to the bottom end and catches some of the sand in his shovel. Debbie, the caregiver, comments, "You saw the sand go down the tube. Gravity pulled the sand out of the bottom. I saw you catch it in your shovel." Mike smiles. Eighteen-month-old Matt chooses a tennis ball from the crate of various toys. He pops it into the top of the tube and watches it roll down, then picks up a shovel and puts that in the tube. It fits in but does not move very far. Debbie says, "How can you get that shovel to move?" Matt scrapes at the outside of the tube, trying to reach the shovel. Mike, watching this, puts a tennis ball down the tube. He laughs as Debbie says, "You figured out how to make the heavy ball push the light shovel down the tube."

Experience Bottles

Clear plastic bottles filled with a variety of solid and liquid material provide opportunities for investigation and observation.

What You'll Need

- Small clear plastic bottles filled, or partially filled, with solid and/or liquid materials. (Commercial water or soda bottles of varying sizes work well.)
- Clear or colored water.
- Vegetable oil.
- Liquid soap or dish detergent.
- Small rocks, powdered substances, colored puff balls, feathers, dry noodles: basically anything nontoxic that fits through the opening of the bottle.
- Everyday items, such as rubber bands, pencils, paper clips.
- Small toys that would be unsafe for children to hold, yet fun to look at.
- Baskets, boxes, or cardboard carriers.

What to Do

- Scrub labels off clear plastic bottles to make the contents easier to see.
- Fill bottles one-third to two-thirds full of water or dry material. You might combine water with vegetable oil, making two differently colored layers, or with liquid soap or detergent, which will make bubbles when children shake the bottles. You could also combine water with waterproof materials, such as sparkles or plastic confetti shapes.
- Glue the bottle caps onto the bottles.
- Make collections of these bottles available to infants and toddlers on shelves or in baskets. Set out three or four bottles per child to provide ample choices.

Limits

- Bottles may not be thrown or banged; encourage rolling or shaking. Use phrases like these to discourage throwing:

    "It's not safe to throw the bottles. You can throw the socks or go outdoors to throw balls."

    "Try rolling the bottle instead of throwing it."

    "What happens to the water when you shake the bottle?"

- Help toddlers with turn taking, using phrases like these:

    "I know you want the bottle with the blue water in it. You've been waiting a long time. Say to Sarah, 'My turn next, please.'"

- Model pretending to drink, holding the bottle away from your mouth rather than inside it.

- Have teethers available as substitutes for infants or todders to chew on.

Other Things to Think About

- Fill large two-liter bottles with liquid for infants to push, roll, and crawl after. These are too heavy for toddlers to manage safely. Fill large bottles with dry materials for toddlers.

- Fill opaque containers with some of the same materials. Use film canisters, or plastic containers with lids that can be glued securely. Can the children identify the contents by sound?

- Consider saving the bottles for special circumstances, such as a rainy day.

- Older toddlers can make suggestions for materials to fill the bottles and can help fill them using a funnel.

- Kitchen or food items in bottles work well for realistic kitchen play.

- Clean bottles that have been mouthed, or put them aside to clean later.

Supporting Play

The strategies shown in these stories support children's play with the bottles:

- Validate the child's experience; "say what you see"
- Offer information; "say what you know"

> *Seven-month-old Samir and eight-month-old Tricia are on the floor surrounded by experience bottles of varying sizes. Chad, the caregiver, says, "You seem to be having lots of fun with those bottles, Samir. You've pushed the one with orange liquid all around the floor. It sloshes around when you roll it. Tricia, you have the little bottle with the bells." Tricia shakes it, smiling. "You can make the bells tinkle," Chad comments.*
>
> ---
>
> *Sixteen-month-old Noel asks, "Zat?" as she points to the contents of the bottle she has. "That's popcorn, before it's popped," answers Grace, the caregiver. Noel returns with another bottle, this one filled with liquid. "Zat?" she inquires. Grace says, "Let's look at it. There are bubbles in there. Shake it again and see what happens."*

Fingerpainting

The sensual delight of squishy paint appeals to all ages and stages. Is there a more direct experience of cause and effect than moving your fingers and hands through the paint, applying marks to the paper, and watching the pattern emerge? Infants can fingerpaint on the floor, lying on their tummies. Toddlers become purposeful in their exploration of pattern making.

What You'll Need

- Finger paint: use commercial paint or mix liquid starch and powdered or liquid tempera directly on the paper.
- Smooth, slick paper.
- Smocks or old T-shirts, if necessary.
- Towels for clean-up.
- Plastic to cover floor.

What to Do

- Have materials ready.
- Remove children's clothing if the room is warm enough. Put smocks or paint shirts on children to protect their clothes if necessary.
- Put a piece of paper in front of each child and offer him his choice of paint color. Or pour 1 or 2 tablespoons of liquid starch on each child's paper and offer him a choice of tempera color to add.
- Let the children mix and move the fingerpaint.
- Allow them their own experience, responding to their comments.

Limits

- Offer infants teethers or other appropriate chew toys if they are putting paint in their mouths.

- Use phrases like these to help toddlers keep paint on the paper:

    "Paint is for your hands and the paper."

    "Please clean the paint off your hands before playing with the other toys."

Other Things to Think About

- Gauge the amount of paint, starch, and tempera to the size of the paper.

- Infants may be more comfortable working on the floor.

- Protect the floor and tape the paper down.

- Place paint and/or starch on the paper for the infant to dabble in. When you have offered this experience a few times, the infants will become more interested in the process than in putting the point in their mouths.

- Infants who can sit up may sit at the table. "Painting" may be done on the table directly. (If you want "evidence" of the experience, take a print of the table design by smoothly placing paper on top of the paint, pressing down lightly, and then lifting it off.)

- Try to avoid snatching an art paper from a child because you think it looks great. Infants are simply experiencing the medium through their senses, and toddlers need to "overpaint" in order to learn when *they* want to stop. Take their papers away to hang up when they give you signals that they are done. With toddlers, say, "Let me know when you want a new paper."

- Plan drying space ahead of time. Newspaper or computer paper can protect rugs and floors from saturated paintings.

- Wet bath towels, wrung out, work well for cleaning paint off skin. Using washable tempera with liquid starch makes it easier to get the paint off too.

- Older toddlers could pour their own starch and tempera from small pitchers. If you do this, be prepared for the focus to change from painting to mixing.

- Many toddlers are tentative about putting their hands in the paint the first time. Let them observe the others and enter at their own speed.

Supporting Play

Use these strategies shown in the following examples to support children's play:

- Provide choices of materials and time to manipulate them
- Validate the child's experience; "say what you see"
- Promote self–awareness

Lying on his tummy on a sheet on the floor, six-month-old Doug waves at the purple paint Lois, the caregiver, is offering him, rather than the orange. Lois pours a bit of purple into the starch on the tray in front of Doug. "There you go; it's for playing with," she tells him. Doug plunges a hand flat into the paint on the tray. He grasps his fingers, but they slide together. He looks at Lois, who says, "It's slippery; that's the finger paint." Doug turns back to the tray and slaps his hand down in the middle of the paint. Paint goes flying. Laughing, Lois says, "Look where the paint went, Doug. Here comes Belle to see what's going on." Lois offers Belle a paint tray too.

Two-and-a-half-year-old Portia chooses green and quickly mixes the starch and paint with her fingers. Then her whole hands are making circles to gather paint for handprints. She covers the paper within three minutes. Nearby, Niles uses one finger to poke at the yellow paint he chose. Vangie, the caregiver, has placed it right in the middle of the starch. "Yellow," he says. "For finger paint," Vangie tells him, "we mix it with the starch; did you need a little more?" Niles sits up straighter, nodding his head. Using two fingers, he mixes back and forth, slowly watching the colors swirl.

Water Play

Infants and toddlers love water. It appeals to them aesthetically. In combination with other materials, it is an ideal medium for investigating cause and effect, exploring the properties of liquids, and discovering the concepts of space and volume. Playing with water indoors is soothing for infants and reduces their exposure to the sun.

What You'll Need

- Water source (faucet or hose).
- Water reservoirs: small water tables, tubs set in tires or crates for stability.
- Toys that may float or sink.
- Water clothes.
- Towels, cornstarch for clean-up.

What to Do

- If you're inside, protect the floor with a plastic tarp.
- Fill small tubs with 1 to 2 inches of water for mobile infants or use a small water table for cruising infants. Provide one tub per infant and place the tubs on towels so they don't slip. You can also put out a shallow tray with up to an inch of water for babies who aren't yet crawling.
- Toddlers can use individual tubs or a small water table. If you're outside, you might also consider hanging a dripping or gently running hose or small wading pools.
- Consider the temperature of the water. On a cold day, warm water is welcome. On a blistering hot summer day, cold water feels good.
- Add a selection of toys to each tub, or place them around or in a water table or wading pool. Be sure to have several of each kind of toy to minimize conflict and have several choices available for each child.
- Strip children down to their diapers if it's warm inside; outside, use water shirts, which can be hung up to dry, to minimize exposure to the sun.

Limits

- Discourage children from drinking play water; provide alternative drinking water.

- Decide ahead of time with other staff members if you will replace the water toddlers dump out from the tubs or water table.

- Use phrases like this one with the children:

  "It's okay to dump water on yourself. Please ask if you can pour some on her."

Other Things to Think About

- Consider providing extra T-shirts and underclothes for wearing when playing in the water. These can be hung on a labeled clothespin for repeated use before washing at the end of the week. Having children wear shirts reduces their exposure to the sun.

- When outside, be aware of cooling breezes and changes in the weather so children don't get chilled.

- Be creative in adding equipment. For example, add sponges, and toddlers can wash trikes and other equipment. Add baby dolls in individual tubs, and children can give them baths. Children can also wash doll clothes.

- Be creative in setting up the water sources. For example, fasten a slow-dripping hose in a tree or hang a sprinkler so the spray just goes over toddlers' heads. Attach multiple short hoses to the water source with interconnected plastic pipe and hang it on a fence.

- Allow for ample transition time. For example, start clean-up in time to get everyone into clean, dry clothes to go home.

- Cornstarch works well to remove sand from wet skin.

- Infants will be very interested in each other and in the other tubs. Expect reaching, climbing, and trading of toys.

- Outside, puddles naturally attract toddlers, who will wallow in them.

Supporting Play

Use these strategies, illustrated in the following scene, to support children's play:

- Provide choices of materials and time to manipulate them

- Validate the child's experience; "say what you see"

- Promote self–awareness

> *Two crawling infants have discovered the tubs Warren, the caregiver, set up on plastic in the middle of the room. There are plastic toys, blocks, and key chains in each tub. By pulling to the edge of the tub and reaching out a foot, Jed balances to reach into the tub. He tosses a block into the other tub, where it floats. "Look what you did—it floats," Warren says. Jed puts both arms into the tub that Roma has climbed into. "That feels pretty cool, doesn't it?" says Warren. Warren has also set up a small tray on the floor with half an inch of water in it, separated from the tubs by pillows, for Dottie. Dottie isn't crawling, but she can enjoy splashing the water while lying on her tummy.*

Cardboard Binoculars

Short cardboard tubes, used singly or taped together, can heighten and enliven sights and sounds. Used outdoors on elements of nature, they can focus and extend toddler senses.

What You'll Need

- Cardboard tubes from toilet tissue or paper towel rolls.
- Cellophane tape or masking tape.

What to Do

- The caregiver can tape the tubes together ahead of time, or toddlers can "help."
- Tape two short tubes (like the ones from toilet paper rolls) together side by side to make a pair of binoculars. Make enough pairs for at least half the toddlers in the group.
- Distribute binoculars to interested toddlers.
- Take the opportunity to share natural interests, such as bird watching, cloud contemplation, or whatever in the area sparks an interest.
- Use a single long tube held to the ear to concentrate sounds—birds singing, dogs barking, babies crying, caregivers whispering.
- One long tube may also simulate a telescope or spyglass.

Limits

- Tubes taped together stay that way; offer single tubes as alternatives. Engage toddlers' help in repairing taped tubes that get torn or ripped apart.

(Cardboard Binoculars from *Trails, Tails & Tidepools in Pails,* Nursery Nature Walks, 1992.)

Other Things to Think About

- You might want to model looking for birds, or squirrels, by moving your head and binoculars together to follow their movement in the sky or trees.

- Toddlers may enjoy looking at each other through the tubes; try covering the ends with colored cellophane.

Supporting Play

Notice how the caregiver in the following story uses these strategies to support the children's learning:

- Validate the child's experience; "say what you see"

- Plan to extend the exploration, using the child's interests as a guide

- Share the caregiver's interests: "say who you are"

The caregiver, Lynn, has a bag of cardboard binoculars and scopes. She distributes them to interested toddlers. Thirty-month-old Roy holds one and pokes his fingers in the holes. Lynn says, "I use binoculars to look at birds or animals, like this," as she models holding the binoculars to her eyes. Roy imitates and says, "I see leaves." Lynn comments, "See how close and big they look when you see them through the binoculars? Can you find that bird on the wire in yours? You can see the birds eating the loquat from our tree."

Bug Study

Toddlers are fascinated by anything that moves, including bugs. They can learn to enjoy and respect bugs when caregivers support their curiosity and model an interest.

What You'll Need

- Small containers.
- Extra leaves or grass.
- Plastic magnifying glasses.

What to Do

- When outside with children, respond to toddlers' interest in bugs. Show them the ones you see that they might miss. Use phrases like these to "say what you see":

  "You found a spider."

  "Oh, you see an ant."

- Share simple information with the children: the name of a bug, how many legs it has, what it eats, if it flies. Ask them questions like "Does it have wings? Do you think it could fly?"

- Speculate with children about the bug when they ask, "What's it doing?" or "Where's it going?" Ask them, "Where do you think it's going?" "What do you think it's doing?"

- You can hold some bugs, such as pill bugs, on your palm, modeling respect and giving simple information (for example, how it tickles your hand when it crawls). Ask if any of the curious toddlers around you would like to hold it. Give a turn to the ones who hold their hands out and keep an eye on their expressions to make sure they are comfortable.

- Older toddlers may want to collect and observe a bug in a small dish or cup.

Limits

- Be aware of dangerous bugs or spiders in your area.

- Discourage smashing bugs. Model respect for life by moving the bug to a safe place when you're finished looking at it.

- Emphasize care around bees. Use phrases like these to caution children:

  "Just use your eyes."

  "Bees are not safe to touch; they have a stinger that can hurt you. It's their way of saying leave me alone."

  "It's best to use your eyes and watch the bug until an adult can tell or show you that this bug is safe."

Other Things to Think About

- Older toddlers may enjoy looking at a bug through a magnifying glass.

- Model an open, respectful approach to other life forms, using phrases like these:

  "I know your dad doesn't like the snails in your garden at home; they are okay here in the bushes. We'll put them over there so we don't accidentally step on them."

- Some toddlers like to have bugs crawl on them or carry bugs in containers. Tell them: "If you can be gentle, it's okay."

- Interested toddlers will say, "I want to find a snail" or a spider or some other kind of bug with which they are familiar. Respond with open-ended questions: "Where is a good place to look? Do you remember where we found one before?"

- It's a good idea for caregivers and children to wash hands after handling bugs.

Supporting Play

Use these strategies to support children's bug study, as shown in the following scene:

- Plan to extend the exploration, using the child's interests as a guide
- Offer information; "say what you know"
- Share the caregiver's interests; "say who you are"

> *Twenty-eight-month-old Leah announces, "I want to find a pill bug." Jillian, the caregiver, asks, "Where's a good place to find one? Do you remember where we found one before?" Leah runs to the fence with leaves piled nearby. Twenty-two-month-old Abby joins the search, backing away when Leah emerges with a pill bug crawling on her hand. Jillian says to Abby, "That bug is afraid of you because you are so much bigger than it is." Abby holds out her hand to hold the pill bug. Jillian says, "It'll just tickle a little on your hand. I love to watch all their legs move."*

Cardboard Tubes Used for Construction

Older toddlers can use cardboard tubes, masking tape, packing material, and/or computer paper edged with holes to experiment with three-dimensional construction.

What You'll Need

- Cardboard tubes of various sizes: paper towel tubes, toilet paper tubes, and wrapping paper tubes may be cut into varying lengths and/or split.
- Ripped edges of computer paper (with holes).
- Packing materials.
- Heavy cardboard for foundation or platform.
- Masking tape, may be colored.

What to Do

- Arrange materials sorted into bins or baskets on a table or other work surface. Make sure there is an ample variety and plenty of each kind of material for children to choose from.
- Gather a group of no more than four older toddlers and present them with the table of three-dimensional materials.
- Offer tape to those who want it. Tearing off pieces and sticking one end on the table for the children to pick off works well.
- Expect the children to combine the materials in all kinds of ways.

Limits

- Use phrases like this one to keep children focused on construction: "The tubes are for building."

Other Things to Think About

- It may be easier for each child to have a basket or tub of materials they can trade from.

- Allow children to explore the materials, rather than expecting finished sculptures. Children may or may not be interested in keeping their constructions. Don't assume one or the other.

- The tape may be very attractive to toddlers. Decide ahead of time whether the caregiver or the toddlers will pull the tape off the roll and, if they do it, how much is sufficient.

- Some children will have difficulty getting the tape to actually hold material together. If they seem frustrated or upset about this, describe what you see happening and help them articulate what it is they want to do.

- Give only enough help to get them past an immobilized point.

- Respond to requests for other media; for example, they may ask for markers in conjunction with this experience.

- Colored tape is available in catalogues and adds a dimension of design to the experience.

Supporting Play

Use these strategies, as Jodanna does in the following example, to support children's learning:

- Validate the child's experience; "say what you see"

- Plan to extend the exploration, using the child's interests as a guide

- Offer information; "say what you know"

> *Four thirty- to thirty-five-month-old toddlers are around a table with tubes, tape, and small boxes. Todd asks for red tape as he attaches a strip of holed computer paper inside a small box. "That's clever how you put that together," reflects the caregiver, Jodanna. Aaron inspects a box in one hand and a piece of tube in the other. Jodanna asks, "How can you get those to fit together?" to extend his exploration. Robert and Maile stand together with one piece of heavy cardboard platform between them. Robert holds a tube on its end while Maile tries to tape a strip of paper to it. Jodanna offers information: "When I use both my hands it helps to hold it still. I like how you are working together."*

Colored Glue

Glue colored with paint enhances gluing projects or may be used itself as paint. Toddlers may participate in the process of mixing the color and glue for cause and effect discovery. They can experiment to see what sticks and what doesn't.

What You'll Need

- White, washable "school" glue.
- Paper.
- Liquid water color.
- Bowl for mixing each color separately.
- Brushes for applying glue, one for each color.
- Collage materials for gluing: feathers, tissue, leaves, pom-poms, etc.

What to Do

- Gather collage materials, either in one central basket or bowl or in individual ones.
- Pour about one-quarter cup of glue into each small mixing bowl.
- Add drops of liquid color until desired color is reached.
- Stir with a brush.
- Offer each child a choice of paper to begin with.
- Let each child choose a color of glue and collage materials to glue to the paper.
- Respond to children's attempts to stick things onto the paper, using phrases like these:

  "Where did you want that red piece?"   "Try the glue first."

  "How does it feel?"   "What happened this time?"

Limits

- Offer alternatives for toddlers who are not interested in this experience. (Some will not like the mess.)

- Use phrases like this to help the children control the glue:

    "Glue is for the paper and collage materials, not the walls or floor."

Other Things to Think About

- Mix the colored glue with the children, so they can observe and then help. They can talk about what they see happening to the white glue when adding and stirring the color in.

- Solicit suggestions from the children for what they would like to glue. Be prepared to honor their requests to glue certain items, or offer choices, using phrases like "Shall we go out and pick up leaves to glue or use the feathers today?"

- If the children are interested, let them use the colored glue as paint. This produces a textured painting with jewel-like colors. The thick glue is manipulated differently than paint, and it also dries differently.

- For clean-up, have wet towels ready to wipe sticky hands. Some toddlers will enjoy using clean sponges to wipe the table down for the next group. Some toddlers will like to let the glue dry on their hands and then peel it off.

Supporting Play

How does the following story illustrate the caregiver's use of these strategies to support children's play?

- Provide choices of materials and time to manipulate them

- Plan to extend the exploration, using the child's interests as a guide

- Promote self-awareness

Roberto says to twenty-six-month-old Ruby, "Oh, I see you chose the purple pom-pom." He then asks, "What's next?" Ruby responds, "Rocks." Roberto says, "Rocks? You want to try rocks? We can go outdoors and collect some to try." Twenty-three-month-old Marcus is rubbing his gluey hands together. "Don't you like the sticky on your hands? We can clean it off or you can peel it off after it dries," Roberto tells him. "Let's go outdoors to find some rocks," he says.

Ice Chunks

Toddlers are fascinated by the transformations they witness in chunks of ice frozen in containers of various shapes and sizes.

What You'll Need

- Containers of various sizes and shapes, such as plastic two-liter bottles with their tops cut off, milk cartons of graduated sizes, plastic tubs; use your imagination and any freezable container that will hold water.

- Clean water for freezing.

- Food coloring.

- Tubs, trays, and a plastic tarp to hold the ice if it's being set up indoors.

- Towels, cornstarch for clean-up.

What to Do

- Fill containers and freeze solidly, at least overnight.

- You might use food coloring to color the water before freezing. It makes some effects easier to observe, such as the crystalline structure of ice. Or freeze the water in colored layers.

- Think about freezing leaves, large rocks, flowers, feathers, etc., in the ice. Suspend heavy items by filling half a container, freezing it, setting the item on the ice, filling the container with water, and refreezing.

- Place the ice chunks in different places around the room or outside. You could remove the chunks from the molds or leave them in. Inside, put them in tubs, on trays, or on tarps, on the floor or on tables. Outside, set them on the sand, on a sidewalk, on the dirt, or on the grass, or float them in a water table; put them in the sun or in the shade; cover them or leave them uncovered.

- Allow children to discover and explore the ice.

Limits

- Provide balls to throw as an alternative to throwing ice.

- Provide drinking water as an alternative to eating the ice.

- Use phrases like these to help toddlers play safely with the ice:

    "I can't let you throw the ice. Can you carry it in your hands or roll it?"

    "Not for licking."

    "Not for eating."

Other Things to Think About

- As the ice melts, toddlers, clothes, and toys will get wet; dress or undress children accordingly.

- Provide enough chunks so that toddlers in small groups can have at least one, and toddlers in large groups can practice taking turns.

- This experience can be repeated for days in a row without toddlers ever getting bored.

- Provide other containers in which the children can carry chunks, such as buckets, sacks, trucks, and shopping carts. Round chunks can be rolled.

- Provide children with spray bottles. Let them experiment with the effect on the ice chunk. How is it different with warm water?

- Infants can also experience chunks of ice if they are placed within reach. Indoors, chunks could be placed on trays on the floor.

Supporting Play

Use these strategies, as shown in the story below, to support children's explorations:

- Validate the child's experience; "say what you see"

- Offer information; "say what you know"

> *On a hot day several toddlers go outdoors to the yard. Two-year-old Brooke sees something different and goes to investigate. She asks, "What's this?" Helen, the caregiver, responds, "Can you tell what it is?" Brooke touches it quickly and smiles as she looks at Helen and says, "Ice." Helen asks her, "How does it feel?" "Cold," says Brooke. Helen offers, "It's frozen water." The other toddlers have discovered other ice chunks. Erma carries a bottle of ice. She sits and looks through the plastic at shapes she traces with her finger. Helen offers, "You see crystals of ice, Erma."*

Painting

Introducing toddlers to brush painting expands their awareness of color and line. They experiment with various colors and textures of paint and paper with a variety of brushes. It takes repeated experience with paint and paper to learn the cause and effect of brushing paint on paper and to absorb the feeling of the paper surface through the brush movement.

What You'll Need

- Paper of various sizes and shapes (big enough to accommodate toddlers' large arm movements).

- Brushes.

- Smocks or aprons.

- Tempera paint in small cups; five basic colors to start (about one-quarter cup of each).

- Clean-up materials: Sponges, paper towels, spray bottles.

- A space for drying finished art; horizontal space is best so that the paper is flat and the paint doesn't run or sag.

What to Do

- Gather a small group of toddlers (no more than four) and offer them the opportunity to paint.

- Offer smocks or aprons to protect children's clothes, or take off their shirts if temperature permits

- Offer each child a choice of two sizes or shapes of paper.

- Offer each child a choice of two paint colors (each toddler uses one color and brush at a time).

- Offer each child a paintbrush.

- Watch how the children experiment with the paint, and offer help if they ask for it, using suggestions like these:

    "Dip your brush in the paint, then smooth it on the paper"

    "Tell me when you want a new paper."

- Help the toddlers trade colors when they are ready, and supply new paper when they request it. Let toddlers decide when they are finished; it is part of the process of learning the effect they can make.

Limits

- Use a tarp or newspaper to cover the floor and under easels.

- It's okay not to wear a smock; find a way of making it possible for children to participate even if they choose not to wear one.

- If you need to set limits about where toddlers paint, use phrases like this one:

    "Paint is for the paper. Use your brush to put it on the paper where you want it."

Other Things to Think About

- After toddlers are used to painting, caregivers may offer a variety of paper, brushes, and colors and texture of paint.

- Painting at an easel offers toddlers an additional spatial dimension and use of their large muscles. It is easiest for the toddler if there is a place to set the paint cup and a procedure is established for trading colors.

- Toddlers like to paint side by side.

- For a collaborative painting effort, cover the table or wall or fence with paper.

- Provide alternative experiences for toddlers to participate in either while they warm up to the idea of painting or to go to after they are finished and others continue painting or get cleaned up.

- Toddlers may indicate they are finished by leaving the table; help them clean up and move on, using words like these:

    "Are you finished painting today? Let's wash your hands before you play with anything else in the room."

- Use spray bottles and paper towels for cleaning hands and bodies.

Supporting Play

Use these strategies, as Matt does in the following story, to support children's painting experience:

- Validate child's experience; "say what you see"
- Promote self-awareness
- Provide choices of materials and time to manipulate them.

Caregiver Matt has invited four toddlers to paint. The toddlers' ages range from eighteen months old to thirty months old. August, an eighteen month old, has never painted before. Dawn, Rosi, and Vicki are all seated or standing by the painting table. Two have removed their shirts, and Matt offers Vicki an old T-shirt. He says to Dawn, "Do you want red paint or blue?" "Blue!" she answers and begins immediately to dip and brush the paint. After four minutes, August is still playing with the Legos, but close observations show him watching the painters. Once when he looks up, Matt invites him to the table, showing him where he could sit. After thirty seconds, he comes to sit. Thirty-month-old Rosi says, "You need a smock!" Matt offers one. August refuses it, but allows his sleeves to be rolled up. Choosing the green paint, August smears the wet brush across the paper. He scrubs the brush back and forth. Dipping his brush again results in big drips and a long line. He grins at Matt, who says, "You made green lines and drops on the paper. Do you want another color?" "No, no," says August. "Oh, you really like green. August, you are painting, painting." "Pantg," August says.

Implement Painting

Painting with various implements sparks toddlers' curiosity and leads to experimenting with cause and effect.

What You'll Need

- A variety of implements to paint with: feather dusters, plastic pizza cutters, rubber band brushes, toothbrushes, combs, sponges of different shapes, whisks, potato mashers, cookie cutters, and so forth. The possibilities are limited only by your imagination.

- Paper to paint on.

- Tempera paint. You may need to mix it thicker than usual to cling to some implements.

- Flat containers for paint, large enough to accommodate implements (meat trays or plastic plates work well), one for each color.

- Smocks or paint shirts to protect clothing.

What to Do

- Gather a small group of toddlers (no more than four). As you put on smocks and/or remove clothes, explain that "instead of brushes, today we're going to use something different to put the paint on the paper."

- Offer a choice of paint colors, a single implement, and one tray of paint to each child.

- When toddlers want to trade colors of paint and implements, help them by facilitating their conversations by saying something like "Ray would like to trade for the pizza cutter when you are finished using it."

- Reflect children's experience: "say what you see" and compare what they're doing to painting with a brush.

Limits

- Help children keep the paint where it belongs, using phrases like "Paint goes on the paper."

Other Things to Think About

- Caregivers should be prepared for some toddlers to enjoy this experience and some not to "get it" right away. Encourage the children to "try it when you're ready" and offer alternatives.

- Younger toddlers or first-time painters may use the implement as a brush, with the same back-and-forth motion. It's okay to allow the children to use their own approaches.

- Try making gentle suggestions such as "Try it softly" or "Try it slowly" or ask, "Now what does it look like?"

- Older or more experienced toddlers might be able to use two different implements at the same time so they can compare the lines they make, how they feel in the hand, what the shapes they make look like.

Supporting Play

Use these strategies, as described in the scene below, to support children's painting:

- Provide choices of materials

- Validate the child's experience; "say what you see"

- Offer information; "say what you know"

Marianne, the caregiver, has four trays of paint colors at the art table. Two trays also hold toothbrushes, and two hold sponges of various shapes. Other implements are available on the shelf. Four toddlers, twenty-one months to thirty-three months old, sit around the table. Angie dots the paper with the toothbrush, then swipes it up and down. "I see you made marks on the paper with your brush," Marianne comments. "Is it heavier or lighter than the regular brushes?" Bruce is dabbing paint onto his paper with a sponge. He turns to the shelf, points, and asks Marianne for the pizza cutter. Marianne says, "I know we usually use this to cut playdough, but I thought it'd be fun to try it in the paint. See what you think." After several back-and-forth manipulations, Bruce pushes the roller wheel through the paint, then onto the paper.

Paper with Holes

Providing a toddler with paper that has a hole deliberately cut out of it is intriguing and sets up a patterned space for the toddler to explore with paint, markers, or other media.

What You'll Need

- Paint, markers, or other media, such as stickers, for applying to paper.

- Paper with holes cut out. Begin with one fairly large hole per piece of paper. Holes may be randomly shaped. Use various colors of paper for toddlers to choose.

- Neutral paper for backing the holes.

- Tape or glue.

What to Do

- Prepare several colors of paint and paper with cut-out holes ahead of time.

- Since "paint goes on the paper," mount the paper with holes onto a neutral background piece.

- Gather a small group of toddlers (no more than four) who would like to paint. As you put on smocks or remove clothing, tell them you have some "new" paper to try.

- Offer each child two different pieces of "new" paper to choose from.

- Have the children sit at a table or stand at an easel to paint the paper. They might also want to color the paper with markers.

Limits

- Help the children keep the paint where it belongs by using this phrase: "Paint is for the paper."

Other Things to Think About

- Have spray bottles and towels on hand to clean up children's hands as they finish painting.

- This is an interesting experience to offer on a monthly basis. Pay attention to the difference between children's approaches to the hole in the paper and how each child changes over time.

- The shapes you cut may be varied. Remember that the focus is on offering a different painting experience, not on learning shapes. Random shapes spark the child's imagination.

Supporting Play

In the following scene, how does Keela use these strategies to support the children's learning?

- Provide choices of materials and time to manipulate them

- Plan to extend the exploration, using the child's interests as a guide

- Offer information; "say what you know"

Cathy, eighteen months old, brushes over her paper, seemingly oblivious to the off-center oval hole. Twenty-two-month-old Allen dots paint all around the edge of the hole in his paper. "What's this?" he asks. Keela, the caregiver, responds, "What do you think?" He says, "Hole." "We all have holes in our papers today," Keela offers. Thirty-one-month-old Samantha carefully pushes and pulls her brush around the hole. "I need some blue now," she says. "Oh, blue," Keela says, giving her the blue paint she asked for. Samantha makes a second line around the hole in her paper. Cathy, discovering the hole, is trying to rip the paper. "Are you all finished painting or would you like a new paper, Cathy?" Keela asks. Cathy stands up. Not wanting to rush the others, Keela provides Cathy with alternative toys after she gets cleaned up.

Ooblick

A mixture of cornstarch and water provides a gooey and messy sensory experience for toddlers to explore with their fingers, hands, and body. This is an opportunity for toddlers to discover the properties of liquid, powder, and suspension: how they are different and/or the same as the more familiar water, sand, and dirt. This experience can be offered indoors or outdoors.

What You'll Need

- Cornstarch: three to four boxes for a group of fifteen toddlers.
- Water.
- Tubs for mixing: one large (18 by 24 inches) for three to four toddlers, or individual dishpan tubs.
- Floor covering (a plastic tarp or towels) for indoor play.

What to Do

- Have all materials ready ahead of time.
- Set up the tubs on a table or on the floor. Each toddler can have a tub of his own, or a large tub may be used for a group.
- Start with half a cup of cornstarch in an individual tub (use more in a large tub) and gradually add water. You want a mixture the thickness of pancake or muffin batter.
- Toddlers could also mix their own from premeasured cups or bowls. Again, give them a small amount of cornstarch to begin with and let them add water slowly. A small squirt bottle works well to control the amount of water they can use. Toddlers who have experience with ooblick can experiment with the mix if you provide small amounts of water and cornstarch to add.
- Get your hands into it to feel the odd quality of this mixture! The cornstarch doesn't dissolve like sugar in water but is suspended. It feels like liquid and solid at the same time.

Limits

- Ooblick is nontoxic, so a curious taste won't hurt. Phrases such as "Not for your mouth" and "Feel it with your fingers and hands" are useful to keep children focused on the sensation of the ooblick.

- Expect the ooblick to drip everywhere. Use phrases like "Try to keep it in the tub." Outdoors, where the cornstarch will quickly disappear into the ground, the concern is mostly about conserving the cornstarch.

Other Things to Think About

- For spontaneous fun outdoors, keep a box of cornstarch and a tub handy to mix with water.

- An outdoor setting frees this messy, fun experience for unlimited manipulation. Don't worry about it mixing with sand and dirt; it's bound to happen. Just describe what you see and let the children experiment.

- Removing shoes and shirts makes the children more comfortable and keeps you from having to brush them off afterwards.

- Add color to the mix. Washable tempera will not stain.

- Clean-up is easy because dry cornstarch quickly brushes off children and clothes and is easily swept up. *Don't* put ooblick down the drain, however—it will clog drains because the cornstarch doesn't dissolve. Let it air dry and then throw it away or save it to use another day.

Supporting Play

Use these strategies, as Pamela does in the following scene, to support children's learning:

- Validate the child's experience; "say what you see"

- Offer information; "say what you know"

- Promote self-awareness

Thirty-month-old Paul stirs the cornstarch into the water, then pats the mixture with his palm. He squeezes a handful through his fingers. Pamela, the caregiver, responds, "You squeezed it, Paul. What does it feel like?" Paul makes a face with a smile and says, "Ooooo, gooey." Nineteen-month-old Robin puts her fingers to her mouth. Pamela says, "Please just feel it with your fingers; it's not for your mouth. Can you feel it slide off your skin?" Twenty-eight-month-old Armando asks, "What is it?" as he moves his index finger through the ooblick. Pamela offers, "It's half liquid and half solid. It's called ooblick—what do you think about it?" Armando says, "It's funny."

Watercolors

Toddlers enjoy watercolors. They enjoy the individual colors and the variety of small brushes. They explore the process of putting the paint on paper, which leads them to mixing color and investigating how different kinds of paper work with the paint.

What You'll Need

- Trays of washable watercolors.
- A variety of small brushes.
- Spray bottles of water.
- Containers of clean water.
- Small containers of water for older toddlers to use.
- Paper in a variety of sizes, colors, textures.
- Old T-shirts or paint smocks to protect clothing.

What to Do

- Have all materials ready ahead of time.
- Let the children each choose a paint smock or remove their shirts.
- Let the children each choose between two pieces of paper.
- Spray the trays of watercolors with water, wet the brushes, and hand out a tray and brush to each child.
- Children may sit or stand at the table to paint.
- Encourage the toddlers to ask for new paper when they are ready.
- Clean brushes and re-spray the watercolor trays whenever new paper is requested or when toddlers ask you to.
- Some older toddlers may be able to use their own small container of water in the traditional manner.

Limits

- Toddlers may sit or stand but must stay at the table with the paint and the brush.

- Tell children that "Paint goes on the paper" rather than on their bodies or the furniture.

- Ask toddlers to respect others by "painting on your own paper." However, if two toddlers agree, they may paint together.

- Toddlers may trade trays or brushes if they both want to. Caregivers can help facilitate a trade by interpreting for the toddlers, using phrases like "Joanne would like to trade trays with you" or "Hal says he doesn't want to trade right now."

- Spraying trays and rinsing brushes are caregiver jobs.

Other Things to Think About

- It is helpful to keep the group small (four at most) and to include a mix of older and younger toddlers.

- Tape the back of the paper to the table for the youngest toddlers, so it doesn't scoot around too much.

- Have drying space for finished work. Watercolors dry quickly, but you may need yards of counter top, depending on the size of paper you're using.

- Provide other experiences for toddlers when they are finished.

- Toddlers new to this experience may not wish to wear a smock or may want to watch for a while. Let them paint without a smock if they wish.

- Good quality paint that will maintain its color when dry honors the children's efforts.

- Offer crayons to color the paper first. When toddlers paint over it, the crayon "resists" the watercolor and shows through.

- An old shower curtain or plastic tablecloth can cover the floor, if necessary.

- Plan to spend time with the youngest toddlers as they learn to manipulate the brush on the solid paint. Allow them to explore freely and don't be too concerned about the colors getting mixed.

Supporting Play

Use the following strategies to support children's play during watercolor painting:

- Provide choices of materials and time to manipulate them
- Validate the child's experience; "say what you see"

> *As twenty-month-old Thomas paints deliberately, his caregiver, Susan, says to him, "I see you're moving the brush slowly. You're working very hard. You made a blue line on the paper." When seventeen-month-old Stella looks frustrated and starts stabbing her brush into the paper, Susan asks, "Is it working the way you want? Try to brush more softly." Twenty-three-month-old Athena wants to trade trays with Thomas, but he shakes his head, and Susan says, "Athena, I know it's hard to wait. You can tell Thomas you want to trade paint trays." She looks at Athena's paper and comments, "You made fat marks and skinny marks. There are lots of colors."*

Encouraging Connections

Young children learn through their connections with the people around them. The connections between parent and child, family and child care center or provider, child and caregiver, and child and other children form a secure web of belonging for infants' and toddlers' explorations of the world. They also form the *content* of what infants and toddlers are learning. Connections are crucial to young children's healthy development.

By empowering even the youngest children with strategies they can use in social interactions, caregivers can help infants and toddlers make solid connections with one another, their caregivers, and the environment. At the same time, children are learning what the world is like from the efforts that adults make to build on those connections.

We know how important it is for infants to attach to people who meet their needs consistently in order to build trust. Parents provide the first experience of attachment for infants, and caregivers support and build on this relationship to extend children's ability to connect. As Erikson points out, it is this security built on trust that supports children's autonomous exploration of the environment, an exploration that they use to figure out how the world works.

The importance of emotional connections cannot be exaggerated in light of the conclusions drawn from research into brain development. We know that stressful situations cause damaging hormones to be released into the child's brain. We also know that the brain is tuned to learn from the emotional context of everything that happens to a baby. Because of this research, caregivers who hear infants crying in distress now know how important it is to promptly relieve their stress and therefore to turn off the hormones which can damage their neural connections. Caregivers also now know that when an infant communicates with a cry or gesture and the caregiver responds with a consoling, comforting touch, nourishment, and/or words, the infant is learning to trust that her communication has meaning to others and that adults will help to relieve her distress. When caregivers act on this knowledge, trustful connections with caring adults grow brain connections in infants and toddlers.

It All Starts with Physical Connection

Think about the womb, where the infant lived for nine months enveloped by a small space of warm liquid. An adult's cradling arms are the first position for the infant outside this comfortable place, so the parent or caregiver's body provides a new safe and secure place for the infant. From there the infant experiences the newness of her body—arms flailing in the air, skin feeling the temperature, a soft cotton shirt or carpeted floor, the billow of a soft pillow, the warmth of a caregiver's body—by beginning to squirm and experience motion.

As infants get older and bigger, they will experience more time away from this bodily connection. They begin to connect with the outside world in small increments of space and time. In a secure bundled warm space of swaddled blankets or a cocoonlike area of soft pillows, they can experience a womb-sized place—just for a few minutes at first, and then for longer as they take in the sounds and sights and feelings of the surrounding environment.

With more space comes more movement. To further develop trust with a crawling infant, a caregiver can be available like an "island" at floor level. This allows the mobile infant to crawl away from the caregiver as she feels comfortable and return to the "island" to touch base as needed. The caregiver becomes a comforting point of connection and reconnection that an infant can rely upon.

Toddlers' new ability to walk brings ample opportunities to connect with the world. Caregivers can honor a toddler's drive for inde-pendence by providing opportunities to make choices and express feelings. Making choices is another way for toddlers to learn that their communications have meaning and that adults will pay attention to them. This allows toddlers to continue to develop trusting relationships with caregivers. From a strong sense of self, the toddler reaches out to peers and adults. Toddlers find friends, just as adults do, through interactions based on mutual interests. The role of caregivers is to facilitate these interactions.

Connections in Child Care

The social arena of a child care program is a natural setting for developing relationships among children and adults. The more information children learn about one another, the more opportunity they have for interdependence. Even the youngest children are able to recognize mutual needs, interests, goals, and various ways of achieving them together. For example, consider the connections between children occurring in this scene:

Nicole and Garrett are both nine months old and have been at the center together for four months. Nicole is a smiley child, usually flashing her dimples at everyone. But today she is tired and hungry and has become loudly upset. Garrett reacts strongly after a minute of her yelling. He stops cold what he is doing and looks at the caregiver, Terry. It is clear that on some level he expects Terry to take care of Nicole. Terry says to Garrett, "You hear Nicole crying, don't you, Garrett? She's probably hungry, and I can feed her now."

Infants and toddlers have an innate empathetic desire to care for one another, which deepens their connections. Garrett looks to Terry for a response to Nicole's crying. He is clearly concerned about her distress and wants Terry to help her. By responding to his concern, Terry is facilitating early interdependence.

Meeting Individual Needs

When caregivers observe individual children closely, they can learn and honor each child's response to given social situations. For example, when caregivers set up a play environment for infants, they must be aware of the sensitivity levels of the infants in their care at the time. Very sensitive infants could be overwhelmed by an environment others find inviting. An experience loaded with color, sound, and light could stress an infant to the point where making connections becomes difficult.

In the same way, caregivers can respectfully honor a child's request for a favored caregiver so that the child's feeling of connection is affirmed. Consider the following scene:

Lunch is drawing to a close, and three caregivers are helping twelve toddlers get ready for nap. Thirty-month-old Malika tells caregiver Vicky, "I want Anna to change my diaper." Vicky says, "Thanks for telling me. Can you find Anna?" Malika looks around, spies Anna, and runs towards her. Vicky facilitates, getting Anna's attention: "Malika has a request for you, Anna." Malika says to Anna, "You change my diaper." Anna responds, "I'll be happy to after I finish helping Poulin take off her shoes."

By honoring Malika's request for Anna to change her diaper, Vicky honors the connection Malika feels with Anna and further develops her trust in both Anna and Vicky.

Trust can also be developed when children communicate a need to connect longer with a play situation. Even when they have been told a transition is coming, toddlers may need more time. Through observation, caregivers learn which children respond slowly to a situation and simply need more time to complete the transition. Caregivers can honor this need by starting the transition sooner. In this way confrontations are avoided and children's connection to what they are doing, as well as to the caregiver, is reinforced through respect. Caregivers can understand the individualizing of responses as helping all young children make their own way in the world; not as treating some children as "special."

The Relationship between Conflict and Connection

Conflict is natural and occurs at all ages and stages of development throughout life! There will never be a time without conflict. When caregivers recognize that conflict and connection occur simultaneously, many possibilities for resolving conflict open up. Caregivers can even begin to appreciate the opportunity conflict brings for *expanding* connection. In order to capitalize on these opportunities, though, it's essential for caregivers to get in touch with their own feelings about conflict, so they can consistently handle conflict with children in ways that promote connection.

Young children literally bump into each other in pursuit of experiences, objects, caregivers, and peers. As infants and toddlers connect with each other, conflict is inevitable and can actually be a starting point for continued connection. The task for the child is learning to resolve conflict when it occurs in order to find the point of connection with the other person involved. The task for caregivers is to accept conflict as a part of life by getting in touch with their personal feelings regarding conflict. Do they experience conflict between children as good or bad? Do they experience one child as the virtuous one and one as the one who misbehaves? Do they just want conflict to go away? Do they believe that young children can learn conflict resolution skills? When caregivers can see conflict as an opportunity for children to build connection, they are more able to help children resolve the conflict in ways that deepen their connections.

Strategies Caregivers Use to Support Connections

We have found the following seven strategies to be helpful in supporting children's ability to connect with themselves, with one another, with caregivers, and with their environment.

- Introduce peers and adults by name
- Include family culture
- Be predictable and consistent in meeting children's needs
- Slow the pace; be an "island"
- Affirm mutual interests to encourage interdependence
- Be aware of one's own inner conflict
- Help children learn to resolve conflicts

Introducing Peers and Adults by Name

Imagine a caregiver saying this to a child coming in for the first time with her parent: "Hi, I'm Maryann, and I'll be your caregiver today." It's a joke, but the connection a "server" attempts to make in a restaurant shows how significant names are in personalizing people's connections with one another. Building relationships and making connections with other people begin early in life as infants begin to recognize and respond with a turn of the head to their given name. Having a name is one way of individualizing a person's identity and separates people from one another. Instead of calling someone with a disrespectful "hey you," people learn each other's names.

When a child begins attending a child care program, he is essentially put among a group of strangers, even though he may have visited previously. Imagine, if you will, being in that situation and not knowing anyone's name. To begin to create connections for young children, caregivers can respectfully introduce children and adults by name as they enter the group care setting and first interact with one another. This strategy acknowledges that even when a child is not yet using language, connections can begin with eye contact, facial expressions, or parallel play. When a caregiver respectfully introduces children who do not yet know each other, connection is supported. Children of this age are drawn to other young children and will find each other based on mutual play interests, but it's easier when the caregiver takes the first step.

In an infant/toddler program there is a mix of different ages and stages of development, from nonmobile infants to toddlers. Whether children are separated by age or mixed together in family-age grouping, they must eventually transition from one area of development to the next during these transitional times, as well as when a child is first enrolled. Children's connections with one another are deepened when children are introduced by name.

It's also important for caregivers to introduce themselves and other adults who enter the program. Often, when caregivers first meet a young child, they ask, "What's your name?" Caregivers can also introduce themselves to a young child, with a phrase like "Hi. My name is

Philomena." Relationships begin when people learn something about a new acquaintance, and names can be that beginning.

Soon after the beginning of expressive language, young children realize that *everything* has a name and begin using a word or phrase like "what it? wast? ist? dat?" to elicit the names of objects from attentive caregivers. Toddlers extend this interest from objects to peers and adults as they move from labeling "baby" to asking "who?" or from "Katie's mommy" to "Pat." It is important that caregivers plan for ways to reinforce this development of communication in order to build these relationships. As children first experience one another, caregivers can provide the personal identity of a name for each so that the first step towards a social relationship is taken. This is a process of inclusion, which develops over time into interdependence.

Notice how Cathy uses introductions to help the children acknowledge each other in the following scene:

Eleven-month-old Melissa is visiting outdoors from the infant room. She is crawling with great agility and beginning to pull up and cruise. She crawls over to a push cart, pulls up, and begins to push it. Her cart bumps into two-year-old Cedric. Nearby, the caregiver Cathy says, "Oh, Cedric, have you met Melissa yet? She's visiting from the infant room. Melissa, this is Cedric." Cedric says, "Baby." Cathy responds, "Yes, that's Melissa from the baby room." Cedric smiles and says, "Missa." Melissa pushes her cart on, but she turns her head when Cedric says her name.

The caregiver, Cathy, provides information for Cedric about the visiting baby, including her name, which Cedric repeats quite naturally. Melissa hears her name several times and shows that she feels a connection with both the caregiver and a new acquaintance, Cedric, when she turns her head to respond to her name.

Including Family Culture

Connection with families begins during the first phone call parents make inquiring about child care. Many centers have a procedure for this initial contact. At ITC, caregivers answer the phone identifying themselves by name as well as the center name. Parents are invited to visit the center. During this tour they can observe caregiving interactions, have questions answered, pick up written information about the program—philosophy statement, schedule, fees—and get on the waiting list if they wish. Part of their decision to seek enrollment is based on finding a good match between their attitude and priorities and those of the center. We believe that extending the philosophy of respect to families is basic to building relationships within the center community.

When a child is actually enrolled, most centers ask parents to complete a packet of information forms, some of which may be required by licensing regulations. These forms can go beyond standard paperwork, however, to reflect the center's intention to be inclusive and respectful. For example, one form used at ITC, called "Parent Information About Their Child," asks parents for their names and addresses. Instead of a place for "mother's name" and "father's name," the form asks for "parent" or "guardian" names so all families are respectfully acknowledged and welcomed. In addition, parents are asked to write down as much information as possible; "no detail is too small" is the phrase used. We ask for information about children's schedules, habits, siblings, favorite toys, pets in the household, and anything else parents think is significant. Such specific information reveals a family's individual culture.

Another form in the enrollment packet invites parents to share any special family cultural customs with the center community. The special connections that children have with their families can be extended to the other children and families of the center. Following are examples of family cultures that have been shared at ITC:

- A celebration of the Chinese New Year: a family provided a snack of pork buns (and made some pork-free, so all the children could participate!) and a gift of red envelopes beautifully designed with tigers to represent the Year of the Tiger.
- The Israeli birthday custom of sitting the crowned child in a chair and lifting her, once for each year of her age, while singing the Hebrew "Happy Birthday" song.
- The Korean custom of using a cut and scooped-out gourd for serving food, which also symbolizes good luck. The gourd hangs in one of the indoor rooms for the children to see and ask about.

Birthdays of family members are another way for the child to connect her own center experience with her family culture. Another enrollment form requests the month and day of relatives' birthdays. Even the youngest infant can participate by making a birthday card for family members. The birthdays are recorded on a calendar in the art room, and caregivers follow through in a timely manner to have the child make a card. Toddlers are delighted to connect their art experience at the center with their family birthday celebrations. Be aware that celebrating birthdays is largely a Western custom and that some families (Jehovah's Witness families, for example) do not celebrate birthdays. Other occasions can be acknowledged in the same way by, for example, making a get well card for a family member who's ill or a card for a new sibling, a visit from grandma, or any other special family event.

An established connection between caregivers and parents opens up more avenues of resolution when conflict does occur. Any cultural differences that may cause conflict to arise are more easily discussed when an open relationship between center and families is already established. For example, here are three cultural conflicts we have experienced and their eventual resolution:

- Charlotte's parents do not want her to go barefoot and ask the staff to exclude her from water play. A caregiver suggests that Charlotte wear water shoes, which is acceptable to her parents and is easily accommodated by the center.
- Elijah keeps getting sand in his hair, and his parents ask the caregivers to keep Elijah out of the large sand area. His mother explains to the staff how much more difficult it is to get sand out of Elijah's kinky hair than straight hair. A teacher suggests that Elijah wear a hat instead of being kept out of sand play. It is an acceptable solution for everyone. In the summertime, Elijah sports a shaved head to match his father's.
- A specific floor area of the center is repeatedly not being cleaned well enough by the evening custodian, José. A note written in Spanish by a Latina caregiver solves the communication problem easily.

Building relationships in a child care community begins with an interest in everyone's cultures and ways of living. It's respectful to acknowledge differences with openness and inclusion. Caregivers can model this social relationship with families so that children of all ages can begin to connect with the wide variety of cultures that exist in the world. When caregivers made an effort to make Sachiko comfortable by including rice at each meal, not only was she able to relax and be curious, but a strong connection of trust developed between her family and the center.

The materials that are chosen for a center or family day care home also reflect the caregiver's attitude toward inclusion. Books that explore human needs such as clothing (Ann Morris's *Hats Hats Hats* or *Shoes Shoes Shoes*), eating (Ann Morris's *Bread Bread Bread* or Norah Dooley's *Everybody Bakes Bread* or *Everybody Cooks Rice*), and living in a shelter (Ann Morris's *Houses and Homes*) point out a variety of ways of meeting needs all people have in common. We approach these differences in culture not as "we do it this way, and they do it that way" but as "we all need hats; we'd wear this hat if we needed to keep warm and that one to keep the sun off." After being sure that all the children and adults in the center community can see themselves reflected in the materials you choose every day, it's good to expand awareness further. For example, books like *Mama Zooms* (about a child whose mother uses a wheelchair) or *Where's Chimpy?* (about a child with Down's syndrome) show people and families in contexts young children may not have direct experience with. Teachers can help children make connections by pointing out the similarities between themselves and the people in the books, people who at first glance may seem completely different.

Being Predictable and Consistent in Meeting Children's Needs

Children's ability to form a strong connection with a caregiver is what gives them the emotional foundation to form connections in the future. Caregivers foster this ability when they are predictable and consistent in the way they respond to children, which allows children to relax in the comfort of familiarity.

In order to be predictable and consistent, caregivers need information. Chapter 2 talks about anticipation as a comprehensive strategy to help children prepare for changes in routine. Here we discuss having the *information* to anticipate a child's needs, in order to be able to meet those needs quickly and calmly. This kind of anticipation enables caregivers to be *responsive* to the child rather than *reactive* to the situation. When caregivers are familiar with the rhythms and patterns of individual children, they can plan for needs ahead of time, rather than react to infants' distress, and avoid the crisis of several infants needing one-on-one care all at the same time.

Upon enrollment, parents can provide caregivers with their child's feeding and napping patterns. From these individual schedules, and from the charts they keep every day, caregivers can plan when to feed the infant or when the infant will need to sleep. When the caregiver knows that feeding or sleeping time is coming, she can be ready to meet the infant's need. She can respond in a caring, calm manner to the child's communicative cry, saying "It's about time to have some food. I have it all ready for you." The caregiver is teaching trust, as well as making her own job easier. By responding calmly, the caregiver is also providing a relaxed experience so that the child's brain may continue to grow, with less stress.

In order to anticipate needs and be dependable, however, caregivers need information. These stories show the importance of daily charting in helping caregivers to be predictable and dependable in meeting infants' needs.

It's noon and Maryann is arriving for her shift in the infant room. After she is greeted by the morning infant person, Maryann reads the infant charts and the bulletin board. She remarks, "I see Jasper woke up at ten this morning. According to last week's pattern, he should be ready to go back to sleep pretty soon."

Katya, the morning infant person, says, "I was just going to write up what he ate for lunch and, yes, he is ready to take another nap. His bottle is all ready to warm up." After Maryann reads about and gathers additional information from Katya about the other infants, she approaches Jasper, calmly saying, "I can tell you're tired, Jasper. Here's your bottle so I can rock you to sleep."

Note how Maryann reads the information available to her *before* she "jumps into" caring for the infants. The information allows her to be *responsive* to Jasper's sleep need rather than waiting for Jasper to get upset and then *reacting* with the question "Why are you crying, Jasper?"

Caregivers build a secure and connected relationship with parents, too, by asking for and using the information they supply to best care for their child. A bulletin board called the "Flash" serves this purpose at ITC, but any central location for daily written information works well as a place for parents to write messages so caregivers know about individual needs.

It's 7:30 a.m., and Pat is arriving for work. After greeting the other caregiver, Pat reads the Flash. She learns that Neil went home with a fever yesterday afternoon and that Meli will be picked up early today. Later that morning, when Neil's mom calls, Pat has an informed conversation with her about Neil's eventual return to the center after a visit to his doctor. And Pat and the other staff who have read the Flash have Meli all ready to go when her dad comes to pick her up early.

A child's feeling of security is partially dependent on the relationship of trust caregivers have with the parents. We can build security for parents when we ask for and use all relevant information. One of the worst positions caregivers can put themselves in is to respond to a parent, "I don't know." Hearing this from a caregiver certainly makes parents feel less secure! If caregivers don't know something, they can make every attempt to find out. Saying "I don't know" when that's the truth is fine, but it's important to add "but let me ask so-and-so" or "but let me find out for you."

As toddlers work on the emotional task of autonomy, caregiver consistency supports their development. Ongoing inconsistency can lead toddlers to doubt that they will ever be able to control themselves or their world. Consider the following two approaches to a familiar scene:

Caregiver: *"Let's get your shoes on so you can play outside."*
Toddler: *"No, no, no. Outside now."*
Caregiver: *"We need to put your shoes on first, then we'll go out."*
Toddler: *"Out now,"* with accompanying writhing and running away.
Caregiver: *"Oh, okay, everyone else is ready anyway."*

Does that sound familiar? What would it be like if the scene played out this way?

Caregiver: *"In two minutes we'll get ready to go outside. You need to have your shoes on today; it's cold out."*
Toddler: *"No shoes."*

Caregiver: "I'll help you put your shoes on now or in two minutes."
(Two minutes later.)
Caregiver: "Here are your shoes; shall we sit on the floor or on the couch to put them on?"
Toddler: "No shoes."
Caregiver: "I know you'd rather not wear your shoes, but we need them on outside."
Toddler: "Outside."
Caregiver: "Yes, we can go out." (Pause.) "Let's get your shoes on and go out."
Toddler: "Outside," as she crawls into the caregiver's lap.

Notice how the caregiver in the second scene anticipates the transition (*"In two minutes it will be time to go outside"*), gives the child information about why shoes are necessary (*"It's cold out"*), offers several choices (*"Now or in two minutes"*; *"Would you like to sit on the floor or on the couch?"*), and acknowledges the child's feelings (*"I know you'd rather not wear your shoes"*).

If the first scene is replayed daily, what do you think will happen when it's raining out and shoes really do have to be worn in order to go outdoors? What about the second scene? What does the caregiver's response tell the toddler

about the effect of his actions? The second interaction takes a little longer, but the caregiver is using a consistent approach that gives the child choices within a dependable framework.

Slowing the Pace; Being an "Island"

Slowing down caregivers' pace of movement near young children creates time for the caregivers to build and strengthen connections with each infant and toddler. To say that slowing down creates time may not make sense at first hearing, but it's true nonetheless. Slowing down does make space for interaction between caregivers and children. Moving slowly to observe what is happening now, in the moment, allows caregivers to pause to respond to children's overtures. Being available in this way builds trust with individual children. It makes the whole day go more smoothly.

One way of slowing down is for the caregiver to sit at the child's level like an island, observing and responding to the movements and interactions of the children around her.

The caregiver, Craig, sits on the floor among three infants: two actively crawling and one nonmobile. As Craig makes contact by gentle touches with four-month-old Amanda, seven-month-old Charles crawls up to touch Craig's knee and squirm into his lap. Craig says to Charles, "I saw you push that noisy ball, then clap your hands." Charles claps his hands and crawls off Craig's lap. Ten-month-old Rohan approaches Craig, pulls to a stand, and pats Craig's back, then lets down and crawls off toward his buddy Charles. Craig says, "Hello to you too, Rohan," as he crawls off.

Craig's availability allows the infants to approach him when they want to. The infants can have a short "conversation" with Craig and then crawl away when they are ready. The caregiver's presence attending to them, instead of doing chores or moving about the room at adult level, is reassuring and refreshing to the infants.

Moreover, a caregiver available to toddlers as an island presents an opportunity for them to further develop their self-concept and autonomy. The freedom to move and follow their own interests allows toddlers to approach or move away from a caregiver at will, rather than being scooped up and carried around at the whim of the caregiver. This strategy also makes caregivers available to respond in specialized cases of need. Consider the contrast between the following scenes:

Fifteen-month-old Felicia has just fallen down and is crying. The caregiver, Jeanne, sits next to Felicia and says, "I saw you fall down, Felicia. I can tell that hurt. How can I help?" As Jeanne holds her arms open, Felicia crawls into her lap and sits there for about a minute. Felicia then gets out of Jeanne's lap and runs off to continue playing.

Because Jeanne was being an "island," she saw what happened and was able to comfort Felicia calmly, at her level. What would happen if Jeanne stayed at adult level instead of being at child level?

From across the yard, Jeanne sees Felicia crying. She sweeps Felicia up to her hip and carries her around the yard. Felicia quiets, but shows no inclination to get down and play again. Then, Jeanne hears another child cry and puts Felicia down abruptly to attend to the new situation. Felicia begins to cry again. Jeanne rushes back to Felicia holding another crying child.

In the first scene, Jeanne makes herself available to Felicia by sitting or stooping or squatting next to her. Jeanne acknowledges Felicia's feelings of being hurt and simultaneously offers help verbally and opens her arms to her. Jeanne also uses this time to visually assess the level of Felicia's injury: Is there any blood? Can she move her arms and legs normally? This is necessary because Felicia can't actually *say* what's wrong. Jeanne is also giving Felicia time to learn to assess her own concept of being hurt. Jeanne's calm response relieves some of the stress for

Felicia, as falling down for young children is usually more emotionally scary than actually physically harmful. Imagine, if you will, your response to seeing an adult fall down. Would you rush over and pick the adult up? Or would you kneel down and offer help? The same calm, respectful assistance benefits young children too.

In the second scene, in which Jeanne scoops her up, Felicia's distress is exacerbated. Being scooped up when she's just fallen is disorienting and confusing to Felicia, and Jeanne doesn't offer her words to describe what she's feeling. Jeanne hasn't seen what happened, so it's harder for her to connect with Felicia about it. Jeanne's motion, carrying Felicia about the yard while she tends to other children, is not comforting to Felicia—Jeanne's attention is not fully with Felicia, and Felicia knows it. Jeanne is also distracted by another crying child, breaking the connection with Felicia. Three people are quite upset at this point—Felicia, the other child, and Jeanne.

When two toddlers are in distress simultaneously, caregivers can support one another. It works well for one caregiver to be an island while another goes to assist the child in need. This teamwork, the connection among caregivers, supports individual staff as they build connection with toddlers, developing security. When caregivers are available to them, young children have opportunities to develop autonomy by making choices of their own. A toddler who needs support can come to the caregiver or allow the caregiver to approach. Then the child can decide when her need has been met by moving away from the caregiver "island." A toddler's developing autonomy flows from this sense of trust. Rather than threatening connection, autonomy thrives on it.

Being available works particularly well as a strategy to help toddlers connect with adults in other ways than through touch. The first connections with infants are made through physical touch, and touch is essential when building trust by meeting infants' needs.

Toddlers are in a different stage of development, however. When caregivers automatically pick up and carry around a toddler who is reaching for connection, it undermines the trust the caregiver established with the toddler as an infant and disrupts the development of autonomy. Being available and allowing toddlers to make the physical connection, as Jeanne does in the first scene when she opens her arms to Felicia without picking her up, gives them the message that it is safe to venture out from the "island" caregiver and that they are capable of making the decision about when and how and how much to seek help.

Affirming Mutual Interests to Encourage Interdependence

Very young children establish connections and budding relationships when playing with a favorite toy. Two infants, for example, will often play the interdependent game of trading a toy back and forth. They are demonstrating that they can have more fun together than if they played separately. They are developing a social relationship. Observe the following scene:

Eight-and-a-half-month-old Adam and nine-month-old Antoine are crawling and romping among the pillows in the infant room. Antoine grabs up a squeaky duck as he crawls down off a pillow and takes two more crawl-steps before he drops it to his right and keeps on crawling. Adam follows Antoine and

picks up the duck. He pulls to a sitting position and claps the duck between his hands. It squeaks, and Adam laughs. Antoine stops crawling and reverses direction to head back to Adam. Adam extends the duck towards Antoine. Antoine takes it, claps it to make it squeak, and holds it for Adam to grab. Adam crawls back onto the pillows with the duck, and Antoine follows quickly, with his eyes on the duck and a smile on his face.

The spontaneous game of connection is the beginning of interdependence between Adam and Antoine. Caregivers can recognize such connections as the infant's first step in the process of developing social relationships. The caregiver, Judy, can affirm the relationship by saying "Look how much fun you two are having trading that duck back and forth."

Toddlers often experience another child's approach when they are holding or manipulating a favored object. Observant caregivers can see these interactions as beginning with a mutual interest, rather than a conflict. Caregivers can facilitate the interaction by helping the toddlers move towards playing together, rather than separating them based on a perceived conflict of possession. Consider how this view influences the following interaction:

Twenty-seven-month-old Brodie is dragging a large hoop, watching the pattern it makes through the sand. Twenty-nine-month-old Cory approaches and grabs Brodie's hoop. Brodie pulls it back and says, "Mine." Nearby, caregiver Jason says, "Cory, I can tell you want to play with a hoop too. There are several; can you find another one? Perhaps you and Brodie can play together with your hoops." Cory looks around and sees an available green hoop, scampers to get it, and runs back to Brodie. They hold their hoops high, laugh, and trot off together watching each other carry their hoops.

Note how Jason doesn't interpret the interaction as a conflict. He could have said, "No, Cory, that's Brodie's hoop; it's not okay to grab...."

Instead, he recognizes that Cory wants to play with Brodie and a hoop. Toddlers often need such help to enter a play interaction, and common objects of play can provide connections for young children that caregivers can affirm as mutual interests. Moments later, for instance, Jason can reinforce the connection by saying something like "I can see how much fun you two are having playing with those hoops." This caregiver expectation that mutual play will take place, even for a short time, is a self-fulfilling prophecy. Over time, as infants and toddlers experience caregivers interpreting their actions this way, they too begin to expect mutual interest, instead of conflict, and they play together more.

On another level, interdependence can be noted in an infant/toddler center setting in which the children are family-age grouped. When children of a siblinglike age range can be together, caregivers can acknowledge connections across the age levels. It is our experience that younger children have a natural attraction to movements of older children and that older children exhibit "helping skills," much as an older brother or sister would try to assist a baby sister or brother. Parents, too, value the connections or relationships their children make: their children have the opportunity to experience being or having an older or a younger sibling, when in fact this interdependent relationship may not exist in the child's own family.

Being Aware of One's Own Inner Conflict

Caregivers and parents meet in the center community carrying past experience that influences their attitudes and behavior. Sometimes adults are aware of their contributions to this atmosphere, and sometimes they are not. Why do your hackles rise when you see a superhero? Why does a child stomping her feet make you uneasy? Number six of the Ten Principles suggests that caregivers "be honest about your feelings around infants and toddlers." However, this doesn't mean that interactions with children or with parents are about *you* as caregiver. Learning to recognize and separate their own emotional reactions from the conflict at hand makes caregivers more respectful and responsive to the children and parents. Remember the story about caregiver Lee welcoming baby David in chapter 1? Because Lee was able to recognize and inwardly acknowledge her own anxiety about leaving her child in child care, she was able to set it aside to support David calmly through a difficult separation.

As that story shows, we all carry family and cultural influences into every interaction. One place they show up quickly is in dealing with conflict. A caregiver's attitude toward conflict is reflected in his ability to help young children face and learn to resolve conflict. It is most challenging for caregivers to be aware of their relationships with conflict and avoid letting them color how they behave with children. Ideally, caregivers at their best can separate themselves from the conflicts they facilitate daily in the child care setting. If a caregiver's "buttons get pushed," she can become aware of attitudes in herself she may not have recognized previously. In this way, young children can be teachers for caregivers as they proceed down their own paths of development and self-knowledge.

"Crossing the line" in a given situation from what's actually going on to a caregiver's own issues may occur when caregivers are not aware of inner conflict. For example, in observing Terrell doing a puzzle, caregiver Ken notices Terrell is getting frustrated. Because Ken himself has a low tolerance for frustration, he is unable to tolerate Terrell's, and so he steps in and finishes the puzzle for Terrell. Ken has reacted to his own frustration by taking over the "problem," when he could have facilitated Terrell's efforts, had he been able to separate his own frustration from Terrell's.

Helping Children Learn to Resolve Conflicts

Since many interactions between young children have the potential to become conflicts, caregivers may have a challenging time deciding not only how to intervene but also when. Of course, safety and preventing injury must be the first concern. Beyond that, caregivers can ask themselves a couple of basic questions when considering whether to intervene:

"What can these children learn at this time?"

"How can I help this connection continue in a supportive way for the children involved?"

Such questions help the caregiver to focus on the child's learning and move the caregiver into the children's frame of reference. This focus helps us separate our personal reactions from the issue at hand.

Beyond those initial concerns, caregivers intervene in interactions between children in order to help infants and toddlers develop their connections to one another and build a foundation of conflict resolution skills. Three skills are essential to resolve conflicts:

- Say what you feel
- Move away physically from the conflict
- Take turns with and trade materials

With practice, supported by caregivers, young children can learn to take responsibility for their own actions and thus become active participants in the resolution of the conflicts they encounter in their lives.

Remember how Judy facilitated the play interaction between Antoine and Adam and the squeaky duck, affirming for them their joy in trading? Let's suppose that like many interactions between infants and toddlers, this one degenerated after a while. What might Judy do then to support the children's skill at resolving conflict? Consider this scene:

Nine-month-old Antoine lies on top of Adam with a playful look in his eye. He glances at Judy. Adam is prone under Antoine's body and peers at Judy with a silent, wide-eyed look. Judy thinks that Adam is probably not enjoying the interaction anymore and asks herself, "What can they learn from this?" or "How can I help Adam and Antoine continue their fun connection?" Adam now begins to squeal a bit. Supportively, Judy calmly approaches, saying "Antoine, I see you lying on top of Adam. Please hear that Adam does not like that. Let's look at his face." Antoine rolls off and looks at Adam's troubled expression. Judy touches Adam gently, saying "That was beginning to hurt you, huh, Adam? You can move your body away next time and say, 'No!' You two were having so much fun trading that duck. Where is that duck?"

Notice how Judy describes what is happening and suggests how Antoine could learn the effects of his actions. Judy wants to preserve the previous playful connection between Adam and Antoine, so she mentions it. She also gives Adam support and an idea about how to act the next time someone should lie on him or begin to hurt him. Clearly, she doesn't expect a not-yet-verbal baby to be able to speak for himself, but knowing that children absorb much more language than they are able to use, she gives Adam the words that he might use when he's ready. It might be another six months or a year before he does, but having heard them over and over again makes it more likely that when Adam is ready, he'll have the words he needs to get himself out of situations that he doesn't like. Judy could also have communicated how to act by actually physically moving the infant away *and* saying the strategy, "You can move yourself away if you are not comfortable." The words become associated with the situation and sensory memory of the movement of the child so that over time as the child hears the words "You can move your body away," the child will know what that means.

Alternatively, without thinking through the questions, Judy could have run over, yanked

Antoine off Adam, and said, "Don't hurt him like that." By seeing this interaction only as a conflict, however, the caregiver would miss the opportunity to link the goodness of a previous playful connection with ways for the children to *begin* self-protection and conflict resolution. Caregivers can learn to facilitate these connections to build on children's natural relationships.

As seen with Antoine and Adam, infants are especially apt to see one another as more interesting play objects than toys are! This interest in peers continues as a characteristic of toddler interactions. As toddlers interact, they often want to play with the same toy that another toddler is playing with or holding. A toy in someone else's hand is much more attractive than an identical toy on the ground or floor and leads to the common conflict of one toddler grabbing a toy from another. Such simple conflicts present a valuable opportunity for caregivers to help toddlers learn the skills of turn taking and trading. Consider the following familiar interaction:

Jessica is holding an experience bottle, tilting it and watching the contrasting layers of oil and water slide over each other. Carley approaches Jessica and grabs the experience bottle. Jessica holds on tight, saying "MINE!" Carley says, "MINE!" also as they both hold on to the experience bottle.

Caregiver Amethyst, approaching the toddlers, says to herself, "This is a great opportunity for Jessica and Carley to learn from this conflict." Down at their level, she says to Carley, "I heard you say, 'MINE!' Would you like a turn with that experience bottle?" Carley says, "Yah." Amethyst says to Carley, "You can tell Jessica, 'I'd like a turn next.'" At the same time, Amethyst says to Jessica, "You can tell Carley, 'Your turn next.'" That might

be enough to solve the conflict. Amethyst might also say to Carley, "You could offer a trade to Jessica for the experience bottle. Maybe she'd like to play with that other experience bottle." Carley picks up a similar experience bottle and holds it out to Jessica. Jessica says, "No, your turn next." Amethyst models for Jessica and reflects back to Carley, "Jessica says, 'No, thanks.' What can you play with while you wait your turn? I know it's hard to wait sometimes."

This formulaic scenario may seem rote or generalized. But it is actually a template to learn and use in order to go beyond seeing the actions of young children as just conflicts and to take the next step. Sure it's a conflict, but its potential for learning goes far beyond the moment. When caregivers support children to see the situation as an opportunity to take responsibility and experience the consequences of their actions, then over time children learn to resolve their conflicts independently. This will probably not happen the first time, or the tenth, or maybe even the twentieth time the caregiver helps children get through a conflict, but eventually, it will happen. We promise.

When a toddler does finally trade of her own accord, caregivers can almost literally see a light go on in the toddler's head. The powerful feeling of connection for both toddlers is very real. When caregivers use this strategy consistently in such common interactions, they will discover how capable toddlers really are of taking responsibility for their own actions in conflicts and beginning to learn to resolve them. When toddlers begin to recognize the consequences that follow from their own actions, they can apply their budding sense of cause and effect to interpersonal relationships. They discover new possibilities for connection.

Promoting Connection during Routines

Caregiving routines in an infant/toddler program go on almost continuously: for the infants, who are on their own individual schedules of feeding, diapering, and napping; and for the toddlers, who transition from play experiences to diaper changes, to mealtimes, to toileting, to naptimes. Meanwhile, nose wiping, shoe tying, hand washing, undressing, and dressing are ongoing. Multiply each of these routines by the number of children in the group and you will see how many routine interactions take place in a day! And each requires some connection between caregiver and child. Part of a caregiver's job is to use these routines to develop trusting connections so that each child's social and emotional development has a strong foundation. From a foundation of trust, the infant or toddler joins with the caregiver to become a participant in each caregiving routine.

We suggest that caregivers flip a switch in their minds and envision children participating as thoroughly in caregiving routines as they do in play. Rather than think of routines as chores to get through, caregivers can focus on the possibilities for learning within the routine: to invest in quality time, to involve the children by working with them and not working around them; to learn their unique ways of communicating; to build security by teaching trust. Routines are a large part of any person's life, and with this new vision of routines children can begin early in life to approach them as valuable opportunities to tune in, rather than monotonous tasks to complete mechanically.

Using Daily Routines to Support Children's Connections

The following scenarios show how the seven strategies to support connections might look

and sound when you use them during routine experiences. Routine experiences with infants and toddlers fall into four main categories: mealtimes, personal care (including diapering and toileting), naptime, and transitions.

Mealtimes

Mealtime can be an experience for promoting caregiver-infant connection on several levels. The caregiver can use information available regarding the infant's schedule and pattern of eating to determine when to initiate the mealtime. The infant's trust is supported when the caregiver anticipates the infant's feeding time in a predictable and consistent manner and has the infant's food ready to offer. On another level, the infant mealtime experience can prompt caregivers' self-awareness about their own feelings toward inner conflict. These may surface toward the end of mealtime when the infant begins to play with the food. For example, remember the story about eight-month-old Emily and her banana from chapter 3? What happens when Emily has had enough eating but is still playing with the banana?

Emily has continued eating at the table. After the second banana slice, she slowed in getting pieces into her mouth. Now she is cheerfully smearing the banana on the table, then on her head. All pretense of eating has stopped. There is banana everywhere—on the table, in her hair, on her clothes under the bib. Consuela, the caregiver, says, "Oh, Emily, you're making a big mess now and that has to stop" as she pulls Emily out of the chair to begin cleaning her up. Emily's face goes into a pout.

Consuela's reaction to Emily indicates Consuela's problem with messiness. Instead of understanding that Emily was communicating nonverbally that she had finished eating, Consuela could only see a messy baby playing with her food. From this experience, Consuela could learn to expect that an infant who can't announce "all done" will naturally start fingering the food everywhere else because her tummy is full. To keep the entire feeding experience enjoyable for Emily, Consuela could use the strategy of acknowledging her own inner conflict without letting it spill into her conversation with Emily. She might say something like "Oh, Emily, it looks like you're not eating the banana anymore. You're enjoying its squishiness, but food is for eating, not for playing. Let's get you cleaned up now." In this way, Consuela could acknowledge all at once Emily's communication of not eating anymore, her tactile experience of the banana, and the end of mealtime. Their connection is more likely to be preserved as both caregiver and infant commence clean-up with a good feeling.

With toddlers, who sit around a table when they eat, the caregiver can involve each child in the serving process by offering pre-meal choices (for example, what color cup each child would like to use), which respects each child's preferences and involves them in the process of serving. By acknowledging common interests, this process also builds interdependence. It may look like this scene:

Seven toddlers sitting at the table have just been served a piece of fruit and a bagel each. Gina, the caregiver, picks up two cups of different colors and holds them in front of fifteen-month-old Theo. "Which color cup would you like, Theo?" He grabs for both, and Gina says, "Please choose one. Would you like the blue one or the clear one?" Theo singles out the clear one. Gina says, "Thank you for choosing" and continues to offer choices to the other toddlers around the table. Two-and-a-half-year-old Maya announces, "I want a red one." Gina says, "Thanks for letting me know, Maya. I'll remember when it's your turn." Penny and Eric, both two years old, are sitting next to each other and proclaim, "I have a green one" and "I have a blue one!" to each other.

Notice how Gina involves each toddler in the serving process by offering a choice of cup color. Theo is given the opportunity to connect with his mealtime experience by revealing his color preference. Penny and Eric make connection and have a social exchange by talking about their cup colors, much like an icebreaker at a party.

Serving meals family style is an exercise in interdependence. Mealtime can be an enjoyable routine experience when the caregiver facilitates each child's connection to the process of serving and to the other children. Remember too that "breaking bread together" has significance beyond nutrition in many cultures. Connecting socially, cementing contracts, and practicing rituals may underlie the serving and eating of food. By treating meals as an opportunity for connection, caregivers can support this social concept of mealtimes as more than food and begin building the practice of social interaction.

Personal Care

With infants, slowing the pace of interaction helps to build connections. One way of doing this is to use games such as finger or toe plays and rhyming phrases in personal care routines, such as dressing an infant. For example, think about this story:

Ten-month-old Jenna does not like the body manipulation necessary to dress her. She particularly squirms when a shirt goes over her head. After the shirt is on that far, caregiver Ginger says, "Arm through, there you go" as she reaches Jenna's right arm through the sleeve. Then Ginger pauses in the dressing to hold Jenna's hand palm up: "Round and round the garden, like a teddy bear. One step, two step, tickle under there!" Jenna wiggles and giggles. "Now we'll do your left arm," Ginger says and repeats, "Arm through, there you go" as Jenna's arm goes through. Then comes the poem again for Jenna's left palm.

Notice how Ginger respects Jenna's discomfort with dressing by slowing the pace and involving Jenna in the process. Jenna puts one hand through the sleeve, then Ginger initiates the teddy bear rhyme before turning to the other arm. For both Ginger and Jenna the routine of dressing becomes a fun, easygoing experience. Because Ginger always uses the rhymes, the dressing process has become ritualized and Jenna knows what to expect. It is consistent and predictable for her, and the parts of dressing that she doesn't like are accompanied by rhymes she enjoys.

Related rhymes could also be used for dressing routines that involve other parts of the body, such as putting on a child's socks:

> This little piggy went to market, this little piggy stayed home.
> This little piggy had roast beef, this little piggy had none.
> This little piggy cried wee-wee-wee-wee all the way home! (tickle bottom of foot)

This connection can continue into toddlerhood. Toddlers especially love "this little piggy." When "roast beef" is left out by the caregiver, toddlers can learn to substitute their own food (or other!) item.

> This little piggy went to market, this little piggy stayed home.
> This little piggy had_____, (child says, "apple pie" or "cheese" or whatever)
> This little piggy had none.
> This little piggy cried wee-wee-wee-wee all the way home! (tickle bottom of foot)

Think of your own favorite rhymes from childhood, or make up chants: "This is the way we pull up our pants, pull up our pants, pull up our pants. This is the way we pull up our pants, early in the morning."

With toddlers, opportunities for connection in personal care often involve diapers. When toddlers let caregivers know that they are interested in using the toilet, caregivers can offer them choices about having their diapers changed. One choice might be "Do you want to lie down or stand up by the potty to have your diaper changed?" Witness the following experience:

Two-and-a-half-year-old Tavor has a poopy diaper, and he and caregiver Joan approach the changing/toileting area. Tavor points and says, "Potty." Joan says, "Oh, Tavor, would you like to lie on the table or stand up in the bathroom to have your diaper changed?" Tavor says, "Stand up" as he walks into the bathroom. Joan assembles the supplies: paper for Tavor to stand on, gloves, washcloth, and clean diaper. While she's cleaning Tavor's bottom, she proposes, "Let me know if you want to sit on the potty when I'm finished cleaning your bottom." Tavor says, "Sit on potty." Tavor sits on the potty for thirty seconds and says, "All done." Joan says, "Nice trying; you can do that whenever you want, just let us know." She finishes putting on Tavor's clean diaper.

Tavor's independent decision to try using the potty is supported by the caregiver, Joan. As a transition between the infant-style of lying down to have a diaper changed and using the toilet, Joan proposes a diaper change standing next to the potty or toilet. Tavor's expression of autonomy is respected when he is given this choice.

Issues surrounding toddler diapering and toileting offer perfect opportunities for learning related to connection. Caregivers can practice understanding their own beliefs, connecting with

family cultures, and responding to children's own interest in toileting. This is further discussed in chapter 7.

Naptimes

Knowing when to step in to help an infant sleep requires knowledge of the individual child. The experience of relaxing to sleep is smoother and more personal when caregivers tailor their actions to the child's individual patterns. Caregivers also need to be aware of how these cues may change as the child grows. For example, consider the changes in Patrick's sleep cues over the six months represented in this story:

When the caregiver, Trudy, picks up four-month-old Patrick, he instantly nestles his head into her neck. She says, "Oh, Patrick, what a nice hug. Are you thinking about going to sleep? Your bottle is ready." Patrick cuddles with his blanket and drinks his bottle and soon is fast asleep.

Months later, Patrick may shake off the suggestion that he's tired, because he's learned to resist sleep. Trudy can build on her early connection with him, noticing his body language and working with him to get the rest he needs.

Ten-month-old Patrick crawls to Trudy's knees, saying "nee nee." Trudy says, "Are you getting tired?" Patrick says again, "Nee nee" and cuddles into Trudy's knees. Trudy picks him up, and he nestles into her neck for a minute but pops his head up abruptly, shaking it back and forth. Trudy says, "Okay, we can wait" and starts to set him down. Patrick screeches and holds his arms up. Trudy says, "Oh, you want to play close." Sitting him on her lap, Trudy goes through his favorite peek-a-boo and pat-a-cake games. "Let's see about a bottle and blanky," Trudy says and carries him around as she assembles the nap items. In Trudy's arms, Patrick pushes the bottle away until Trudy has sung two verses of a favorite lullaby. When Trudy offers the bottle again, he takes it and snuggles in to go to sleep.

Note how Trudy knows Patrick's main cue for sleep: wanting to be held close. After he screeches to communicate a need to stay close, Trudy plays calming games with him on her lap to help him move gently toward sleep. By honoring his feelings (being tired, wanting to be close, not quite being ready for his bottle and blanket), she guides him toward sleep. Patrick's cues provide Trudy with the information she needs to help Patrick settle down and sleep.

Older toddlers who nap on cots are able to focus for longer periods of time. This means that they can sit for a ten- to fifteen-minute story time prior to naptime. This transition from lunch to play to sleep gives a small group of toddlers a relaxed connection with the caregivers. They also connect with each other as they share the story.

Eight two- to two-and-a-half-year-olds sit on the floor in the nap room facing Jill, who is reading stories today. Johanna sits among the toddlers, one on her lap, two others leaning comfortably on her legs. Jill says, "Ossie suggested we do 'Miss Polly' today. What other finger play shall we do before I read these two books?" Alex shouts out, "'Hickory Dickory Dock'—fast!" The group settles in to the experience with many smiles and creative movements.

The social and emotional connections that toddlers can make during a short story time are invaluable. Trust is demonstrated as caregivers provide for and honor individual choices and personal expressions. The group of young children learns interdependence as caregivers respond to each of them. Ossie's choice and Alex's imaginative request to do the finger play "fast" were honored.

Transitions

The transition times between experiences are as important as the experiences themselves—it's true even in your adult life. For example, think about how you feel when the ride to work is rushed, or there's an accident, or when you get a disturbing phone call before leaving the house. The tension, anxiety, and distress are bound to affect your adjustment to work that day. How much more true must this be for young children, who are not in control of the circumstances surrounding them and who have no way to understand intellectually the source of their stress?

When and how a transition occurs for an infant is entirely up to the adult, and it's a good example of how caregiver attitude affects the quality of the interaction. Infants' experience of the transition depends on the mood and behavior of the adult involved. When the caregiver feels stress, the infant experiences the same anxiety. When the caregiver's pace is slow and predictable, the infant experiences a sense of relaxation and trust. Consider the following scenario:

Zoe and her mother arrive Tuesday morning. Eight-month-old Zoe is wide-eyed, and Mom is breathless. "I'm really late. She's fine," says Zoe's mom. "Hi, Zoe, hi, Sharon," Phoebe says to greet them, holding her hands out to Zoe. Zoe fixes on Phoebe and turns her body toward the caregiver, who slowly takes her in her arms, rocks her, and says, "Have you had breakfast?" "Oh, some bagel in the car," says Sharon, and she hurriedly turns away to begin walking out to the parking lot. "Tell Mom bye-bye, have a good day," Phoebe says. Sharon turns back from walking out to give Zoe a quick kiss and pat. Phoebe says to Zoe as her mom leaves, "Let's get your coat off and think about food. Your friend Jon hasn't eaten yet either. You can have some banana together. And I'll fix you some cereal."

As Zoe and her mom breathlessly arrive, Phoebe calmly greets them and slows the pace by holding her arms open for Zoe. Phoebe transitions Zoe from the hurried, jerky movements of her rushing mother to a gentle rocking while Phoebe gathers information from Sharon. The information will enable Phoebe to be predictable and consistent in meeting Zoe's imminent need to eat some more food and then take her morning nap. The transition for Zoe from hurried drop-off to calming mealtime with a friend smooths this experience for Zoe and lessens any anxiety she feels.

Short of picking up a child, the transition of moving a toddler from point A to point B can sometimes be challenging for caregivers. Yet it can also be a connecting experience when a caregiver respectfully engages a toddler in the transition. The first step is to respect a toddler's current play by *anticipating* the needed transition, using phrases like "In two minutes, it'll be time to…." Following through as close as possible to the announced time is important to maintain trust and give real meaning to the communication between child and caregiver.

The next step is to help toddlers bridge the gap between what they have been doing and what's going to happen next. One of the easiest and most effective ways to do this is by giving them a choice. Caregivers can create any number of choices to match the situation, the child, or the moment. The principle to remember is that children always get a choice, but the caregiver chooses the alternatives she offers the child. Two choices at a time are sufficient. For example, consider the possible choices found in a single transition from play to diaper change for a young toddler:

- "Aviram, you have poop in your diaper. Do you want Jan or Theresa to change your diaper?"
- "Now, or in two minutes?"
- "Aviram, it's time to change your poopy diaper now. Do you want to walk or be carried to the changing table?"
- "Do you want to hold my right hand or my left hand?

Of course, all the available choices might not be offered during any one transition. But thinking of and articulating possibilities help children identify what needs to be accomplished and understand how they can be involved.

Caring Responses to Hurtful Behaviors

Some possibly hurtful situations, such as biting, require yet another level of thoughtfulness from the caregiver. In their quest for experience, sensory stimulation, attention, autonomy, and connection, infants and toddlers literally run into each other. They are often actively involved in ways to connect with a peer, and a physical approach gets a grand response from both the other child (crying) and a caregiver (attention). When caregivers assume such collisions to be normal and respond calmly, such hurtful approaches may occur less often.

When caregivers maintain a caring attitude and recognize the child's actions as investigative rather than malicious, they understand that the child is not intending to hurt. The child's "animal brain" is simply protecting possession, territory, or self. When adults model a calm response, they are offering the child an opportunity to learn appropriate expressions of her normal feelings.

As soon as infants are mobile, they interact in a physical way. Most of these interactions are harmless, resulting in smiles, toy exchanges, and peek-a-boo games. Sometimes mobile infants will crawl over, lie on, or grab at one another. These behaviors call for a response from the caregiver in order to prevent injury.

Here are the steps to effectively intervene in these situations:

1. Intervene calmly to stop the hurtful behavior. Use words to describe the situation, and offer comfort to children who are upset.
2. Empower the "victim" to move away. Even crawling infants can learn to move away. For older toddlers, offer words they can use, such as "Tell her you don't like it" or "Say 'Please touch me gently.'" Caregivers can discourage victim behavior by simply acknowledging, and therefore respecting, the feelings of all involved. Use an empathetic phrase like "I can tell that hurt" or ask, "What would make you feel better?" so the child can begin to move past the "woe is me, poor little me" stage.
3. Offer alternatives for hurtful actions. For example, provide a doll for hair pulling, a teether for biting, and a pillow for climbing on or crawling over. Or suggest alternative actions that match the muscle action being used: a cart or truck to push; a ball or tire to kick.

A calm response by the caregiver is best because it does not reinforce the hurtful behavior by overemphasizing it. A caregiver's response should not be emotionally stronger than the child's response. Authentic, calm empathy both acknowledges the real feelings of the child and soothes them. Here are some possible phrases caregivers can use to acknowledge feelings and provide alternatives:

- "I can tell you are very upset. Let's sit for a minute and think about what would help."
- "When you are finished crying, we can talk about it."
- "I cannot let you hurt (punch, kick, hit, pinch, scratch) people or animals."
- "You can kick the ball, punch the pillow, throw the sock, butt the big bear, push the cart...."

- "Did you want to say hi to...."
- "Please blow kisses. It's not healthy to spit; it spreads germs." (Caregiver may need to demonstrate this technique to encourage its use instead of spitting.)

Real language that describes what the toddler might want to communicate will help replace the hurtful action. Often a toddler's need to physically move collides with others, and language can provide the bridge for respectful communication, interaction, and connection.

Biting

One way young children may literally connect with each other is through biting. Biting is one of the most difficult behaviors in infant/toddler group care. It is very scary for all: for the child being bitten, for the child who is biting, for the caregivers, and for the parents who hear about it later. Parents whose child is being bitten may be enraged; parents whose child is biting may feel horrified or embarrassed. Biting taps into adults' deepest fears and can easily "push their buttons." Before caregivers can deal effectively with hurtful situations, particularly biting, they must acknowledge their own feelings. Then they can learn from child development and brain research to establish realistic expectations and help children who come to rely on biting and other hurtful behaviors in order to get their needs met.

Why Do Children Bite?

Theories about why biting occurs abound. Some believe people carry tension in various parts of their body—for example, in their arms, legs, neck, or jaws—and act accordingly to relieve the stress. Another idea is that some children don't give clear facial cues to their feelings. These children may resort to biting when other toddlers push them to the point of response; it is a bite in self-defense.

Children who are nonverbal may also bite to defend their personal space or possessions. Young children may become frustrated in the midst of other children. If a reaching arm or other body part is nearby, a child may bite because she has few, if any, words to express her frustration.

Many children in group care may try biting, but only a few adopt it as a regular strategy. It seems to "work" for some children by relieving stress or gaining attention. A caregiver's job is to consistently give the child alternatives so that the child finds other ways to communicate or meet needs.

Guidelines for Responding to Biting

It is critical for caregivers to prevent children from hurting other children. With an understanding and respectful attitude, caregivers can empower toddlers to seek help for themselves by asking for a teether and begin to control themselves in order to prevent injury to other children. A consistent approach from all staff is necessary.

- Accept biting as normal behavior for most children to try, and for some to rely on longer than others.
- Through observation, caregivers can note a child's early use of biting as a strategy to respond to and interact with others. This would be more than the normal mouthing of objects we expect in infants and young toddlers. For example, biting an inappropriate object: books, wooden blocks, people. Biting others sometimes begins as open mouthing when kissing others.
- Immediately and calmly offer a choice of two teethers as an alternative to biting a person or inappropriate object. At our center, we keep a variety of teethers in refrigerators and cold boxes so they are always available in every room and outdoors. Caregivers can keep one or two in their

pockets and have enough available to foster healthy sanitation practices.

- Provide language or specific words to describe what is happening; "say what you see," using phrases like these:
  - "I can tell you are teething; which teether would you like to chew on?"
  - "Does your mouth hurt today? Here's a teether to bite on."
  - "Teeth are for chewing our food or teethers, not biting other people."
  - "That's not for your mouth. This teether can go in your mouth."

- If a toddler uses biting or other hurtful behavior often, a caregiver can shadow that child to prevent injury to other children. Consistent shadowing and offering language and teethers to replace biting other people will help the toddler not hurt others. Eventually, the child can and will ask for a teether and hence begin to develop self-control and gain autonomy in satisfying a personal need without hurting other people.

A calm response is necessary, starting with the very first incident. This approach to biting turns a crisis into a real learning opportunity that enables young children to move respectfully through their world.

Helping Toddlers Learn Manners

Adults recognize the value of manners in society, to smooth interactions and express respect for others. We would prefer to interact with polite people. We want children to learn these niceties and use them appropriately at the earliest age. Experienced caregivers also recognize that some adults become very anxious around "unruly" or impolite children. This anxiety often leads an adult to prompt or demand that children share, say "I'm sorry," or use "please" and "thank you."

Adults prompt a child usually when they, the adults, are uncomfortable. The prompting adult is making assumptions about the child's behavior and projecting internal feelings of discomfort onto the child. People who do not understand child development or how young children learn just want kids to "play nice." Some think that by simply saying the words, toddlers will know what is meant by them. The goal is for young children to understand their own true feelings and then learn how to communicate and act on them in ways that respect others. Forcing them to parrot words they don't understand and express things they may not feel is not effective.

Basic politeness is best learned by children through authentic adult modeling. When caregivers model saying "I'm sorry," "excuse me," "please," and "thank you," they are modeling that they have internalized these feelings for themselves. The more caregivers model polite responses in real and appropriate situations, the more likely children will learn to use them as well.

Young children think differently from adults and yet have the same feelings. The point of manners is to make all interactions authentic, respectful, and comfortable for everyone involved. The next time you are tempted to prompt a young child's manners, ask yourself if you would feel more or less comfortable in the situation if someone said that to you. It's more effective to learn to read children's emotions and help them communicate their feelings honestly, while setting clear limits about respecting other people and modeling the kind of politeness we want to see in children.

"Sharing"

When caregivers or adults force children to "share," it demeans the spontaneous act of sharing that can occur between young children when they choose to offer a toy to another. It also reflects a lack of respect for that child's true feelings and valued possessions. How would you feel if you were forced to share your car? Or a sentimental piece of jewelry? Can sharing be taught by being forced to give up something that means much to us? On the other hand, is it really sharing to give up something that means nothing to us? And how can we know how special something is to someone else?

Adults share out of a learned politeness or out of a true mutual feeling. We want another person to have the same response to an object or experience. Young children learn to share by seeing others model sharing and by being given the opportunity to do it on their own. When children do it naturally, they are learning the genuine good feeling of connecting with others. The most important aspect of this process is that the child is allowed to determine *when* a possession or turn is given away. The caregiver gives the children words to help them understand one another. We have found phrases such as these particularly helpful:

- When a child grabs another child's toy and that child responds with displeasure: "I can tell you want that toy back, Amy. Tell Sarah, 'Mine, your turn next.'"
- When a toddler grabs for something held by an adult, the adult says, "I'm using this right now; I'll give it to you when I'm done" or "Your turn next."
- Follow through soon, saying something like "I'm finished with this—your turn now."

The adult is modeling self-respect for possession and reinforces the toddler waiting for a turn. In this way, the process of taking turns is internalized.

Saying "I'm Sorry"

As adults, we routinely say "sorry" or "excuse me" when we accidentally bump into someone. This inconsequential act actually has nuanced overtones. By saying we're sorry, adults are taking responsibility for an action. (This is different from the empathetic "I'm sorry," meaning "I'm sorry that happened; I understand; I'll try to help.") We believe that by having children parrot "I'm sorry," the connection between their real feelings and real language expression is short-circuited. Often, the child who has learned to parrot "I'm sorry" will hit another child and immediately say "sorry" as if that will make hitting excusable. The links between feeling, its appropriate expression, experiencing the consequences, and taking responsibility are surely missing, if not lost.

Actually, the hitting toddler has done nothing to feel sorry for! She probably is attempting to enter play, express feelings of anger or frustration, or practice a skill. By assigning blame and implying wrong behavior that should make the child feel bad, adults start the child down a path of denial and shame that leads her away from natural development. This practice of blame and shame has nothing to do with helping children learn about their own feelings or interact with others in an authentic way. Children simply need adults to model these real life interactions.

When accidents happen between children, caregivers can "say what you see" and describe the incident. "Oh, Joshua accidentally bumped you with his cart." When accidents happen between a child and a caregiver or other adult, caregivers can model an authentic response by saying, for example, "Excuse me, you tripped over my foot" or "Sorry, I did not know you were right behind me."

"Please" and "Thank You"

"Please" and "thank you" are *not* "magic words." It is basically insulting and manipulative to insist children ask for something using "please" or to withhold the item until it is said. How confusing it must be the first time the child asks, "Please let me have a sip (of coffee or beer)" or "Please let me stay up late," and it doesn't work! "Please" and "thank you" naturally used by young children are, without exception, the result of appropriate adult modeling behavior. It is much more effective for caregivers to model these niceties as part of daily routine interactions, using phrases like these:

- "I need to change your diaper; thanks for lying down."
- When infants play trading games, model "thank you" and "you're welcome" at appropriate times.
- "Thanks for holding still while I wiped your nose."
- "Excuse me, I'd like to tie your shoe so you don't trip and fall."
- "It's time for lunch, please come now." (Following five-minute anticipation, of course!)
- "Excuse me, I need to get by; Billy needs my help."
- "Thanks for listening to my words."
- "It's nice to hear a please when you ask for more."

Caregivers can model please and thank you as part of scripting for toddlers, using phrases like these:

> *Toddler: "Wanna swing. Push."*
> *Caregiver: "You want a push, please?"*
> *Toddler: "More."*
> *Caregiver: "More apple, please?"*
> *Toddler: "Mine now, mine now."*
> *Caregiver: "You want a turn next, please?"*
> *"Let her know you want a turn next, please."*
> (Describing a turn-taking sequence)
> *"Oh, thank you for my turn. You're welcome."*

Caregivers can also model please and thank you when interacting with one another, parents, or other adults, using phrases like these:

- "Could you please hand me a sponge, Maggie."
- "I need more paper towels. Thanks, Jill."
- "Please remember to sign in."
- "Thank you for visiting our center."
- "Thanks for being here today." (To a substitute)

Young children can learn to use please and thank you naturally and appropriately when they are consistently modeled in daily exchanges.

Basically, respectful responses beget other respectful responses. When adults model respect of possessions, children can and will learn to share naturally. When adults model politeness in everyday interactions, children can and will do the same. They possess keen observation skills and can quickly understand how and when to use sorry, please, and thank you when these words are spoken to them and around them. All children deserve such respect.

Communication
(relates to Language Development)

Honor both nonverbal and verbal communication, and respond with respect to child-initiated interactions.

The attitude we communicate determines the quality of each interaction.

Curiosity (relates to cognitive development)		Connection (relates to social-emotional development)		Coordination (relates to physical development and integration of skills)
Child Tasks	**Caregiver Strategies**	**Child Tasks**	**Caregiver Strategies**	
Use senses to explore environment to construct own reality	Provide choices of materials and time to manipulate them.	Develop self-concept	Be predictable and consistent in meeting children's needs.	
	Validate the child's experience ("say what you see").	Trust		
		Autonomy	Slow the pace; be an "island."	
Discover cause and effect	Plan to extend the exploration using the child's interests as a guide.	Build relationships with peers, family, caregivers	Introduce peers and adults by name.	
			Include family culture.	
	Offer information ("say what you know").		Affirm mutual interests to encourage interdependence.	
Assimilate knowledge				
	Promote self-awareness.	Learn to resolve conflict Taking responsibility and experiencing the consequences of actions	Be aware of one's own internal conflict.	
	Share the caregiver's interests ("say who you are").	With self With others	Help children learn to resolve conflicts.	

Comprehensive Strategies That Support Caring Interactions

- **Observe** individual children; provide for **Optimal Stress**
- **Model** the behavior you wish to see
- **Acknowledge Feelings**
- **Anticipate** transitions, unusual events, and changes in routine
- Help Children **Articulate** their **Needs and Wants**
- **Offer Real Choices**
- **Set Consistent Limits**

6

Playing with Connection

As illustrated in the previous chapter, the intimacy produced by routine is essential to supporting children's connections with one another and with caregivers. But once a caregiver has slowed the pace of the program and made room in her day for closeness with children during routines, what comes next? The experiences in this chapter further support children's abilities to connect with each other and with the adults around them. They are deliberately set up to make it easy for children to come together around something interesting: materials, people, language, music, and so on. In order to support children's connections, we suggest that caregivers think in terms of exploring the experience together with the children, rather than entertaining them.

Babies Love Balls

Watch a baby respond to a rolling ball. Crawling or rolling infants chase it, and nonmobile infants bat it as it rolls by. When the ball rolls to a caregiver and he rolls it back, the exchange is like the beginnings of conversation. Older babies will often roll a ball back and forth or play a loose game of catch.

What You'll Need

- Balls of varying textures, sizes, and qualities. For example, clear balls with spinners inside, plastic balls with openings, soft squishy balls, nylon stocking balls stuffed with quilt batting, plain plastic or rubber or tennis or golf balls, musical balls, rattling balls.

- Baskets or containers to put the balls in.

What to Do

- Put other toys away or on shelves.

- Fill the room with all the balls, and let the infants discover them.

- Watch how the infants connect through the balls, and comment on their play.

Limits

- Inside, balls should be rolled, not thrown, unless they are very light and soft. Model rolling, not throwing.

Other Things to Think About

- Be sure that the balls are safe for infants: large enough not to fit into their mouths, safe if they chew on them.

You can use this same idea with any toy you have a number of: busy boxes, containers and loose objects to fill and dump, foam blocks, towers, and rings. Many different versions of the same thing are often better for a group of babies than a lot of different toys.

Supporting Play

Use these strategies, as Katie does in the following story, to support children's connections while they play with the balls:

- Slow the pace; be an "island"
- Affirm mutual interests to encourage interdependence

Seven-month-old Raoul is on his tummy on the floor. Both hands are in front of him, one palm on top of a ball, rolling it side to side. When his hand slips, the ball is propelled two feet to where the caregiver, Katie, sits. She says, "Raoul, did you want to play catch?" and slowly rolls back the ball. The movement of the ball draws the interest of nine-month-old Abby, who crawls over to Raoul. "Abby, you like balls too. Here is another one," says Katie, and she rolls it to Abby. Five-month-old Kisha lies on her back on the carpet, her head turned toward the action with the balls. A ball rolls into her sight, and her eyes follow it. As her arm reaches out toward it, Kisha rolls over and taps the ball a little bit further. She smiles and looks around, perhaps for more balls.

Experience Table or Tubs

Tubs full of interesting materials placed on the floor or in a sensory table can be a gathering place for infants, who then connect with each other through their exploration of the materials.

What You'll Need

- Small individual tubs, perhaps 12 by 18 or 24 inches. Dishtubs work fine.

- A sensory table, or a frame that the smaller tubs fit into (this is optional).

- Materials that appeal to the senses, large enough not to fit into children's mouths. For example, lids from frozen juice cans or baby food jars; strings of wooden beads; pine cones; small balls or textured shapes; pop beads; wooden clothespins (the old-fashioned kind without a spring), and so on. Use a choke tube to test materials if you aren't sure whether or not they are large enough.

What to Do

- Set up two or three tubs together, each full of a different material. You could use a sensory table to hold all three tubs, or use a frame that the tubs fit into.

- Let the infants discover the materials on their own, and watch to see what they do with them.

Limits

- Expect that the babies will remove the materials from the tubs, mix them together, and strew them around the room. That's okay.

- Limit children's play with the materials only to keep them safe.

Other Things to Think About

- Watch the babies to see what they are interested in and how they play with the materials.

- Use their interests to choose further materials to use for this experience.

Supporting Play

Can you see how Ana uses these strategies to support children's play in the following scene?

- Slow the pace; be an "island"

- Affirm mutual interests to encourage interdependence

"Oh, Jennifer, you found the tub of lids!" caregiver Ana says to the crawling infant. Ten-month-old Jennifer is kneeling by the tub, raking her hands through the lids. She grasps a handful and drags them out of the tub. A few roll by five-month-old Steve, who is lying on the floor next to Ana. He grabs at them as they go by. Jennifer stops to watch Steve, placing a lid on his tummy. "Thanks, Jennifer, now Steve can get that lid," says Ana. Jennifer moves to another tub. "Oh, you like the beads," says Ana, as Jennifer hangs them on her forearm and crawls away.

Peeking and Hiding

As infants become aware that objects and people exist even when they are out of sight, peek-a-boo becomes a favorite game. Purposely setting up the physical environment to provide opportunities for hiding and peeking enhances children's connections with one another and with caregivers.

What You'll Need

- Large cardboard boxes with "windows" cut in the sides.

- Pieces of lightweight fabric (12 by 12 inches is a good size).

- Snap-together plastic wall blocks with holes in the sides.

- Other ways of making structures for babies to crawl behind—perhaps a shelf turned on its side. They don't have to be very big to provide a hiding place for babies!

What to Do

- Using wall blocks, shelves, or a cardboard box, arrange pathways in the room for infants to crawl through and around.

- Make little nooks and crannies children can hide in.

- Observe how children use the environment to hide, and change it to provide the kinds of spaces they're most interested in.

Limits

None needed if the structure is set up safely

Other Things to Think About

- It may be possible to rearrange existing furniture to provide hiding spaces.

- Securely hung curtains provide instant peek-a-boo.

Supporting Play

Can you see how this experience can give you opportunity to use the following strategies to support children's connections, as Hanne does in the scenario below?

- Slow the pace; be an "island"

- Affirm mutual interests to encourage interdependence

Caregiver Hanne has introduced into the infant room two three-dimensional triangular structures made from snap-together wall panels. Three infants from seven to eleven months of age are crawling in and around the openings. As two infants appear at opposite ends of the triangle tunnel and spot each other, Hanne says to one of them, "You see Melony at the other end of the tunnel." Seven-month-old Dee crawls into Hanne's lap and looks back at the other two infants in the tunnel. Hanne says, "You see Melony and Lael peeking at each other? What do you think about that?"

Gathering Table

When infants begin pulling up and cruising, a sturdy table in the center of the room acts as a gathering place for infants to see one another from a new upright perspective.

What You'll Need

- A sturdy table about 18 inches high (high enough to keep children from climbing on it, just the right height for cruising infants to hold on to).
- Pillows, cushions, foam mats, or other padding.
- A variety of interesting toys for the tabletop.

What to Do

- Set the table in the center of the room for the infants who are beginning to pull up and cruise.
- Surround the table with padding, placing it far enough away from the table to provide a clear walkway around it. The padding needs to be where an infant would fall if she lost her balance and fell sideways, or if she sat quickly and fell backward.
- Place a few interesting toys on the tabletop to attract the infants' attention.

Limits

- The table is for cruising around. Adjust the height or push back the padding if it is possible for the infants to climb up on it.

Other Things to Think About

- The correct table height may vary with the ages and heights of the children— a table that works with one group of children may not work with the next.

- Toys that stick on the table with a suction base are great. For other toys, think about whether you want them to roll off the table or not.

- You could also group toys in a basket on or beside the table.

Supporting Play

Use these strategies, as Betsy does in the scene below, to encourage children's connections with one another around the cruising table:

- Affirm mutual interests to encourage interdependence

- Help children to resolve conflicts

Nine-month-old Julia is standing at a table in the center of the infant room. She is reaching across the table toward a toy stuck to the table with a suction cup. She raises herself up on her toes and reaches across, trying each hand in turn. Caregiver Betsy says, "Julia, you are trying hard to reach that red toy. Oh, here comes Eleni." Eleni crawls across the room at a fast clip, pulling up near the toy. She bats at it. After ten seconds of watching this, Julia begins to sidestep around the table. Eleni stops batting the toy and grins at Julia. They are face to face, both upright. Julia reaches for the toy and bats it. Eleni grabs it. "You both like that red shaker," says Betsy. "Julia, you walked around the table to get to it. Eleni wants to play with it too." Julia drops down and crawls off, and Eleni follows her.

Infant Massage

One way of connecting with infants during playtime or during routines is to use simple massage techniques on infants' hands or feet.

What You'll Need

No materials are needed for this experience.

What to Do

- Notice which infants are particularly sensitive to touch during routine dressing experiences.
- Start with the finger play "Round and Round the Garden" on an infant's palm.
- Continue rubbing the infant's palm gently with your thumbs, moving them up the center of the infant's palm and out along the base of the fingers.
- Go slowly, and note the infant's reaction. Continue as long as the infant seems to be enjoying the experience.
- If the infant is enjoying the massage, do both hands, and then sit quietly together for a moment.

Limits

None needed

Other Things to Think About

- Some infants might prefer to have their feet massaged. Foot massage follows the same pattern, using the thumbs to press gently up the center of the infant's sole and out the base of the toes.

- This intimate contact must respect the infant. If the infant is uncomfortable or squirming away, it's time to stop.

- Using the same technique, but barely touching, on other parts of the body like the back of the neck may give clues about where this baby carries tension.

Supporting Play

This experience gives you the opportunity to use these strategies to promote connection in infants, as Laurie does in the following scene:

- Be predictable and consistent in meeting children's needs

- Slow the pace; be an "island"

"And this little piggy cried wee wee wee wee all the way home!" Laurie tickles Angela's foot at the end of the rhyme. Nine-month-old Angela kicks her foot, so Laurie tickles again. Angela kicks out, smiling. Laurie smiles back and begins to massage Angela's foot with both thumbs. Angela visibly relaxes as Laurie begins to massage the other foot.

Photo Display

Displaying family photos behind Plexiglas at children's level provides opportunities for sharing about life outside of the center. Families provide photos upon enrollment and may include cultural designs and celebrations.

What You'll Need

- Plexiglas cut to fit your space (see below).

- Plexiglas screws to secure the Plexiglas to the wall. Use anchors if you are attaching the Plexiglas to drywall or plaster. Different sizes of anchors and screws are available at hardware stores.

- Tagboard in different colors for mounting the photos.

- Photos of families from parents and staff. You can also use photos of the children, photos cut from magazines, photos of natural objects, children's art, and so forth.

What to Do

- Measure the space where you want to put photos (low down on the wall where infants can see them). Bring the measurements to professional glass cutters and have them cut a piece of Plexiglas to size. Ask them to smooth the sharp edges left from the cutting. They may also carry a special drill bit you'll need to use to drill holes for the Plexiglas screws.

- Attach the Plexiglas to the wall using screws and anchors. Use a special drill bit to keep the Plexiglas from cracking when you drill holes in it. Place two or more screws on each side and several across the bottom for the tagboard to rest on when you slide it in. Space screws across the top far enough apart (12 to 14 inches) to be able to slip in the photos mounted to tagboard.

- Cut a piece of tagboard to slide in between the Plexiglas and the wall. It should be just small enough to fit between the screws on the right and left sides of the Plexiglas. You want it to slide down far enough to rest on the screws across the bottom of the Plexiglas without any tagboard sticking out the top, so that the infants can't reach it. (Adults can use tweezers to reach down and pull it out when it's time to change the photos.)

- Mount photos or other memorabilia to the tagboard.

- Slip the tagboard behind the Plexiglas.
- Allow the infants to discover the photos.

Limits

- Use phrases like this one to redirect children who pull on the edges of the Plexiglas: "Please use your eyes to look at the photos. Pulling will break the frame. Thank you."

Other Things to Think About

- Include a request for family photos in the enrollment packet.
- Ask for updated photos as children grow and change.
- Display photos of center happenings: potlucks, camping trips, water play, visitors.

Supporting Play

Use these strategies to support children's examination of the photos, as Julie does in this example:

- Introduce peers and adults by name
- Include family culture

Twenty-six-month-old Malika has just finished snack. She kneels on the pillow to look at the photo display on the wall. "Look, there's my mommy, my daddy, and my Dylan," she says. Fourteen-month-old Linda peers over Malika's shoulder and plops down on the pillow next to her. Linda looks at the photos with Malika. Nearby, caregiver Julie asks, "Linda, can you see Malika's dog, Dylan?" Malika points to Dylan as Linda looks at the photo. "That's my Dylan," she says again. Julie adds, "And your mom, Sheila, and your dad, Brian."

Note how Julie included Linda in Malika's reconnecting with her family photo by introducing her entire family. When the children learn other parents' names, the community of a child care program grows and expands to include all.

Classic Rhymes

Caregivers can use nursery rhymes, made-up chants, or quotes from well-known storybooks to make connections during routines or playtimes. Infants will initiate peek-a-boo or pat-a-cake or hold a foot out for "This Little Piggy." Toddlers learn the rhymes and request them for fun and comfort. This is the perfect experience to have ready when caregivers are available as an island.

What You'll Need

- Children's books and stories.

- Reference books, such as *A Child's Garden of Verses* by Robert Louis Stevenson or a Mother Goose book.

What to Do

- Let your mind be free to make connections between the subject or idea at hand and the infant. Often, a poem or rhyme will come to mind that is related to what you are seeing the infant do.

- Say the poem or rhyme playfully for the children. Usually there will be key words that connect with the experience.

- When children ask for a favorite poem, song, or rhyme, say it for them and invite them to join in. Recognize cues from infants, like initiating a game of peek-a-boo by hiding behind a scarf or holding out a foot for "This Little Piggy."

Limits

- None needed for infants.

- If toddlers interrupt while waiting for their turn to be named in the rhyme (for example, "Throw it in the oven for ____and me!"), caregivers can talk about waiting and taking turns, using phrases like "Your turn is after Kevin's."

- If toddlers lose interest in the game, take this as a sign that it's time to stop. They may simply wander away.

Other Things to Think About

- You probably know more rhymes than you think.

- Make up chants or stories about what is happening: use familiar tunes or rhythms, but add your own words. For example, sing, "This is the way we put on shoes, put on shoes, put on shoes…" to the tune of "This Is the Way We Wash Our Hands."

- Use rhymes to slow down routines so that you can connect. Putting on shoes and socks is more fun with a round of "This Little Piggy."

- Accept children's refusal to participate.

- Older toddlers make "jokes" and tell stories. Be the kind of audience you would want.

- After saying "This Little Piggy" a few times, you could ask the toddler what the third little piggy had to eat!

- It's fun to pretend to read a book that is so familiar that everyone knows how it goes. Hold out your hands as if holding a book and pretend to turn the pages while you recite the words. Toddlers can often remember large chunks of text!

- Many images of infants and toddlers at play call to mind familiar rhymes or quotes. Here are the ones we use most frequently:

  Riding on a horse: "Ride a cock horse to Banbury Cross…"

  Crying for Mommy or Daddy: We use a made-up chant which goes like this:

  Driving driving driving. Red light: stop; green light: go.

  Driving driving driving. Here's a stop sign; let's look both ways. Okay!

  Driving driving driving. Here's ITC! Let's open the door, close the door, go in and get_____!

Digging in sand and water: "Dark brown is the river and golden is the sand…" from Robert Louis Stevenson's *A Child's Garden of Verses*

Clapping hands: "Pat-a-cake, pat-a-cake, baker's man…"

Seeing a bird: "A birdie with a yellow bill hopped upon my window sill…"; or a bee: "Here is the beehive, where are the bees?…"; or a fly: "Shoo fly, don't bother me…"

Toddlers acting strong and "puffed up": "The night Max wore his wolf suit and made mischief…" from Maurice Sendak's *Where the Wild Things Are*

Supporting Play

Can you see how this experience can help you use the following strategies, as Marcia does in her conversation with Ariel or Chuck and Patrick do with the toddlers in the stories below?

- Slow the pace; be an "island"

- Affirm mutual interests to encourage interdependence

- Help children to resolve conflicts

Seven-month-old Ariel is crawling on the grass outside and sees a fly. She moves toward it, and caregiver Marcia notes, "Oh, you see a fly, Ariel." She pauses for a second or two and then sings softly, "Shoo fly, don't bother me, shoo fly, don't bother me, shoo fly, don't bother me, for I belong to somebody." Ariel points and waves at the insect as it flies away.

Children can learn to relate calmly to insects with help from this rhyme and a calm approach by the caregiver. Note how calmly Marcia acknowledged Ariel's interest in the fly and supported it with the accompanying song.

Chuck, an afternoon caregiver, has set up the yard for water play. He is sitting close to the action, beaming back at toddlers gleefully digging in wet sand. Thirty-five-month-old Lamar is digging vigorously, making a trench. Sami, thirty months old, has a bucket of water ready. After barely a minute, she dumps the water into the trench. Chuck watches with them as the water flows down the trench. Chuck spontaneously recites:

> *"Dark brown is the river, and golden is the sand;*
> *It flows along forever, with trees on either hand;*
> *Green leaves are floating, castles on the foam;*
> *Boats of mine are boating, where will all come home?"*

Lamar says, "A river! It's a river!" Sami says, "Again." Chuck repeats the verse.

Chuck uses rich and varied language to describe what Sami and Lamar are doing with the sand. This helps children connect poetry and rhyme to their real experience with sand and water.

Three toddlers are sitting on a rocking boat; a fourth approaches and puts his hands on the handle. The caregiver, Patrick, says, "Your turn next, Buddy." Patrick begins singing, "See saw, Marjory Daw, Jack shall have a new master. He shall have but a penny a day because he can't work any faster." One of the three climbs off and Buddy climbs on. "Thanks for trading so Buddy could have a turn," says Patrick.

Note how Patrick is available and makes a connection with the three rocking toddlers by singing the song. He not only facilitates turn taking, but he also acknowledges a connection among the three toddlers who are rocking together and the fourth waiting for a turn.

Musical Instruments

Infants and toddlers love the cause and effect of their actions making sound through an instrument. When they play together, they can experience connecting with others who also enjoy it. Toddlers enjoy being part of a "band," where they play with others, or a "parade," when they combine playing with walking or marching.

What You'll Need

- Musical instruments. These may be commercial or homemade, such as drums (especially popular), shakers, tambourines, bells, cymbals, rain sticks, or toy pianos.

- Tape recordings of music to accompany, if you wish.

What to Do

- Place a collection of small musical instruments on the floor, at least one for every infant. With toddlers, you might gather a small group of children who want to play music. Have at least two of every type of instrument to use with toddlers and more than enough instruments for each toddler to have one.

- Name the instruments as the infants come over to investigate or as you pass them out to toddlers.

- Begin with your instrument, modeling a rhythm and gentle noisemaking.

- Follow the children's lead in matching rhythm and sound.

- Facilitate trading and turn taking of the instruments.

- With toddlers, talk about which sound they like the best or what the different sounds remind them of.

Limits

- Infants can begin to learn how to be gentle with the instruments. Use words like these to help them understand how to use the instruments: "I can't let you break the tambourine. Bang it with your hand. Please hit the pillow or the floor if you want to punch."

Other Things to Think About

- It works well to be an "island" with the instruments; let infants come and go as they are interested.

- Introducing musical instruments to infants offers them an opportunity to connect around a mutual interest.

- Infants will need lots of experience investigating. Caregivers can point out when two play together or enjoy the same instrument.

- With toddlers, this experience works best in small groups.

- Observe the exuberance level of a particular group and their past experience with instruments. Some groups need focus, such as a leader or music to follow; others experiment on their own without resorting to inappropriate banging.

Supporting Play

Use these strategies, as shown in the following scenes, to support children's play with the instruments:

- Include family culture
- Slow the pace; be an "island"
- Affirm mutual interests to encourage interdependence

Three infants, seven to ten months old, are inside with their caregiver, Penny, on a rainy day. Penny brings out bell shakers—multiple bells sewn onto rings of cloth. Joel crawls over to look, then takes and shakes one of the rings. Mo turns at the sound and crawls over. Sitting, she laughs out loud at Joel, then grabs for the ring. "Here's one for you too," Penny tells her. "You both like that sound."

Kelly has chosen a tape of Peruvian flute music, shared by a family, to accompany the toddlers' exploration of musical instruments today. Four toddlers have chosen their instruments and are sitting with her on the floor. Ben is rapidly turning the rain stick back and forth, holding it close to his ear. Melinda shakes a large maraca, using both hands to hold it. Kelly says, "This flute music is a tape that Cam brought to us. It's very soft here at the beginning." She pats very lightly on her drum to model "soft." Ginger and Cam, who also have drums, play similarly. "We can all play together," Kelly says, and they fall into a shared rhythm during the flute song.

Bird Feeding

A bird feeder near the yard where infants and toddlers can watch for and talk about birds builds connection between caregivers and children who like birds and between children and the natural world.

What You'll Need

- Bird feeder: Use either a standard seed feeder or a hummingbird feeder, which is less messy, or both.
- Supply of sugar to make nectar for refilling the hummingbird feeder.
- Birdseed for the seed feeder.
- Interested caregiver who will maintain the feeder.

What to Do

- Purchase a bird feeder with a large capacity to make it easier for the caregiver who has taken on this chore.
- Fill the feeder and place in a tree or on a deck where children can easily see it.
- Wait for the birds to find it.

Limits

- Make sure the feeder is out of reach of children.
- Model kindness toward and interest in the birds. "He's very little; please speak softly."

Other Things to Think About

- Research the birds that frequent your area to determine what kind of feeder would attract birds you wish to see.

- Think of relating bird watching or any natural observation to the changing of the seasons and the natural year.

Supporting Play

Use the following strategies, as shown in the scene below, to support children's exploration of the birds:

- Slow the pace; be an "island"

- Affirm mutual interests to encourage interdependence

The tiny bird swoops through the yard to the feeder. "They found it," calls Heather. It's been more than a week since she put up the feeder, and she's glad to see a bird drinking from it. "We can sit here and watch," she tells Jake. The twenty-eight month old has been watching for the hummers too. Jake and Heather have talked about it every day. "What's that?" Jake asked a few days ago. Heather replied, "A feeder for hummingbirds. I'm hoping they will come to eat so we can watch them." After three days, Jake told his mother about it at pick-up time. Now she too asks every day about the birds, and today they can tell her the hummer came. Heather is planning further connections; in the spring they will put out cotton for the hummingbirds to line their nests.

Cameras from Home

Asking parents to bring in disposable cameras works well to create connections between home and the center. When staff take photographs of kids in action, parents can see "what they do all day," and caregivers pay attention to the children's play. Staff should plan to accommodate photography, as well as observe and recommend "photo-ops" to one another.

What You'll Need

- Disposable cameras. Some centers ask parents to bring one in when they enroll their children. You could also set aside money in the budget for a certain number of disposable ones. You might label each with the child's name or keep them in one general pool to be used communally. Either way, be sure to make this experience accessible to all children and families by having extras, if necessary, for families who can't afford to supply cameras.

- Basket or container to store cameras for easy access by staff.

- Play cameras (real cameras that don't work, but click) to make available to children.

What to Do

- Suggest to parents that if they provide the cameras, staff will take the pictures.

- Collect the cameras in a basket or container to carry from room to room or outdoors. Put the play cameras in the same basket so they are readily available for children to use.

- Plan to photograph children's special interests, games in action, playmates, and staff connections.

- When the film is exposed, the cameras can be returned to the parents to be developed, or the center can develop them. Even if cameras are not assigned to individual children, parents may be willing to "donate" developing.

Limits

- Toddler's curiosity will lead them to ask to try the camera, look through it, and take pictures. This is when the play cameras come in handy!

Other Things to Think About

- These photographs are valuable as a way to begin conversations between staff and parents.

- Take photos of routines, too: drop off, pick up, mealtimes, birthday parties, story times, visitors for music or stories.

- Taking photos as unobtrusively as possible keeps the focus on the children and the importance of their play. Respond to their interest and questions, but don't take too many pictures of them making silly faces or "mugging" for the camera.

- You might ask parents to have double prints made when they develop the film and keep one set at the center to display. If the center is developing the film, you might have duplicates made and then use one set to give away to parents. Toddlers especially enjoy these displays of real life at the center.

- Small books made from plastic sleeve pages and notebook rings allow toddlers to carry around and look at the photos of themselves and their friends.

- Be sure everyone is mindful that it may take two or three months to use all twenty-four exposures in the camera.

Supporting Play

The following scenario describing a camera experience illustrates the following strategies:

- Include family culture

- Affirm mutual interests to encourage interdependence

Caregiver Naomi has been observing Gregg and Jessica playing in the playhouse for about ten minutes. They are cooking, and she is jotting down their conversation for an anecdotal record. She remembers the cameras and moves quietly to get them. Putting a play camera in her pocket, she approaches slowly to capture the moment. She is able to snap a picture just as Gregg hands Jessica a pot with a spoon. They both look up when the flash goes off. "What you doin'?" twenty-month-old Jessica asks. Naomi answers, "I took a picture of you and Gregg playing in the house. Your folks gave us this camera so we could take pictures of you here at the center." "Take me, take me!" Gregg says. Jessica says, "Me do it," and Naomi hands her the play camera. Stooping down, Naomi points out the viewfinder and the shutter button. "Push that button to take the picture," she says. Jessica snaps away, Gregg smiling, and Naomi takes the opportunity to take another photo with her camera.

Naomi observes a special scenario with Gregg and Jessica playing together. She thinks, "How nice it would be to show their parents" and remembers to take a photograph with the camera provided from home. One of the toddlers is interested in taking a photo, so Naomi facilitates her interest by giving her the play camera.

Cars and Trucks

Small handheld vehicles offer an introduction to interactive pretend play for toddlers. They connect with each other as they manipulate the vehicles. A commercial mat or carpet illustrating a town scene is great for this, but "roads" made with tape on a tabletop or floor are just as good.

What You'll Need

- A collection of small handheld vehicles (six to eight per toddler).

- A mat or carpet showing a town scene, at least 3 by 5 feet; or tape to make "roads" on a tabletop or floor.

What to Do

- Set out the mat on open floor space, or use the tape to make roads on the floor or tabletop.

- Set out vehicles in random groups equal to the number of toddlers in the group. Respond to individual requests for specific vehicles as much as possible.

- Offer four toddlers at a time the chance to come play with the vehicles.

- Allow toddlers to explore the various vehicles on the mat or taped roads.

- Be available to facilitate interactions between toddlers.

Limits

- Have soft balled socks or other appropriate soft things available for indoor throwing, and use phrases like this to discourage children from throwing the cars: "Cars are for rolling or pushing, not for throwing."

- Encourage children to keep vehicles on the mat or roads. Play elsewhere is okay if it's safe and respectful of others.

Other Things to Think About

- Collections of vehicles may vary: You could sort them and have collections of emergency vehicles, travel vehicles, farm vehicles, or collections around other related themes to bring out at different times.
- It may be helpful to have toddlers experienced in this kind of play join the group of younger toddlers.
- Younger toddlers will hold, roll, and carry the vehicles and practice trading them.
- In addition to the vehicles, older toddlers may be interested in the town scene. When a caregiver sits with them and talks with them about the town, they will stay interested for longer as the new information stimulates their imagination.
- Try a different mat (for example, a forest scene with appropriate wildlife props).
- Use a favorite book, story, or song with this experience. For example, "Wheels on the Bus" or "Hurry Hurry Drive the Fire Truck."
- This experience may be saved for special times, such as a rainy day.
- You could make a mat that is a map of the center yard.

Supporting Play

Use these strategies to support children's play, as in the example below:

- Slow the pace; be an "island"
- Affirm mutual interests to encourage interdependence
- Help children resolve conflicts

Twenty-month-old Shira squats and clutches a train car. She reaches over toward sixteen-month-old Jamie, who is pushing another train car on the mat, and says, "Train." Caregiver Rafael notes, "I can see you especially like the trains, Shira. You can ask Jamie for a turn. Say, 'My turn next, please.' I see a blue hopper car that no one is playing with, or you can wait your turn."

See how Rafael supports Shira's interest in trains by observing her holding one and reaching for another. He facilitates Shira asking for a turn with Jamie's train. Rafael also presents another choice of train that is available to Shira, one that no one else is holding. Noticing what each child likes and wants helps a caregiver facilitate connections between toddlers.

Collage of Faces

This special gluing experience uses cutout pictures of children's faces, including all ethnic variations, all hair and eye colors, glasses, and hearing aids, if possible. The variety inspires toddlers to comment on similarities and differences and make connections. (Thanks to Johanna Leni for originating this experience.)

What You'll Need

- Photos of children's faces cut from magazines or photos.
- Choices of paper for gluing onto.
- Glue in shallow bowls and brushes (water-soluble school glue aids clean–up).
- Trays (approximately 12 by 18 inches).

What to Do

- Have the materials ready ahead of time.
- Give each toddler a tray to focus his attention and contain the materials. Each tray should have a glue container, a brush, and the child's choice of paper.
- Let the children choose from many cutout faces accessible to them on the table.
- Respond to the toddlers' comments and reactions to the faces. Expand their recognition of physical characteristics with comments like "Yes, she has brown eyes like you do" or "That does look like Sami's mom!" Don't be afraid of questions about skin color or other visible physical differences, but respond matter-of-factly, using phrases like these: "Yes, her skin is lighter than yours" or "Those are hearing aids. He wears them to help him hear better."
- Help children with gluing if they ask you to, doing just enough to get them "unstuck" so they can complete it themselves.

Limits

- Facilitate turn taking and/or trading when toddlers request an item someone else is using.

- Provide alternative toys or books for toddlers not wishing to participate or who indicate they are finished by trashing the materials.

Other Things to Think About

- Consider ahead of time what your response will be if toddlers make negative comments about the pictured faces. For instance, children may say they "don't like that hair" or find a child's glasses "funny," and so on. These comments are important clues to biases that children may be developing. It's often helpful to gently ask questions such as "Why do you think so?" or "What makes you think that?" or "How do you know?" or "Do you know anyone who wears glasses?" to discover what children are thinking. Then you can offer simple, accurate information to help dispel stereotypes ("I bet he wears glasses to help him see better"), share your own experience ("I like to have many different kinds of friends. Some of my friends wear glasses, and some don't"), or point out to children someone they know who also has that characteristic ("Did you know that Anne wears glasses to read? They help her eyes see the words better"). Often children do not make the connection between the stereotypes they absorb and the people in their own lives. Be prepared to follow through by bringing stories and visitors into the classroom to counter misinformation and so children become more comfortable with a variety of people.

- Children may focus on the experience of gluing instead of on the faces. That's okay. We're focusing on the faces here to illustrate one of many ways to expand connection.

Supporting Play

Use these strategies to support children's gluing experience, as shown in the following scene:

- Introduce peers and adults by name
- Include family culture

Two-year-old Leticia moves her hand across the several dozen cutout faces on the table. She points to one and exclaims, "Glasses!" Caregiver Allen says, "Yes, that little girl is wearing glasses so she can see more clearly. Who do you know who wears glasses?" Leticia looks at Allen and points with a smile, "Allen." Thirty-month-old Noah shouts, "Sarah! She's my friend."

Leticia chooses a picture that interests her. Allen helps her to make a connection between it and the people she knows.

Drumming

The rhythm and resonance of drumming are attractive to children of all ages. When caregivers begin by drumming on objects in the environment, children will gather quickly and form connections with each other by playing off each other's rhythms, as well as through the sheer joy of making big noises together!

What You'll Need

- Objects in the environment that have a flat surface: jugs, buckets, tubs, baskets, thighs! Be exploratory and try anything to drum on: tables, floor, couch, pillows, fence.

- A children's gathering drum for small-group experiences.

What to Do

- Just start drumming on something!

- Interested toddlers will listen, gather around, and drum together.

- Sometimes toddlers will start the drumming session; caregivers can imitate them or join in by adding their own rhythms.

Limits

- Use phrases like this one if toddlers start drumming on one another: "Objects or your own body are for drumming; not other people."

- If a toddler attempts to take away your drum, say, "I know you want to drum. This is mine right now, but your turn next." Or, "Can you drum with me?" or "I see another drum over there—see that red bucket?"

- If sticks or other objects are used as drumsticks, remind the toddlers of the following: "Sticks are only for hitting the drums, not people." You may decide not to allow sticks, in which case you could remind children to "Use your hands" (or fingers, or palms).

Other Things to Think About

- Children are likely to notice the different sounds that different materials (metal, wood, plastic) make when drummed.
- Be creative in adapting objects in the environment to use; encourage the children to observe, experiment, and find their own drums.
- Try matching the rhythms the children use.
- Babies love to drum and especially enjoy taking turns drumming.

Supporting Play

Use these strategies to support children's drumming, as shown in the following scenes:

- Slow the pace; be an "island"
- Intervene as appropriate to facilitate interaction

> *Thirty-month-old Dejon initiates drumming one day by beating on an upturned tub. He looks up at caregiver Hannah, and she imitates his beat for two or three drumbeats. He drums another series of beats; she follows him. They go back and forth for about thirty seconds.*

Note that the responsive caregiver recognized a toddler's invitation and followed his lead to connect without "teaching" or taking over the experience.

Caregiver Fran sits on a milk crate and reaches for a nearby sand jug. She places it between her knees and drums a staccato beat. Several nearby toddlers lift their heads and turn to look and listen. Twenty-month-old Danisha smiles as she approaches Fran. Danisha grabs for the jug and Fran responds, "I know you'd like to have this drum, but I'm using it right now. We can drum on this one together, or you can use that white bucket over there. I'll give you this one when I am finished. Thanks for waiting." Fran drums a few more rhythms. Danisha grabs again. Fran suggests, "We can trade drums if you bring me the white bucket."

Notice how Fran is sitting at the children's level on a milk crate, like an island. Note too how Fran models waiting turns by not allowing Danisha to grab her drum away. It's just as respectful to not allow kids to grab objects from caregivers as it is to keep them from taking things from one another. This provides a great opportunity to reinforce a toddler's ability to wait a short period. The caregiver can drum for twenty more seconds and say, "I'm finished. Your turn now. Thanks for waiting."

Farm Animals

Toddlers enjoy manipulating small versions of real things. They may name them, line them up, lay them down, or act out an imagined scene. A small group of toddlers "farming" in close proximity provides opportunity for caregivers to facilitate interactions.

What You'll Need

- Small model farm animals.

- Related support figures: farm families, trees, barns, and so on.

- Fences.

- Masking or other colored tape.

What to Do

- Offer the experience to a small group of no more than four toddlers.

- Use masking or colored tape to divide the table top into "farms."

- Distribute animals and figures, naming them as they are handed them out. Be sure each toddler starts with a similar set of figures.

Limits

- The tape divisions on the table are simply guidelines. Toddlers will inevitably reach for one another's animals, so treat it as an opportunity to promote connection between toddlers by teaching conflict resolution strategies. Use phrases like "Maybe he would trade animals with you" or "Say 'my turn next'" or "I know you want another cow. It's hard to wait, but Cameron says he's not ready to trade yet" to support the children's problem solving.

- If children chew on the animals, say "Animals are not for chewing" and offer teethers instead.

- If children throw the animals, say something like "Animals are not for throwing. There are soft socks to throw inside."

- If it's important to you, remind children, "This is a table game; try to keep the figures on the table."

Other Things to Think About

- A mix of experienced toddlers and those new to this experience works well; they learn a lot from one another.

- A small group (four toddlers) is best suited to this experience.

- Playing farm is usually very popular. Plan a time limit and a way for others to participate. One way is to repeat the experience on consecutive days in order to provide opportunity for both extended exploration and participation by all who are interested.

- Don't be surprised if some children focus on things other than the farm animals. The tape on the table may be more intriguing to some. (Offer other, smaller pieces of tape for manipulation.)

- This is a good experience to offer at the end of the day during pick-up time. Parents love to participate, and it's a good opportunity for them to see how caregivers interact with children.

- Add fences or other related equipment, such as trucks, carts, wagons, or people, as play becomes more sophisticated.

- Relate the play to stories or songs about farms or farm animals.

- This format is applicable to any manipulative toy used with a small group. For example, you could use dinosaurs, zoo animals, families, city workers—the possibilities are endless.

- These special manipulatives could be saved for rainy days or for other special times.

- A trip to a farm or petting zoo could accompany this experience.

Supporting Play

Can you see how this experience gives you room to use these strategies to support children's connections with one another?

- Affirm mutual interests to encourage interdependence

- Intervene as appropriate to facilitate interaction

Chuck intervenes when Tran reaches for Gavin's chicken. "Please ask first if Gavin is finished with that chicken. You can find one that no one is using or wait your turn." After Tran has waited for a few seconds, he says, "I can tell you really want that brown chicken that Gavin's using. You're waiting very patiently." Looking around the table at the other children, Chuck comments, "Oh, Kevin, you have lots of pigs. Do you especially like them?" Kevin reaches for Tran's pig and says, "Mine." Chuck says to Tran, "Tran, you can tell him 'My turn, your turn next.'" Kevin looks at Tran and pulls his hand back. Tran says, "Fens." Chuck replies, "You'd like a new fence? Let's see if Bridget will trade." "You can have my fence 'cause I'm done with it," Bridget volunteers.

This experience provides particularly important practice in verbal communication necessary for turn taking and trading. Chuck gives children the words to voice their own needs and supports them in negotiating with one another. As he talks with children, he behaves the way he wants them to behave. Providing consistent limits allows the toddlers to focus on their strategies for conflict resolution, rather than on testing limits.

Flannelboard

Many toddlers are not ready to just listen to a flannelboard story when faced with enticing figures, characters, and manipulation. When given their own flannelboards and pieces, they can control some of the magic. It is also helpful to involve them when the caregiver is telling the story.

What You'll Need

- Small flannelboards: 12 by 12 inches or 12 by 18 inches. (You can make these by covering pieces of cardboard with flannel.)
- Flannel pieces in various shapes (animals, people, geometric shapes, characters in a story, and so on) and colors.
- Scrap pieces of flannel or interfacing cut in random shapes, at least 2 by 3 inches.
- Glue.
- Collage materials: yarn, cut fabric, large buttons.

What to Do

- Gather a small group of toddlers (no more than four).
- Tell them a short flannelboard story. When the story's over, give each of the children a small flannelboard and some shapes. They could take turns telling others their story or play separately with their flannelboards.
- The next day, offer pieces of felt, collage materials, and glue.
- Let them make their own flannelboard pieces by gluing collage materials on the felt.
- When they are dry (which may take another day), gather the children again and give them the flannelboard pieces they made. Let them put the pieces on the big board if they want to, inviting them to "tell us about your flannel piece" as they do. Or they could play with their pieces individually on smaller flannelboards.

Limits

- Provide alternative toys for children who are not ready to use materials appropriately. Use phrases like this one to help children find something else to do: "The flannelboard pieces are not for throwing. We have socks to throw indoors."

Other Things to Think About

- This experience may be altered to match the developmental level of the group. For example, you could vary the length of the story to match children's interest or start by giving children their own flannelboards to play with.

- Fabric interfacing makes durable flannelboard pieces. They may be drawn on, they stick to the flannelboard, and they don't wrinkle up as easily as plain felt.

Supporting Play

Can you see how Edna is using these strategies to support children's play in the following scene?

- Affirm mutual interests to encourage interdependence
- Help children to resolve conflicts

After introducing a group of toddlers to the use of flannel pieces on a board, caregiver Edna sets up an art experience for them to make their own pieces. Four toddlers sit around a table filled with yarn, fabric pieces, and glue. Edna holds irregular pieces of felt in various colors and sizes. She passes them around and asks, "Which piece would you like, Ali?" Ali chooses the purple one. Kiko says, "Purple too," and Edna gives her a purple one. Jerry wants a red one, and George takes blue. "Remember the flannelboard story? Today we can make our own pieces for the flannelboard. You can glue decorations onto your piece."

Another day, when the pieces have dried, the toddlers gather again. Edna has the flannelboard set up. "Today you get to tell the flannelboard story with the pieces you made. I have them right here. Here's your red one, Jerry; you can come up and put it on the flannelboard. What would you like to tell us about it?" "It's an ant," Jerry says. George stands before Jerry has finished, and Edna says, "Do you want to be next? Here's your blue piece." George takes it and freezes. "Did you want to tell us about it? (pause) I can see it's blue with red yarn glued on it. (pause) You can hold it while Ali tells us about hers."

Photo Albums

Toddlers enjoy looking through small photo albums that they can sit with, carry, and manipulate. Filled with photos from the center community of themselves and their peers, they delight the toddlers, who frequently connect friends and photos.

What You'll Need

- Small photo albums holding twenty-four or thirty-six photos.
- Photographs of children at the center or with their families.

What to Do

- Take pictures around the center. Be sure to get a good mix of the children and all the things that you do in a day or a week. You can also use photos that families bring in.
- Put the photos into small one-photo-per-page albums. You may want to organize them by types of experience: water play, saying good-bye to a mom or dad, naptime.
- Set them out on tables or shelves where toddlers can discover them. Expect interested questions such as "Who's that?"
- Be available to talk about the photos. Ask questions that lead to conversation, such as "Who does it look like?"

Limits

- It is probably best to keep these albums indoors, unless someone is very watchful.
- Use phrases like this one to help children take care of the photo albums: "Please be gentle with our album of pictures."

Other Things to Think About

- It's fun to see photos even a few months old because of the changes in young children's appearance.

- Photographs of center events, such as potlucks or work days, remind children of community connections.

- Some small albums are not sturdy. Consider making permanent fabric and acrylic albums to rotate photos through.

- It is also possible to laminate photographs so the toddlers can carry them around.

Supporting Play

How is the caregiver in the following scene using these strategies to support children's connections?

- Slow the pace; be an "island"

- Introduce peers and adults by name

- Affirm mutual interests to encourage interdependence

> *Cristiana is sitting looking through the photo album. She stands and goes to Van. "Look, there's Sidney." Van looks and says, "He's in the box," and they both laugh. Cristiana continues, "And here's Tran, and here's…." Turning to the caregiver Nu, who has been listening, Cristiana asks, "Who's that?" Nu says, "She was a baby then, now she's grown. Can you tell? (pause) It's Mildred!" Almost three, Cristiana understands. "I was a baby once," she says.*

Rock Game

This game evolved in response to toddlers bringing caregivers small rocks or items they found outdoors. We find that toddlers are very interested in the seeming "disappearance" of the object!

What You'll Need

- Small rock or object that can be hidden inside a closed adult hand. You can use a special one you bring in or something a child brings you.

What to Do

- Start the game when a child brings you a small rock or other object, or show him something you have brought. Ask the child, "Do you want to play the rock game?"

- If the child says yes, say something like "Let me show you; may I have your rock? I will give it back to you." Hold open both hands, palms up, for the toddler to place the rock in.

- Shake the rock in your cupped-together hands. Then close each hand into a fist, with the rock in one. Ask the child a question like "Where did it go?" or "Which hand is it in?"

- Have the child turn one hand over and open your closed fingers. Some kids will close the hand back up and repeat with the other hand, but if they don't, prompt them by asking "Is it in the other hand?"

- After the toddler finds the rock, you can start the game over and continue as long as the toddler is interested. If other toddlers are interested, you can help them take turns.

Limits

- If children have trouble keeping their rocks out of their mouths, remind them to "Please hold your rock in your hand or put it in your pocket. Rocks are not for your mouth." Offer toddlers teethers to put in their mouths.

- If many toddlers become interested at the same time, help them take turns or suggest they play the game with one another.

Other Things to Think About

- Observe the toddlers' responses and match their level of glee, using phrases like "You found it!" and "Want to do it again?"

- Switch the hand into which the rock disappears. Observe any pattern in the toddlers' guesses and play with it.

- Older toddlers relish an added challenge: as they attempt to open your closed fingers, keep them shut tight and say, "Oh, they're stuck." Their eyes will light up. As they pry open your fingers, make verbal sounds of effort. Gauge how much resistance to use depending on the toddlers' interest.

- Often toddlers don't want to find the rock on the first try.

- Several toddlers may gather to play the rock game with one caregiver. As you are shaking someone's rock, say, "You'll be next" to whoever is waiting. Respect whoever has been waiting the longest and follow through in the order you set.

Supporting Play

How would you use these strategies to further children's connections during this experience?

- Slow the pace; be an "island"

- Intervene as appropriate to facilitate interaction

Eighteen-month-old Hadar presents a small rock to Fran, who is sitting on a tire. "You want to play the rock game? Let me show you." Fran shakes the rock, then hides it in one hand as thirty-three-month-old Otto reaches in to grab Hadar's rock. Fran says, "This is Hadar's game right now. I see a seed over there under the bushes. Can you find it? And then you can have a turn next. Thanks for waiting." Hadar finds her rock as Otto returns. Fran says to her, "You can have another turn after Otto." Hadar watches Otto's turn, and they both laugh when Fran declares, "You found it!"

Fran is being an "island" as she sits on a tire in the yard. Note how she responds with the idea of a game to Hadar's presentation of a rock. This is a special one-on-one time of interaction. Other toddlers observe and want to participate, and Fran helps Otto to find his own small object and then to take turns with Hadar.

Story Time

Older toddlers enjoy a daily story time before lying on their cots to nap. This experience is slightly more formal than the spontaneous book reading that occurs throughout the day and usually lasts ten to twenty minutes, depending on the developmental range of the group.

What You'll Need

- Children's books.

- Adult resource books with finger plays or simple rhymes.

What to Do

- After readying toddlers for naps (toileting, changing, undressing), settle down with a small group of toddlers (could be one caregiver and four toddlers or two caregivers and eight toddlers).

- Sit with caregivers and toddlers in a group. Encourage toddlers to sit.

- Introduce the finger plays or books to the children, using phrases like these:

  "Today we're going to do the eentsy weentsy spider."

  "Alex wanted to do the three bears."

  "We have two books. This one is *Each Peach Pear Plum.* We'll read it first."

  "This is the last book; then we'll lie on our cots and go to sleep."

Limits

- Help children find places to sit, using phrases like "Please sit so everyone can see, or you may stand behind the group."

- Help children take turns talking about the book; let everyone who wants to make a comment.

Other Things to Think About

- Read requested books or do requested finger plays at the time they are requested, if possible.

- Sometimes children who can hear a story in a small group are too excited or distracted by a larger group. These children may be invited to go to a quiet corner or another room to play until it's time to take a nap.

- Flannelboard stories may be effective with an older group of toddlers (see page 169).

- Sometimes books may be chosen to coincide with a family interest, happening, or current developmental issue, such as a new sibling, toilet learning, or camping.

Supporting Play

Use these strategies to support children's connections during story time:

- Include family culture

- Slow the pace; be an "island"

Rita has chosen stories for the day and knows that there will be time to do a finger play that involves individual children. When the toddlers are gathered, she says, "Today we'll do 'Candlestick,' with Little Mousy Brown. Everyone will have a turn. Candlesticks ready? An, what kind of candlestick would you like?" An answers, "Red."

> *Up the red candlestick ran Little Mousy Brown.*
> *All the way to the top, but he couldn't get down.*
> *So he called for his friend, he called An, An, but she was out of town.*
> *So he made himself into a ball and rolled himself right down.*

"Vince, what kind of candlestick do you want?" says Rita when An's turn with the finger play is finished. Vince replies, "Brown." Rita says, "Brown? That's your last name, too." Rita continues until all the toddlers have had a turn. When she asks, "What kind of candlestick would you like?" there are responses such as "my mommy," "train one," and "blue and purple." Rita uses all of them in the rhyme.

Swinging

Rocking and swinging are essential for the development of balance and sensory integration. Swinging and other physical experiences can advance a child's development and even promote good emotional growth.

What You'll Need

- Swings safe for the developmental ages in the group: belt swings are the easiest for young children to get into and out of by themselves.

What to Do

- Outside, offer a push on the swing or respond to toddlers' requests for pushes.

- Use a poem like "How do you like to go up in a swing?" while spacing two or three good pushes through the poem.

- At the end of the poem, say, "Last push" and push once more.

Limits

- Have the toddlers get on and off the swings by themselves.

- Let toddlers who swing on their tummies propel themselves. Adult pushing is safest when the toddler is sitting on the belt swing and grasping the chains with both hands.

- Encourage toddlers to wait at the side of the swings or find something else to do while they wait for a turn.

- Let the child who is swinging determine the end of his turn. A turn is as long as a swinging toddler wants. When he leaves the swing, the next toddler waiting gets it.

Other Things to Think About

- Adjust the level of cushioning material under the swings so they are at the right height for all toddlers to be able to swing by themselves on their tummies.

- Any rhyme or made-up chant may be used.

Supporting Play

Use these strategies, as shown in the following scene, to support children's development of connections while swinging:

- Be predictable and consistent in meeting children's needs
- Help children resolve conflict

Toddlers and caregivers tumble out the door to the yard after lunch. "Push?" inquires twenty-five-month-old Jamal of caregiver Barbara. "Sure, I can do that," says Barbara. Jamal runs and sits on the swing by himself. Several other toddlers run over, saying "Wanna swing." Barbara says to them, "You can have a turn next. You can sit here and wait or do something else while I say the swing poem." Barbara asks Jamal, "Are you ready? Are you hanging on tight?" Jamal nods with a smile. She begins pushing and reciting the poem:

> *"How do you like to go up in a swing, up in the sky so blue? (push)*
> *Oh, I do think it the pleasantest thing ever a child can do.*
> *Up in the air and over the wall, 'til I can see so wide (push)*
> *Rivers and trees and cattle and all over the countryside.*
> *'Til I look down on the garden green, down on the roof so brown, (push)*
> *Up in the air I go flying again, up in the air and down!" (pause)*

She announces, "Last push!" and pushes Jamal one last time. She backs away from the swing; Jamal flops on his tummy to swing himself a couple of times. Barbara stays near the swings in order to reinforce any waiting toddler by saying "Nice waiting. Okay, your turn. He's all done now."

Note how Barbara responds to Jamal's request. She also responds to other interested toddlers by encouraging them to wait their turn. Barbara anticipates the last push consistently and predictably for Jamal; she always limits her pushes to the narration of the poem.

Weather

Caregivers can spontaneously notice or respond to children's interest in weather phenomena: wind, clouds, rain, snow, hail, rainbows, thunder, lightning, sun, and shadow. The shared experience connects children and adults through their exploration of the natural world.

What You'll Need

No materials needed—just the ability to pay attention to what's happening outside.

What to Do

- When outdoors with children, or looking out the window, comment on what's happening outside or respond to what children notice about the weather. Use phrases like these: "You see the clouds. Look at those billowy clouds. What shapes can you see?" or "What does it look like to you? I see a rabbit."

- Collect rain, snow, or hail for kids to hold and see. You can bring snow inside to fill small individual tubs or a water table. Children can also watch snow or ice melt.

- Set up windsocks or banners to show the motion of the wind, and then talk about it with children, using words like these:

    "See the wind moving in the maple tree?"

    "I see your hair moving in the wind."

    "Can you feel the wind on your skin?"

    "Look, the wind is blowing that ball across the sidewalk."

    "See the drops in the puddles?"

    "Dark clouds usually have rain in them."

Limits

None needed

Other Things to Think About

- If you can't go outside, sit in a doorway to watch and listen to the rain, wind, or snow.

- Introduce new detailed language: billowy clouds, blustery wind, showers of rain, gusts of wind.

- Notice and talk about how clouds move through the sky with wind and how tree leaves and branches move in the wind.

- Sing songs that reflect what is happening outside (for example, "Rain Rain Go Away") or make up a song reflecting what is happening. Any words put to music notes will catch toddlers' interest.

Supporting Play

How do the caregivers in this scene use these strategies to connect with children through the weather?

- Slow the pace; be an "island"

- Affirm mutual interests to encourage interdependence

One spring afternoon, an intense rain- and hailstorm caught a group of toddlers and two caregivers outside under a fiberglass roofed enclosure. It was an exciting experience as they all watched the marble-sized hail bounce on the sidewalk and listened to the deafening sound of it hitting the fiberglass roof. Caregivers Tom and Christina modeled putting their hands over their ears if it was too loud to be comfortable. Christina noticed two-and-a-half-year-old Daniel curled up on a mat, eyes wide open, watching and listening. She went to him, softly touched his shoulder, and asked, "Are you all right?" And his eyes got bigger as he answered with a huge grin, "Yeah!" Christina gave him a hug and said, "Isn't this fantastic?"

Note how the caregiver made herself available to Daniel without assuming he was uncomfortable or traumatized. Her comfort and excitement about the hailstorm helped Daniel have a trusting experience as well.

Wheelbarrow

Toddlers "walk on their hands" while the caregiver supports their bodies by the ankles. This is a great experience to offer to a particularly energetic toddler. Much verbal and nonverbal communication takes place as the caregiver encourages, listens, and feels each toddler's large-muscle efforts.

What You'll Need

- A soft, cool surface for the palms of toddlers' hands. Grass is perfect, while sand makes the experience more challenging for an older toddler.

What to Do

- Ask the child to "stand on the grass with your hands" or "put your hands down on the grass," and show him how to do it if he seems confused.

- Say, "Now I'm going to lift your feet up, and you see if you can walk with your hands." Lift the child's body by the ankles, being sure the toddler is able to support the lower body with arms extended and hands on the grass.

- For toddlers, "walking on the hands" is a tricky challenge that may take a few tries. Give them simple directions and encouragement, using phrases like "Now, walk with your hands" or "Move one hand, then the other." You will feel their feet move as they think about it and try it out. Once toddlers move one hand forward, they usually get it and keep moving on their hands.

Limits

- For safety, keep other children from pushing, shoving, or otherwise getting in the way of the toddler who is being the wheelbarrow.

Other Things to Think About

- Each child's upper body strength and stamina is different. Be sensitive so that this experience is successful and fun for the child. It might vary from two or three hand steps to ten yards!

- If you think it will be fun for the child, set a goal by picking out an object that the toddler can see from the hands-down position. Tell her, "Try to walk on your hands to that ball" or tree or whatever they can see. Remember that success and fun are the main ideas!

- Some toddlers will try to do this for themselves by backing up to a wall, balancing on their hands, and "walking" their feet up the wall.

Supporting Play

This experience gives you an opportunity to use these strategies to support children's connections:

- Be predictable and consistent in meeting children's needs

- Intervene as appropriate to facilitate interaction

> *Janie is running around the yard, haphazardly pushing toys and bumping into other children. Nancy notices her high energy and issues an invitation: "Hey Janie, would you like to be a wheelbarrow?" She responds by running over to the caregiver. Nancy says, "Now put your hands down on the grass, and I'll lift and hold your feet up." As Nancy begins the experience for Janie, two to three other toddlers approach to watch and say, "Me do it." Nancy facilitates turn-taking by saying "Alex, it'll be your turn next, then Stephanie; thanks for waiting." She turns her attention back to Janie. "Janie, now walk with your hands. Walk, walk, walk—can you make it to the tree over there? Walk, walk, you can do it, you're almost there, just two more steps, you did it! Look how strong you are," she says to validate Janie's experience.*

Once started, this experience is very popular. Turn taking happens quite easily as turns are usually quick and short, depending on individual toddler strength and stamina. Note how Nancy clearly communicates what will happen and follows through, both for Dejon and for those waiting. Being predictable and consistent develops trust.

7

Fostering Coordination

In addition to being warm and comfortable, infants' experience in the womb is one of motion as they move with their mothers' bodies. In this way, their brains have been practicing orientation in space since before they were born. Many caregivers have had the experience of holding a crying baby who stops crying the instant they stand up! This comfort in movement or in a given orientation is the beginning of a young child's journey to find her place in space, negotiate her relationship with gravity, and move towards physical balance, strength, and control of her body. This process is especially important because literal hands-on, feet-on learning is the way infants and toddlers give feedback to their brains. They can't just think about an action in order to understand it—they have to play it out. Coordination enables them to investigate their world in this manner. Driven by curiosity and supported by connection, coordination is the combination of skills that allows young children to work their will in the world.

The sensory experiences of touch and the sense of movement in space give young brains feedback about where motion is taking them and help the child to decide what body part to move next in order to attain a goal. Children ask to be picked up or put down and seek out these experiences again and again to practice using the feedback, which then makes more permanent connections and pathways in their brains.

The last of the Ten Principles states, "Don't rush infants and toddlers to meet developmental milestones." Milestones of coordination are often uppermost in adult minds, as shown by frequently asked questions such as "Does he walk yet?" or "Does she use the toilet?" This emphasis on one specific task, as if it happened by itself rather than as a part of a process, ignores children's individual approaches to development and the effort they put into each tiny new capability along the way to the big milestones. Attempting to push infants and toddlers to meet milestones isn't advantageous.

Human bodies and brains are designed to interact, with the brain receiving feedback from the body. Often it seems as if one day a baby is barely rolling over and the next day she's sitting up. But close observation can reveal all the tiny steps along the way to this achievement, as well as the effort expended in a baby's drive to be mobile and then to be vertical, in order to interact with objects and people in the environment. Adults who focus only on the milestone will miss all these little triumphs along the way.

For these reasons, we wouldn't say, "She *should* be walking" any more than we would insist that a fourteen month old *should* wear size six shoes! Children naturally practice the movements that they are developmentally ready for and that will strengthen their bodies in the ways that they need to tackle the next developmental step. When caregivers pay attention to what children are doing physically in each moment, they can observe this process for themselves. Movement is one of children's first means of communicating their needs or intentions.

Coordination as a Way of Thinking about Physical Development

Like other kinds of development, physical development is sequential, meaning that it happens in a predictable order (for example, babies roll over before they crawl, and crawl before they walk). Physical coordination follows a developmental sequence that caregivers can observe, and individual differences are expressed within this predictable sequence. Some children scoot instead of crawling, others cruise only briefly before walking, and young children often spend differing lengths of time in each stage. Because of these differences, there will be a wide range of normal development in a group care setting with children of similar ages. For example, three ten month olds with birthdays within days of each other may have four, six, or zero teeth and be crawling, cruising,

or walking. Two year olds may also exhibit a range of development, even if they are actually only a week apart in age. Only one of the three might be able to pedal a trike, while another has the fine-motor coordination to successfully manipulate a zipper, though all three could be able to run fast.

This knowledge of developmental sequences can assure caregivers that a child is within the "normal" range or signal if she is not. Being secure in this knowledge allows caregivers to be enchanted by infants' and toddlers' individual expressions of development—the special aim Will puts on a ball, the astounding agility with which Tomasine runs, the deep concentration Chapin shows when trying to cut with scissors, Ravi's affinity for being up high.

In addition, each increase in an infant's physical skills allows the infant's development to blossom in other ways. This relationship is evident from the infant's first movement. Holding one's head in balance, for example, allows the eyes to focus steadily on a target, such as identifying a toy to reach for or move toward.

For a toddler, coordination has two levels of meaning. The first is actual physical coordination or the process of combining physical movements toward a goal or end point. Climbing up stairs or a ladder is rewarded by a new perspective. Climbing down takes equal effort! The next level of coordination is that of integrating skills—using more than one skill at the same time. The child forms an intention that requires both complex bodily control and extended concentration to achieve. Examples of activities that require children to integrate skills include toilet learning, throwing a ball at a target, pedaling a trike, screwing lids onto jars, pouring without spilling, dressing and undressing, completing puzzles, and stringing beads. Integrating skills calls for "putting it all together" so that physical coordination and mental efforts can be combined to solve problems encountered in daily life. How to balance this ball on this block? How to stop pushing the cart in time to keep it from hitting Julio? How to make the sticker stick to the paper? These questions foreshadow the more complex ones children will encounter as they get older. The process of trying to solve them leads to discovery and knowledge, but more importantly, it develops a child's problem-solving technique.

If human brains are a marvel, contemplate the wonder of human bodies. Consider all the ways in which adults use their bodies without thinking, relying on muscle memory instead of their brains. For example, think of making a bed, which requires throwing the covers out over to cover the bed. How many times did you have to do that before you could do it predictably? When you put away leftovers, can you reliably choose a container that matches the volume of the food? How much practice did you need? If you have recently taken up a new hobby—line dancing, drumming, cooking, a craft, shape-note singing—then you have experienced again the joy of making your body work the way you intended. In much the same way, children are engaged in experimenting with making their bodies work the way their minds envision.

Going up steps, rising from a sitting to a standing position, running on uneven ground, and balancing while carrying objects are feats caregivers see children master every day. Adults have been capable in these ways for so long that it's easy to forget what complex skills they really are. Through close observation of children's efforts and understanding child development, caregivers can not only appreciate children's practice of physical skills but also learn how to support it.

Strategies Caregivers Use to Promote Coordination

There are some specific ways that caregivers can interact with infants and toddlers to support their efforts toward physical development. These strategies allow infants to feel safe as they reach out to explore, and they allow toddlers to control their own rate and level of skill practice. The strategies work well to help children with coordination because they take into account the long-term learning that is necessary to build a reliable skill from everyday practice. Use the following strategies to support children's experience with physical coordination:

- Provide opportunities for practice at varied levels of skill
- Promote body awareness by coaching
- Make room for trial and error and repeated investigation
- Allow for innovative use of materials
- Facilitate problem solving with observation and open-ended questions

Provide Opportunities for Practice at Varied Levels of Skill

Caregivers can set up the infant and toddler environments so that infants and toddlers will be able to practice skills they're most comfortable with, try something new, and then revisit an already mastered skill in order to consolidate all of their experience before moving on. Infants and toddlers naturally use this "two steps forward, one step back" approach, and caregivers can support it by making sure opportunities for skill practice are present for all the developmental levels every day. It's not up to caregivers to say to a group of toddlers, for example, "Let's move on to jumping today." Rather, caregivers can provide a safe mat and platform, and the children will use them when they are ready to practice jumping.

When a toddler has the opportunity to visit the infant room, for example, caregivers can observe the toddler's glee in revisiting the infant toys. Consider the following scene:

Fifteen-month-old Janie is walking well and has been out of the infant room for nearly three months, and loves to visit now as a toddler. Before she was walking, one of her favorite toys in the infant room was a pop-up box. Caregiver Samantha remembers how long she would practice sliding, pushing, squeezing, and flipping each lid open. Now, in the infant room, Janie toddles to one of the pop-up boxes and with coordinated speed and agility pops open each lid in quick succession. She shuts the lids quickly and repeats the exercise even faster a second time. Samantha comments, "Look how fast you can open those lids now."

When she was an infant, Janie's skill practice focused on the individual muscle and finger movements of pushing the button, sliding the bar, squeezing the knob, or flipping the switch to open each lid purposefully and slowly. Now, as a larger and stronger toddler, she has moved on to a new challenge, consolidating and extending her skills by challenging herself to repeat the sequential motions faster and faster.

Recognizing the need for young children to test themselves, caregivers can set up the indoor and outdoor environments to allow infants and toddlers to practice skills related to balance, knowledge of their positions in space, strength, and control of their bodies. Through observation, caregivers can provide experiences that are designed as "optimal stress," those that provide a bridge from one task to the next.

Close observation of individual children leads caregivers to anticipate the next stage and respond to it. For infants, this might mean providing floor space needed for rolling, sturdy furniture for pulling up on, and shape boxes for small-muscle exploration. For toddlers, caregivers can offer riding toys as well as push toys, gluing activities in addition to ones that involve paintbrushes, and scissors as well as squeeze bottles.

For example, consider what caregiver Scott has done in the following scenario to support Leeza's development of coordination:

Twenty-two-month-old Leeza is very fast at scooting on a trike with no pedals. She and her friends chase each other round and round the cement path, slowing just enough to negotiate the curves. Trikes with pedals are also available in the yard, and today Leeza is sitting on one. She rocks back and forth, pushing the pedals but never quite rotating them the full turn. "Push hard, Leeza, you're moving the trike when you push the pedals," caregiver Scott encourages her. By straightening her knees, Leeza succeeds in moving the trike backward in short spurts. After ten minutes, she rejoins her friends scooting around on the little pedal-less trikes. Scott continues to include both kinds of trikes in the yard and notices that it's three or four days before she attempts the pedals again.

Promote Body Awareness by Coaching

After setting up the environment, caregivers can respond to children's actions and efforts by coaching. In coaching, caregivers act as a reference point for the children as they move through time and space. Caregivers can give children the security they need to venture down new paths and learn new skills until they no longer need an outside reference point.

The first step in coaching is to monitor and encourage children's skill practice. One way to do this is for caregivers to point out to children what they see children do, and then go a step beyond the validation used to promote curiosity. Standing close by, caregivers can put what the child is doing into words by describing her actions; interpreting what she might be thinking, feeling, or wondering; and suggesting specific possibilities for what she might do next. For example, a caregiver might say something like "I see you're standing on top of the slide. Did you want to sit to slide down or climb back down the ladder?" By focusing on what they might do next, caregivers help children identify their intentions and do the necessary planning to carry them out.

Caregivers can expand infants' awareness of their motion by describing what they are doing as they move. Coaching helps guide children by pointing out where they are in relation to the ground, others, and objects. For example, a caregiver can say to a four month old who is turning over, "You're throwing your legs up to turn onto your tummy—that's it, push with your feet." To an eight month old who is backing down off a cushion, a caregiver might say, "Put your feet down first—reach with your feet and push with your arms." A cruising infant learning to go up stairs might hear "Hold on with your hands, reach with your foot, and pull with your arms."

When focused on an objective, young children don't realize they can't go directly to it.

Infants crawl over others or reach across a table rather than go around. A toddler's perspective is similar. Crawling over a table, going through a fence, getting inside a box, climbing up on a shelf—toddlers have to try these spaces out for themselves to see how or if they fit in them.

Magical thinking is evident when small-muscle coordination lags behind a toddler's intention and understanding. Having climbed up onto a couch, a child will want to magically be back down on the ground without having to climb back down. This type of thinking is Maddie's difficulty in the scene below. How does Lupe coach her to help her figure out how to use her body to solve her problem with the puzzle?

Nineteen-month-old Maddie has a puzzle piece in her hand. She tries repeatedly to set the piece into the matching hole, but it isn't quite aligned and won't fit in. Caregiver Lupe suggests, "Try rotating the piece, Maddie." Maddie looks at her and then at the piece. Lupe adds, "Turn it around." Maddie quickly turns over the piece. She continues waving the piece over the hole and then starts banging it gently. Lupe takes a different puzzle piece and puts it on the table. Demonstrating with the new piece, she explains, "Rotate it, turn it around and around, then try it in the hole." Maddie sets her piece over the hole and turns it. "That's it," Lupe says. It takes five more turns for the piece to settle into place. Maddie smiles and says, "I did it."

Coaching is tailored to a specific process of learning. It is respectful of what children are really working on at a particular time. Lupe offered Maddie a new technique and the language to describe it. Her coaching was successful because she had observed Maddie enough to offer a technique that met Maddie's need and was a good next step for Maddie. In another example of a similar problem, what happens when a newly walking toddler experiences an upright perspective? From his new height he literally sees new tasks to try to accomplish. Consider the following scene, in which fourteen-month-old Niko approaches a ladder that leads up to a platform and slide.

Niko flops his extended body against the steps of the ladder. His hands reach toward the top step. He repeatedly lifts his right foot and swipes it in the air as he blindly searches for the bottom step. Observing Niko's efforts, the caregiver, Sita, approaches him. "I can tell you want to climb that ladder, Niko. Here's the first step," she says as she taps it with her hand to make a sound. Niko looks down to the step and places his foot on it. Holding his foot down on the step with her hand, Sita continues coaching: "Here's a place to pull yourself up with your arms." As he pulls with his arms, Niko's left foot steps up onto the bottom step. "Hold tight here," Sita says as she places her hands on Niko's. Then Sita repeats, "Here's the next step, Niko," tapping it with her hand. He lifts his right foot up to the next step. "Nice holding on, Niko. You're climbing," Sita says. Sita continues to coach each move in Niko's process of climbing. He makes it to the top platform and beams proudly. Sita says, "You made it to the top! Way to go, Niko! Do you need help to slide down or can you do it by yourself? I'll stay nearby."

Note how Sita observes and supports Niko's initial efforts to climb the ladder. Her coaching begins by having him look at the bottom step. The sound of her tapping on it helps him locate it. To help him maintain his balance, she holds in place first his foot and then his hand while he moves his other foot. Step by step, Sita coaches Niko up the ladder, letting him pull up and move his body. This initial coaching will help Niko feel successful and want to practice climbing. The repeated feel of success will build his body's muscle memory so that eventually he will be able to climb without looking at the steps.

Make Room for Trial and Error and Repeated Investigation

Caregivers can support self-discovery by letting children do as much as they can safely do by themselves. This allows them to gain a full understanding of their actions that is not possible when adults skip them over the hard parts or do things for them. Caregivers can honor a child's lengthy, prolonged process, knowing that it is the way children learn the natural consequences of their interactions with the environment.

Self-discovery is an area in which a caregiver can clearly observe children building one skill on another. As one muscle group strengthens, it can then be applied in the service of the child's quest for combining skills. For example, infants often begin crawling by going backward. Pushing off with the hands enough times exercises their arm muscles and gives their brains information about how this specific movement works. Then they can start crawling forward with the combination of strength and intent developed by the experience of crawling backward.

The perseverance shown by toddlers belies their reputation of having short attention spans. When an eighteen month old spends all day digging sand to fill pails, the caregiver's job is to support this effort, not interrupt with artificial directives, abrupt breaks, or forced transitions.

The caregiver observes how she tries using various shovels before settling on the most efficient and actually dumping out some pails to refill them using this favored shovel. In the next weeks this new arm strength will serve her ability to throw balls.

Placing the emphasis on the process changes the focus for caregivers and allows them to see the child's process of learning as more important than reaching a certain arbitrary point by a certain time. When caregivers take on a role as facilitator, it allows infants and toddlers to go through their process with support rather than interruption. Caregivers can understand that babies' brains are not the same as they were yesterday or last week; as children literally make connections, they have to retest their perceptions. Coordination is the basis of this process, because children practice with their bodies first, then carry out investigation of objects outside themselves. Many caregivers have seen babies "practicing gravity" by dropping objects repeatedly and watching them fall until they are sure that's what will happen.

Supporting this process means gauging the child's interest and intent at any time and encouraging practice. Infants may pull up many times before getting a knee bent under them to give them a strong enough push to stand stably, and they may have to renegotiate this balance when drawn by a ball they want to pick up from the floor. Toddlers continually go through this process of reassessment with physical tasks, as shown in this scene:

After many fillings and dumpings of buckets, two-and-a-half-year-old Stephanie has filled a big bucket with wet sand. Dragging on the handle with one hand, she says, "Help!" The caregiver, Nic, says, "What is it you want to have happen?" Stephanie says, "Turn it over." "Try using both hands," suggests Nic. "Too heavy," says Stephanie. Idly, Stephanie kicks at it, and the bucket falls over. Nic says, "Now what can you do?" Steph uses both hands to empty the bucket. Her face shines with delight.

Reinvestigation of previous skills builds on new strengths and perception. This is the reason playdough doesn't get old or boring for toddlers; it can grow with them as their new capabilities provide new ideas of how to manipulate it. Playdough and other open-ended materials and environmental setups provide numerous possibilities for this reinvestigation. Toddlers who began swinging on their tummies, and then learned to sit holding on, can later straddle the swing to swing side to side or finally attempt to stand in the swing.

This long-term experience with many materials allows the infants and toddlers to begin to draw conclusions about how the world works. As we have discussed previously, children develop this understanding in a progression from simple to more complex concepts. For example, "practicing gravity" occurs in infancy and then is revisited when balls are thrown. Language enhances this progression as children learn that there's a name for where they are in space, beginning with up and down and building to words like here, there, fast, slow, over, under.

Allow for Innovative Use of Materials

Individuals show consistent preferences in choice of materials and approach to the world as early as four months of age. When caregivers honor these preferences, infants and toddlers internalize a sense of inquiry rather than a dependence on external interpretations as a way of gaining knowledge about the world. One such individual approach is expressed by infant Sami in the story below.

Sami loved strings since before she could crawl. She would pull strings to bring toys closer as she lay on her tummy. She pulled them with her as she crawled, cruised, and walked. At sixteen months old, she is still drawn to strings. Her alertness to strings organizes her approach and leads to discovery in new environments.

Toddlers refine their own approaches when given the opportunity as well.

As an experienced caregiver, Diane has long presented puzzles to toddlers in an orderly way. Gauging the skill level of each child, she offers each child puzzles that will lead to the next level of difficulty. Twenty-one-month-old Galen begs to try a sixteen-piece puzzle of a barn, though it seems too hard for her to Diane. Diane finally gives it to her because it seems so important to Galen. As Diane watches, contrary to her expectations, Galen doesn't dump out the puzzle. Instead, she carefully lifts each piece and lets it back down. She repeats for the four pieces in one corner. The next day, Galen asks again for the barn puzzle. She repeatedly lifts each piece slightly. She works for five minutes or more. Every time the puzzles are out, Galen works on the barn. After a few days of practicing like this, Galen begins taking pieces out, one at a time, then in twos and fours and sixes. After three weeks, Galen can do the entire sixteen-piece puzzle.

After this experience, Diane rethinks her belief that there is a logical way to present puzzles to every child. This is also a reminder of what caregivers can learn from children when they pay attention.

At ITC, we largely allow children to mix toys and move materials from place to place, though we do separate indoor and outdoor toys, mostly to keep the indoor toys clean. Recognizing how important multiple brain connections are, we allow children to "mix and match," and caregivers applaud safe innovations as evidence that "their brains work." Baskets used as baby cradles, stuffed animals placed in the fire engines, Lego blocks as pretend food in the kitchen area all provide opportunities for interesting juxtaposition and new possibilities for skill practice. The children can decide if it's working the way they intend; we don't dictate their explorations with statements like "That animal's too big for a fire engine."

Facilitate Problem Solving with Observation and Open-Ended Questions

How can anybody accomplish anything when everything is falling down? If you think about it, humans and the objects they act upon are all in the process of balancing against gravity. The problems encountered by infants and toddlers in working their physical wills center on this fact. Caregivers facilitate children's approaches to problem solving by carefully joining their space to see what it is they want to do, reflecting what they do, identifying what problems they are having, and asking open-ended questions that might illuminate how the child can accomplish the task.

An infant's body in balance leads to mobility—rolling, creeping, crawling—each of which requires a relearning of holding oneself in relation to the earth. Manipulating small cars, trucks, brushes, spoons, or cups requires a child to determine how much strength it takes to overcome inertia—otherwise the cup goes flying to the ceiling when it is picked up. Toddlers often want to stand to do tasks like cutting with scissors or solving puzzles. It could be their balance is better, giving them one less thing to concentrate on if they can be literally grounded.

What people call "problems" are really opportunities to learn to fulfill their intentions. All of the physical experiences that children have during their play—moving a stuck trike or pushcart, adding the block to the tower that makes it fall, jumping without falling, fitting things into other things, watching spherical or cylindrical objects roll—move young children towards powers that can be brought to bear on new problems they encounter.

Sometimes toddlers say to caregivers, "You do it." This may be evidence of their feelings of self-doubt. Caregivers can help toddlers through the doubt side of autonomy by modeling a belief that they *can* do it. Sometimes it helps to break a task into very small "doable" steps. If caregivers don't make an effort in this area, toddlers may become dependent on adult help. After all, they may think, why else would she be helping me except that I can't do it myself? Young children may cease to see themselves as competent if caregivers fail to facilitate their problem-solving abilities.

Open-ended questions help children focus in order to think about and articulate what it is they want to achieve. Open-ended questions also can broaden children's ideas of how to move past barriers by broadening their perception of possibilities. An open-ended question is any question that can't be answered by yes or no. "Did you want to make the tower taller?" is a yes-or-no question. "What did you want to have happen?" is an open-ended question. To form an open-ended question, build on the strategy of saying what you see by opening with a reflective statement (for example, "I see that the blocks fell down") and continuing to comment, pausing for responses from the child. Then respond to the child's remarks, helping her to build ideas and see possibility. Here are some examples:

- "I see you're working hard with that bucket. (pause) What is it you want to have happen? Oh."
- "What do you see?"
- "Thanks for showing me. What's next?"
- "How else could you use that? What do you see around it? Please tell me more."
- "Please tell me about it." (Use when a child offers an item for your consideration.)
- "What will you do next?"
- "What else could you try?"
- "What does it remind you of?"
- "What do you think would happen if you…?"
- "What does it feel like?"
- "Remember yesterday, when the ball rolled under the couch? What did we have to do?"
- "Is there anything else you could use?"
- "How can your friend help? What can your friend do?" (Problem solving offers many possibilities to encourage interdependence by focusing on what children can do together.)

It makes sense to start with the simplest questions and then use more complex ones as children's language develops. For infants, a caregiver can expand the strategy of "say what you see" and simply describe alternatives, such as "Did you want to roll the ball or pick it up?" Toddlers whose language is more complex can respond to more complex questions, and when they have had enough experience of choosing from alternatives, toddlers will begin to offer alternatives to others or ask for possibilities not yet mentioned. As their concentration increases, older toddlers can see possibilities before acting them out and can engage in "What do you think would happen?" discussions. Their experience is limited, so the answers may seem outlandish, but it is the *process* of observing and assessing using trial and error, reinforced through the use of open-ended questions, that leads them to problem solving.

Using the Strategies during Caregiving Routines

Caregivers can carefully plan their approach to daily routines in order to be alert to opportunities for children to practice physical skills during these everyday experiences.

Mealtimes

Children's drive to refine physical movements in order to accomplish what they intend is evident during mealtimes. A four-month-old infant is able to hold a bottle, and some infants communicate this preference by reaching for the bottle. When infants are spoon-fed solid foods, they may grab for the spoon. Let's revisit eight-month-old Emily with her banana.

Emily has been feeding herself at the table for a couple of weeks, but Maggie continues to spoon-feed her at the same time. Today, Cheerios cereal and bits of banana are on the table in front of Emily. She expertly pinches a Cheerio between her thumb and forefinger, conveying it directly to her mouth. Maggie waits with some rice cereal, knowing that if she tries to put something else into Emily's mouth immediately, Emily will spit out the Cheerio. After Emily swallows, Maggie offers the spoon of food, and Emily grabs at the spoon! "Oh, you want to try it?" Maggie asks. She gives the spoon to Emily, who waves it in the direction of her mouth. Maggie has another spoon ready and continues feeding. Emily trades spoons, dropping one and grabbing the other. Once, she gets a good bite off her spoon into her mouth. After two more trades, she drops the spoon and returns to the Cheerios.

Note how Maggie was prepared for this developmental step and had a second spoon handy, demonstrating her willingness to engage in Emily's approach to self-feeding. Emily is building up a variety of foods to self-feed, beginning with the banana and now Cheerios. This respect of practice and providing for self-discovery learning will promote Emily's consolidation of skills and feeling of competence. Over the next months she will master spoon-feeding because she wants to practice and is given the experience to do so.

There are many opportunities for toddlers to practice physical skills at mealtimes. For example, toddlers can practice hand-eye coordination by pouring their beverage from a small (one cup) spouted measuring cup into their cup. This is a real *process*: practicing, missing the cup, and practicing again at the next snack until the toddler can eventually pour spill-free. It might take months for young toddlers to master this skill, but they do love to practice.

Twenty-two-month-old Lizzie says, "Milk?" Jen says, "Not milk; we're having juice today. It's your turn to pour your juice." Lizzie moves her cup near her right hand, picking up the pitcher handle with her left. Her eyebrows are drawn together, her lips compressed into a tight line. Lifting the pitcher, she moves it through the air, pauses over the cup, and tips the pitcher so the juice flows into the cup. "Nice pouring, Lizzie!" Jen says. Eighteen-month-old Tim is wiggling in his seat. "Thanks for waiting. Your turn, Tim," Jen assures him. She fills the pitcher barely one-quarter cup. Tim pushes her hand away when she hands him the pitcher, so she verbally coaches, "Try pointing the spout of the pitcher into the cup." Tim lifts and dumps in one swift motion; half the juice spills on the table. Jen takes a sponge and wipes up the puddle. Tim drinks the juice from his cup.

Mealtimes offer toddlers practical experience in learning to coordinate small muscles for feeding and serving themselves. Caregivers can prepare for this practice without hurrying or having unrealistic expectations. By having a sponge handy as spills occur, Jen can accept the toddlers' spills as a part of their process of learning.

To prevent or decrease the spread of germs, it is important to limit the child's practice of pouring from a pitcher. After the toddler has put her cup to her mouth, there are now germs on that cup: if the pouring pitcher is used again, it may very well touch the edge of the cup and become "infected." So it's best to offer the pouring pitcher to each child only at the first serving of the beverage.

Naptimes

What a delicious feeling to wake in the middle of the night and be able to go back to sleep! Learning to relax may seem elusive, but it is an important part of coordination. As far as possible in a group care setting, caregivers can allow infants to practice calming themselves. Working closely with parents, caregivers learn the individual habits and patterns of infants. Caregivers can then coach them to become aware of the state of their bodies and assure them it's safe to relax.

"Allowing practice" also means that caregivers do not expect immediate success. Recognition of the effort made by the infant is an important step in the process of practicing. Consider this napping scene:

Meli is whimpering quietly. She is six months old and has been at the center about two weeks. Ted, the caregiver, says, "Oh, you're a tired girl, huh. Mom said you woke up early this morning." Holding her while gathering her pacifier, Ted speaks slowly. "Here's your soft blanket, your pacifier, let's get you comfortable. There, all snuggled." Ted carries Meli to rock and sing. Nearly asleep, Meli startles awake at the sound of another baby with a telephone toy. Ted moves slowly to pat Meli gently to bring her back to relaxation, stroking the tenseness away. "Let yourself sleep," he whispers. With Ted's singing and rocking, she relaxes again and stays asleep. Today she sleeps thirty minutes.

One month later, Meli barely rouses at the sound of other children. She often sleeps an hour. When she is rested, she is much more verbal and active in the environment. The trust and relaxation she feels from her naptime carries over to her play experiences.

Ted recognized Meli's sleepy signs. Knowing that an infant new to group care may have difficulty relaxing enough to sleep, he builds trust by responding and coaching with the phrases "Oh, you're a tired girl" and "Let yourself sleep," without expecting immediate success. He knows it will take Meli practice at relaxing before she will settle in and stay asleep.

It takes an integration of skills for toddlers to ready themselves for sleep. Identifying what they need, acquiring it, taking responsibility for it, and learning to relax are all done through conscious effort, and toddlers may need coaching help to acknowledge the personal signals their bodies are sending them.

Sixteen-month-old Kiana is next to go into the crib room for her nap. As Marion picks her up, Kiana pats her mouth and lets out a cry. Marion says, "Oh, you want your pacifier." Kiana says, "Yes." Marion asks, "Do you remember where it is?" Kiana says, "Cubby," as she points in that direction. When Marion finds it, she hands it to Kiana, who puts it in her mouth herself. With smiling, relaxed eyes, Kiana heads to the nap room with Marion.

Twenty-eight-month-old Nicholas runs to join the nap group for stories. At the door, Tammy reminds him, "Do you want to bring your sleeping friends, Nicholas?" Nicholas says, "Oh yeah, my blanket and koala" as he points to his cubby, and then carries them to the nap room.

At the end of story time, Tammy says, "Let's all pretend to be balloons. Fill up with air, and hold it!" In five seconds Tammy says, "Let the air out of your balloon." Having modeled taking a deep breath (chest expanded, cheeks blown out), Tammy now pushes the air out of her mouth and droops "just like an empty balloon, with no air."

Toddlers are capable of relaxing to sleep with personal aids or sleeping friends. Remembering where such items are kept and putting the pacifier into and out of their own mouth are vital steps to coordinating the whole process of relaxing themselves to sleep. In the above example, Kiana places the pacifier into her own mouth, and Nicholas carries his own sleeping friends. He and Kiana are becoming responsible for their personal care. "Be a balloon" is a useful modeling exercise for coaching toddlers to relax. We've observed that some toddlers will adopt this as a personal strategy, taking a deep breath between efforts to climb or as they sit down to read a book.

Personal Care: Cleaning Up and Diapering

Routines are often performed on a schedule that is not related to children's preferences or interests. In order to respect their interests and involve them in things that concern them, caregivers can apply the strategy of allowing their own approach to a routine situation. This approach also respects their skill practice by interrupting their effort as little and as respectfully as possible. Consider diapering a nine-month-old infant:

Rob is pulling up on a table in the middle of the infant room. Turning his right foot parallel to the edge of the table, he steps to his right, bringing his left foot over as he balances on his right foot, all the while holding on to the edge of the table. Caregiver Andrea comments, "Are you going after that bear? It's on the other side of the table." Rob continues around the table, ignoring the bear. "I need to check your diaper. I can do it while you're standing at the table." Bringing over a piece of computer paper, Andrea places it so Rob steps on it next. Andrea continues, "I have the new diaper. This is the dry one. The one you've got on is wet." Andrea takes off the wet diaper and places the new one on, securing it with the tape. Andrea disposes of the diaper wrapped in the paper. She models washing her hands using a spray bottle and paper towel, then follows through by washing Rob's hands.

Changing wet diapers while children stand up accommodates the cruising infants' developmental drive to be vertical and honors their coordination practice. What Rob is doing is just as important as a diaper change; Andrea can accommodate him by changing his diaper in a way that allows him to keep doing it.

A matter-of-fact approach to problem solving is useful when the caregiver is not sure if a toddler's refusal to do something is because the child doesn't know how or doesn't want to. For example, in this scene, toddlers are getting wet paper towels to clean their hands and faces after lunch.

"All done," Dorian says as she leaves the table. Caregiver Natasha says, "Please get a wet towel and wipe your face." This comment is met by a blank look. Natasha repeats, "Can you get a wet towel for your face?" When Dorian doesn't respond, Natasha moves close to her and says, "Look at the spaghetti sauce all over your face. How shall we get it off?" Dorian grins but doesn't move. Natasha gently directs her attention to the wet towels and helps her to get one. "Let's look in the mirror to clean your face," Natasha suggests.

Because Natasha suspends judgment about why Dorian is resistant, she is able to successfully use a direct approach to work through the resistance, rather than complaining or blaming Dorian. Observing what is actually happening is the first step in defining the problem.

Toilet learning is a process of coordination for a toddler that integrates autonomy and muscle control. As with other aspects of physical development, a child's progress is dependent not only on her body being mature enough to allow control over her need to poop or pee but also on the child's interest, practice, and experience. It is a perfect example of a child's "integration of skills" during a routine experience.

The topic of toileting raises a lot of discussion in the child care field. Approaches vary from culture to culture. In some cultures, the ways that children are trained reflect the opportunities that an adult has to interact one on one with a child. As Janet Gonzalez-Mena discusses in *Multicultural Issues in Child Care,* there are some cultures in which infants are held a majority of the time. Interdependent partnerships between adult and child occur as the child exhibits physical cues to be held away from the mother's body in order to urinate or defecate. As a result, both adult and child are trained, to a certain extent, to respond to each other's cues.

Cultural conflicts may occur when there are differing ideas about what is meant by toilet training. If the adult's goal is to train the child away from using diapers, then the adult introduces the idea to the child, but if toileting is seen as an independent process for the child to explore, the starting point is left up to the child. There really is no right or wrong perspective to the toileting approach. What we want to illuminate is the effect of the process on the child. Is it supportive or punitive? Does it foster development or slow it down?

In the United States there are at least two common approaches to toileting. One is the training approach, where a child is introduced to the idea of using the toilet by an adult, usually the parent. Cues for when to begin, under this approach, seem to be the child's age in relationship to a parent's experience ("*My* mother says I was trained at one year!"), parent convenience ("I'm tired of changing diapers"), or pressure to meet a requirement to enroll in preschool ("She can't go to that preschool unless she's toilet trained").

Standing-Up Diaper Changes

At ITC we often change wet diapers while a child is standing. Of course, poopy diapers are changed where there is running hot water. Lying down is usually necessary to clean all areas of the body thoroughly, but older toddlers can stand firmly and squat to allow a caregiver to clean their bottoms. It is more challenging to change cloth diapers on a standing infant or toddler, but practice helps the caregiver develop strategies for doing this successfully. Cloth diapers secured with clips rather than pins make this process entirely safe. Or, if a wrap is used, cloth diapers may be masking-taped in place before placing the wrap on.

If a caregiver is not comfortable with this standing-up method, she can still make changing a diaper a rewarding interactive experience and an opportunity to practice physical coordination. While the child is prone the caregiver can emphasize the physical help the child can give, using phrases such as "Please lift up your bottom," "Now I need you to bend your knees," "Roll to the side, please," "Thanks, that helps a lot."

The respectful caregiver response is to follow the child's lead. If she resists lying down, respect this effort to stand and accommodate it if at all possible. If an ointment or cream needs to be applied, try doing it while the infant is standing, especially if that is the child's expressed preference. When you think about it, is it any easier to apply cream to a writhing, fighting child who does not want to lie down?

A different approach to toileting is a developmental one, which takes into account the individual child's interest, capability, and coordination. Here, to begin the process, an observant parent or caregiver observes cues from the child that she is interested in transitioning from wearing a diaper to learning how and when to use the toilet. Such cues include

1. tugging at her diaper
2. going to a private area to pee or poop in her diaper
3. wanting to observe an older toddler practicing the process or a parent using the toilet
4. practicing taking steps backwards to sit on a potty-chair (even fully clothed)

When adults observe any or several of these cues over a period of time, they can begin to offer the opportunities for the child to experiment and practice with the physical skill of using the toilet. Like crawling or walking, toileting is a complex process that a child learns over time. When children tug at their diapers after releasing urine or moving their bowels, they are letting caregivers know that they experience the difference between a wet or poopy diaper and having a dry one. This is a step in the process of early learning about elimination. The child experiences a different sensation "down there" and communicates it. The widespread use of disposable diapers has certainly affected toddlers' abilities to perceive that difference. As the technology of paper diapers enhances or prolongs dryness against the child's bottom, she may not feel different or uncomfortable enough to want to do anything different like using the potty.

Consider the following scenario:

Twenty-three-month-old Norman has shown some curiosity about using the potty-chair for several months. He stands close to the potty-chairs and watches thirty-month-old Jack pull his pants down to go pee. Occasionally Norman sits on the potty-chair, *fully clothed. The day after his second birthday, Norman's mother, Betty, brings a pair of underwear ("training pants") and says, "Norman needs to be toilet trained so he can be ready for preschool next year. I want you to take him to the potty every hour." The first hour, Tina says to Norman, "It's time to go potty, let's go," as she takes his hand. Norman looks at her wide-eyed and says, "No!" Tina pulls his arm, saying "Oh, come on. Your mommy wants you to go potty." Norman begins to cry and screams, "No, don't want to go potty."*

Norman obviously does not want to use the potty just because someone else wants him to. To push or pull him beyond this point would be a disrespectful battle between Norman and Tina and stressful for all others to observe.

In a child care setting where children of different ages are together, advantages exist for a learning process such as toileting. As seen in the above scenario, Norman was beginning to be curious about using the potty naturally and on his own. He was using his sense of vision to observe an older child going to the potty, and he was practicing the task of sitting on the potty-chair when fully clothed. But when someone else decided for him that he should start using the potty, Norman declared, "No." Consider an alternative approach to Norman's toileting that is respectful and involves him:

When Norman's mother presents the underwear to the caregiver, Tina says, "It'll be nice to have the unders here when Norman feels ready to wear them." To Norman she says, "You **are** *showing some interest, aren't you? I've seen you watch Jack use the potty, and I've seen you practice sitting on the potty-chair, too." Norman smiles, points, and says, "Potty," as he runs off. His mother says, "I want you to take him to the potty every hour." Tina responds, "I know you would like us to do that, but it's not possible with the staffing ratio. What we* **can** *do that has worked well is to continue following his interest and invite him to go potty with Jack. We do this on a regular schedule after meals, snacks, and naps. We can let Norman* *know his unders are in his cubby." Norman runs back to hold his mother's leg. Tina says to him, "The unders will be in your cubby; you can let us know when you want to put them on. You can practice wearing them on the outside of your diaper if you want." Norman runs off again. To his mother, Tina says, "If you'd like, we can discuss with you how toilet learning can work here in the center with Norman's involvement. I know you must feel a lot of pressure since most preschools require children to be out of diapers. Norman is interested now, and I'm sure he will learn to use the potty in time for preschool. Either Isabel or I would be happy to talk further with you."*

As Tina respectfully acknowledges Norman's mother's feelings, she also shares the center's approach to a child's process of learning to use the toilet. She acknowledges that Norman's curiosity is a step in that process.

The third principle of respectful caregiving reminds caregivers to learn each child's unique way of communicating. This includes body language. When a child moves to a private place or scrunches up her face with a pronounced body position of pushing, she is probably having a bowel movement in her diaper. These communications provide a connection for a caregiver, who can comment, "I can tell you might be pooping; let me know when you're finished, so we can change your diaper." The toddler's communication is acknowledged and her continued involvement in her process is encouraged. Likewise, when a child is busily playing and may be reluctant to give up an area or object of play, a caregiver can take a portable potty-chair to that location and assure the toddler that she'll "save" the item or space so the toddler can "go potty." Respect, trust, involvement, and modeling for other kids are happening all at once in such a caregiving experience.

For parents' involvement with their child, we suggest they take their toddler shopping to choose which unders to wear when she is ready.

The parent can determine the choices if some commercial options are unacceptable. To further involve the toddler in the process, we suggest she wear elastic-waist pants so she can pull them up and down herself. Overalls make it difficult for the toddler to undress on her own in order to use the toilet.

Transitions

Body language is the first language. During transitions, caregivers can respond to signals that the infant communicates to them. Mobile babies use their physical coordination to tell us when they want a change. Sometimes movement is coordinated with language, sometimes not. For instance, a crawling baby will go to the eating table, and a caregiver might say something like "Oh, are you hungry now?" When caregivers recognize a child's individual approach, they begin to involve the child in how to accomplish a transition from one activity to the next together. Consider what the following scene might mean:

Lasana, ten months old, has been cruising around the table in the middle of the infant room. With barely a pause, he has walked around it, stooping to pick up toys and moving on after six minutes. Now he drops to the floor on all fours and quickly crawls to the eating table. Pulling himself up in one motion, Lasana picks at the tabletop with his fingers and looks at the caregiver. Taphne responds, "Oh, did you want something to eat? It's almost snack time, but you can eat now if you want. Let's get a bib." Lasana allows the bib to be put on thirty seconds before bits of cheese and melon appear on the tabletop.

Taphne's response to Lasana's initiation of snack time confirms for him that he can communicate and use his coordination to get his needs met. What if he declined the bib and refused the food? Taphne could model problem-solving techniques to find out what he really wanted. Some possibilities to explore: Different food? No bib? Something to drink first? Investigation of the table? Lasana can still be assured that Taphne will respectfully work with him when he indicates he wants a change.

Getting a toddler from point A to point B is either complicated or enhanced by her growing coordination. Sometimes it seems her impetus to practice is only active when there are other things to be done! Planning for time in transitions to include these opportunities to practice skills respects the toddler's efforts and reminds caregivers of their role as facilitators. Dressing and undressing practice, for example, takes up much time and energy at transition times for toddlers.

Personal care is important to toddlers. Caregivers often hear "I do it myself" or "Me do it" during the caregiving day, as toddlers practice and expand their coordinated efforts. For example, this may emerge as an interest in removing shoes and socks as a transition to naptime or to barefoot comfort on a warm day. If caregivers observe closely, they can understand the complexity of the skills toddlers push themselves to practice and acquire.

Twenty-six-month-old Claire is visiting the infant room before nap. Caregiver Cheryl is sitting in the rocking chair feeding six-month-old Jimmy. Claire approaches and asks, "Baby Jimmy?" Cheryl says, "Yes, this is Jimmy." Claire asks, "Jimmy feet?" "Yes, inside his socks are Jimmy's feet," Cheryl answers. Claire holds up her foot and says, "Socks." Cheryl says, "Yes, I have my socks on too." Claire pulls at Jimmy's socks, interrupting his eating. Cheryl says, "Oh, let's not take off his socks; his feet might get cold. You can take off your own socks." "Shoes," Claire answers. Cheryl confirms, "Yes, your shoes come off first." Claire sits on the floor, expertly

ripping the Velcro straps up and pulling off her shoes. The socks take a bit longer. First she struggles, trying to just pull them from the toe, but her arms aren't long enough with her legs out in front of her. Cheryl suggests, "Take your time; try pushing your sock down and around the heel of your foot." This works, and Claire gets up to walk around the room barefoot. Cheryl asks, "How does the floor feel?" Claire answers, "Cold." "How can you get your feet warm?" Cheryl asks. Claire makes a circuit of the room and, coming upon her socks and shoes, sits down to put them back on.

Claire's investigation begins with her curiosity about the baby's socks. When Cheryl suggests that Claire remove her own socks rather than Jimmy's, Claire follows through her exploration with some coaching by Cheryl and repeated attempts to push her socks off. Cheryl's open-ended question "How does the floor feel?" allows Claire to feel the floor and assess that socks and shoes on would be warmer and more comfortable. Again, undressing involves a process of coordinated movements. Consider the complexity of this task for a toddler:

- balancing body in sitting position while reaching foot
- fine motor grasp of shoelace or Velcro strap
- pulling knot loose
- pushing shoe off heel
- pulling/pushing sock off or around heel

Dressing oneself is complicated too. Getting clothes aligned right side out and frontwards with body requires lots of practice. When older toddlers are given practice time and coaching help along the way, they can master this skill as well.

This chart summarizes the behavior caregivers see expressed by young children in routine and play experiences and presents coinciding approaches for caring interactions. Please note that development of the whole child is a continuing and an overlapping process.

Communication
(relates to Language Development)

Honor both nonverbal and verbal communication, and respond with respect to child-initiated interactions.

The attitude we communicate determines the quality of each interaction.

Curiosity
(relates to cognitive development)

Child Tasks	Caregiver Strategies
Use senses to explore environment to construct own reality	Provide choices of materials and time to manipulate them.
	Validate the child's experience ("say what you see").
Discover cause and effect	Plan to extend the exploration using the child's interests as a guide.
Assimilate knowledge	Offer information ("say what you know").
	Promote self-awareness.
	Share the caregiver's interests ("say who you are").

Connection
(relates to social-emotional development)

Child Tasks	Caregiver Strategies
Develop self-concept	
Trust	Be predictable and consistent in meeting children's needs.
Autonomy	Slow the pace; be an "island."
Build relationships with peers, family, caregivers	Introduce peers and adults by name.
	Include family culture.
	Affirm mutual interests to encourage interdependence.
Learn to resolve conflict	Be aware of one's own internal conflict.
Taking responsibility and experiencing the consequences of actions With self With others	Help children learn to resolve conflicts.

Coordination
(relates to physical development and integration of skills)

Child Tasks	Caregiver Strategies
Negotiate relationship with gravity and space Balance Mobility Control Strength Large/Small motor	Provide opportunities for practice at varied levels of skill.
	Promote body awareness by coaching.
Integration of skills	Make room for trial and error and repeated investigation.
Problem solving	Allow for innovative use of materials.
	Facilitate problem solving with observation and open-ended questions.

Comprehensive Strategies That Support Caring Interactions

- **Observe** individual children; provide for Optimal Stress
- **Model** the behavior you wish to see
- **Acknowledge Feelings**
- **Anticipate** transitions, unusual events, and changes in routine
- **Help Children Articulate their Needs and Wants**
- **Offer Real Choices**
- **Set Consistent Limits**

8

Playing with Coordination

Planned play experiences for small groups of infants and toddlers give caregivers opportunities to focus on children's physical development and the integration of skills used in problem solving. The strategies we discussed in chapter 7 can be used to support children's development of coordination during these planned play experiences as well as during caregiving routines.

Boxes for Babies

One way to provide for large-motor practice for babies indoors is to turn over a toy shelf. As a platform, it can be a base for more challenging climbing or a place to sit with a new view. Using the shelf on its back makes "boxes for babies."

What You'll Need

- Shallow toy shelf with two or three shelves.

- Pillows, cushions, bedspreads.

What to Do

- While the infants are sleeping or before they come in the morning, turn a toy shelf on its back to make "boxes" or on its front to make a platform if it has a solid back.

- You can put one side against a wall or place it in a corner if you are worried about infants falling off the platform. It's also fine to put it in the center of the room with space all around it.

- Surround with pillows or other cushiony material.

- Let crawling, cruising infants discover the new arrangement.

Limits

None needed

Other Things to Think About

- If you choose to make a platform, use pillows to make "steps" up to it.

- Adjust the height of the platform to infants in your care by using a deeper or shallower toy shelf and more or fewer pillows around it. Ask yourself questions like these: Do they have good balance sitting? Can they back down from a height? Observe to see what they are capable of, rather than assuming.

- If "boxes" are made, consider the height of the infants and the depth of the boxes. Cruising infants will usually climb over into a "box" of the right height. If it's too tall, they may try to go in headfirst. If this is the case, you might want pillows on the inside too.

Supporting Play

Can you see how Roya uses these strategies to support baby Ilene's coordination in the following story?

- Provide opportunities for practice at varied levels of skill

- Promote body awareness by coaching

On the fifth rainy day in a row, the room where the infants spend most of their time feels very small to caregiver Roya. While the babies nap, she enlists the help of a colleague to set one of the toy shelves on its back. This makes four open boxes! She puts a pillow and a toy in the bottom of each box. As the babies awake they discover the new space. Ten-month-old Ilene pulls up by the side of the box. Spying the stuffed elephant at the bottom, she reaches for it. "You want to have the elephant," Roya says. Ilene lifts her knee up. "That's it; you can climb into the box and be with the elephant." Roya moves closer in order to coach Ilene. "Hold on with your hands, reach your foot," Roya gently guides Ilene. She'll try this again, whether it rains or not!

Pillow Mountain

Infants who are efficient crawlers will enjoy this extra challenge. Imagine a soft mound to crawl over, with interesting dips and ridges. What might an infant see anew from the top?

What You'll Need

- A variety of covered foam, cushions, and/or pillows in various shapes.
- Large sheet or bedspread (optional).

What to Do

- Build a mountain with the pillows you've collected, taking care to see that it is stable. Base the steepness and height of the mountain on your observation of the infants who will use it.
- You may choose to cover the mountain with a sheet or bedspread to help keep its shape.
- Be sure there is a soft landing area for infants who roll off.
- Let the babies discover and freely explore the mountain.
- Respond to the infants making eye contact with you, squealing, or making other vocalizations and gestures. "Say what you see" and reflect their experience back to them.

Limits

- Caregiver may need to "direct traffic" as babies climb over pillows and each other.

Other Things to Think About

- By observation, a caregiver can tell when infants would enjoy this experience. Observation will also help the caregiver modify the mountain.

- It's probably easier to set up the mountain while infants sleep or prior to their arrival. It is fun, but takes longer, to build it together with them.

- Beginning crawlers may find a simple half-cylinder pillow a good challenge.

- This will work outdoors. When the age groups are combined, it's easier if the toddlers can have their own mountain. Toddlers might enjoy a mountain of tires covered with small carpets.

Supporting Play

Use these strategies to support babies' crawling over the mountain:

- Provide opportunities for practice at varied levels of skill

- Promote body awareness by coaching

Katya has built a pillow mountain for three crawling infants, ages eight months to eleven months. "Alex, you pulled up on the pillow! Here comes Maddie. You can climb up on the pillows," Katya says, patting the pillow beside her. Maddie starts up, pulling up with her arms. The next step takes her to a depression in the pillow where she can't get her knee up. "Oh, Maddie, you're stuck. Push your foot against my hand to move up. See where your foot can go here?" Meanwhile, Julia has climbed right to the top and now is trying to head down. "Try turning around and backing down that pillow. I'm here to help if you want," Katya says. "See, Maddie is right there. Let's go around her."

Katya coaches so the babies begin to learn where their bodies are relative to the objects and one another. Next time, she can reconfigure the mountain to maintain an "optimal stress" experience of further challenges for the infants.

Puzzles

Puzzles offer infants and toddlers focused practice at hand-eye coordination in conjunction with developing a problem-solving approach. From simple shape sorters to single-piece knobbed puzzles to simple interlocking puzzles, young children can build their skills when caregivers guide and encourage them to keep trying different strategies.

What You'll Need

- A variety of puzzles, increasing in complexity, such as

  Three-dimensional shape sorters or stacking toys

  One-piece puzzles with knobs

  Two- to four-piece puzzles with knobs

  Interlocking puzzles with two to sixteen pieces for toddlers.

What to Do

- Make simple shape sorters of various kinds available to infants or toddlers on open toy shelves.

- Invite small groups of toddlers (no more than four at once) to do puzzles at a table.

- From a variety of puzzles, offer a choice of two to each toddler.

- Encourage the toddlers to look carefully at the puzzles before taking them apart.

- Give the children lots of verbal encouragement and suggestions if they need them, using phrases like these:

  "Try taking it out and putting it back."

  "Try a different hole."

  "Try another piece."

"Rotate it." (Demonstrate.)

"Look for the curves and points."

"Put them together." (or "Match them.")

"Try using both hands."

Limits

- None needed for infants; none needed with simple shape sorters that are put out on toy shelves.

- Generally, encourage toddlers to finish one puzzle before starting another. You can help to complete one they are all finished with. If they don't help or leave the table, ask if they are all done with the puzzles for now.

- This is a table experience; pieces stay on the table.

- Make sure there are alternative materials for children who are not ready to use puzzles appropriately.

- Provide soft balls for throwing inside if toddlers throw pieces, and teethers for biting or chewing if they put the pieces in their mouths.

Other Things to Think About

- Homemade shape sorters may be fashioned by cutting a hole in a plastic lid of a coffee or similar can. Cut the hole to fit the lids from frozen juice cans. When the babies become adept at the circle, substitute a lid with a slit cut. Large food jar lids offer an alternative size.

- Note shape matching in other experiences: lids on pans, small figures in cars or trucks, baby toys involving objects or figures set inside holders.

Supporting Play

Use these strategies to support children's play with shape sorters and puzzles, as shown in the following scene:

- Make room for trial and error and repeated investigation

- Allow for innovative use of materials

- Facilitate problem solving with observation and open-ended questions

When caregiver Rich notices ten-month-old Reuben putting toys back into the basket he dumped, Rich gets out a simple shape sorter for Reuben. Juice lids go through a cutout circle in the lid on a coffee can. When Rich drops one in, Reuben is drawn by the sound. Rich leaves a basket of lids next to the can. Reuben quickly sees that the round lid fits easily through the hole. He puts all ten of the lids in and shakes the can. Cheerfully, he dumps it out. "I'm glad you enjoyed that," Rich says. He brings out another can with two slits cut in the lid. Reuben sets about banging the lids against the top while Rich observes.

Thirty-one-month-old Erika is sitting down and doing a simple puzzle of wild animals. Caregiver Eve is aware that Erika can do more difficult puzzles, and she is aware that coordination of skills is as important as hand-eye coordination for Erika right now. Erika suddenly picks up a puzzle piece with a panda on it and takes it to the basket of wild animal figures on the shelf. "This goes there," she says. Eve comments, "You put that panda with the other wild animals." Erika says, "The lion and tiger." Sitting back down, she asks for another puzzle. Eve makes a mental note to retrieve the puzzle piece when it's time to pick up the puzzles. Eve helps Erika to problem solve the new puzzle with phrases like "Let me know if you need help," "Look, you figured out how that fits," "I like how you're sticking to it to finish that puzzle," "Look at the outline," "Do you see the pointed part? Is there a hole that looks like that?"

Beads, Strings, and Nail Boards

Beads, strings, and nail boards are fascinating to toddlers when used in combination with one another. Children will string the beads and put them on the nails in the nail board, practicing hand-eye coordination and making patterns at the same time.

What You'll Need

- Large wooden or plastic beads (1 inch minimum in diameter) in small baskets for each toddler. Have at least 100 beads for every 4 toddlers.

- Small baskets, bowls, or trays—one for each toddler.

- Strings for bead stringing (long shoelaces work well, also), each with a knot tied at one end.

- One nail board for each toddler. These are commercially available, or you can make them with finish nails and pieces of scrap wood. Use rectangular pieces of board or plywood in various sizes, but at least 8 inches on a side. Sand the wood, particularly on the edges, until it is smooth enough to ensure that children will not get splinters. Use finish nails (which don't have wide heads) 1½ or 2 inches long (depending on the thickness of the board) and thick enough not to bend easily. Hammer the nails securely into the board about an inch and a half apart to make a grid, with about an inch of the nail sticking out of the board.

What to Do

- Offer a basket or small tray with beads, a string, and a nailboard to each toddler in a small group around a table.

- Younger toddlers may simply want to fondle the beads or place them on and off the nails.

- Older toddlers will often string the beads. Sometimes they will request that caregivers tie the string to make a necklace.

- Some toddlers may build with the beads, using the nail board as a foundation.

Limits

- "Beads are not for throwing." (Provide soft objects to throw.)

- "Beads are not for chewing." (Provide teethers.)

- This is a table experience; generally, materials stay at the table. (If wearing necklaces they strung, toddlers may move away from the table.)

- It's not safe to swing the string of beads. "Let me tie that up into a circle for you, or you can leave it on the table."

Other Things to Think About

- Have sufficient materials for each toddler to fill a string and a board.

- The stiff string ends can be extended by wrapping them with tape to make a longer "needle."

- Let toddlers do as much as they can for themselves; assist when asked.

- Have alternative toys to play with in the room for those who are not interested or who finish with the experience.

- If toddlers wish to keep their necklaces or beads strung to show their parents, let them if at all possible.

- Use thin, flat beads with short holes for younger toddlers learning to string beads. The process is easier if they can see it happening. They may also choose to observe others.

- Place one large-headed nail on the board among the others. How does this change the experience? Observe children's comments and problem solving.

- Place a block (no hole) the same size as the beads in the bead basket. How does this change the experience? Observe children's comments and problem solving.

Supporting Play

Can you see how Nell uses these strategies to support children's play in the following scene?

● Provide opportunities for practice at varied levels of skill

● Make room for trial and error and repeated investigation

Two-and-a-half-year-olds Amelia and Frank, two-year-old Mara, and sixteen-month-old Daniel each have a nail board, a basket of beads, and a string at the table. The caregiver, Nell, sits at the table and observes Mara tapping and pushing a bead against a nail. Nell acknowledges, "You're working very hard, Mara. Try turning the bead...see the hole?" Frank has chosen three red beads and puts them in a row. Amelia stacks two green beads on top of each other. Nell remarks, "I notice you're using green beads and Frank is using red ones." Daniel has the smallest nail board, 8 inches by 8 inches, lifted off the table and upside down. A barrel-shaped bead is upright on the table as Daniel slowly and carefully lowers the board aiming one nail towards the hole of the bead. Nell watches his sure approach silently. Daniel lays the board down on top of the bead so that the nail goes through the bead hole! Nell says, "Look at how you put the nail through the bead! Wow!"

Notice how Nell has a wide age range of toddlers for this experience. She notes various developmental expressions of skill. She verbally appreciates Daniel's innovative approach.

Decorating Cardboard Tubes or Cylinders

Paper towel or toilet paper rolls offer an unusual surface for toddlers to decorate. Coordinating small muscles to hold the tube, mark it with crayon or marker, and keep it from rolling offers children a focused challenge.

What You'll Need

- Cardboard cylinders like paper towel or toilet paper rolls or cut-up wrapping paper tubes.

- Paint, stickers, crayons, markers, colored tape, glue and collage materials, or other art materials

What to Do

- Collect cardboard tubes from families and staff members until you have a good assortment of different kinds. You want enough to be able to offer each toddler a choice of two tubes.

- Set the other art materials out on a table. If you're using glue or paint, you may want to cover the table with newspaper first. You may want to keep it simple the first time you offer this experience and offer a choice of two materials to decorate with. You can always make it more complex later, as the children get more experience with the challenges.

- Gather a small group of toddlers (no more than four). Offer each a choice of two tubes to decorate.

- Let the toddlers choose how (or even if!) to decorate their tubes. Observe their efforts and support their problem solving as they work with the curved surfaces of the tubes.

Limits

- Rolls are for decorating rather than hitting people or throwing (offer appropriate alternatives).

- Markers, glue, tape, etc., are for the rolls, rather than tables, floor, or walls.

Other Things to Think About

- Make suggestions only if children are "stuck" or ask for help. They can learn from each other how, for instance, to slip the roll over two fingers of one hand in order to reach all the way around it. (Try not to deprive them of this valuable self-discovery experience.)

- Decorated rolls may be hung as mobiles or strung as necklaces.

- Children may suggest materials to use for decoration.

Supporting Play

This experience is well suited for these strategies:

- Make room for trial and error and repeated investigation

- Allow for innovative use of materials

- Facilitate problem solving with observation and open-ended questions

Four toddlers ranging in age from fifteen to thirty-two months enter the art room to find various lengths of cardboard cylinders (5 to 10 inches) and baskets of stickers on the table. The two oldest toddlers run to grab the larger tubes; they sit and roll the tubes as they investigate the stickers. The youngest toddler, Shea, bangs a tube on the table. Caregiver Nina says, "I know that may be fun to do, but this tube is for decorating." Shea looks across the table at Jackie, who is removing stickers and placing them on his tube. Shea removes a sticker from its backing paper and pushes it on the tube as it rolls away. She reaches with her other hand to catch the tube. Nina asks as she observes Jackie looking for something, "What else would work to decorate the tube?" Jackie responds, "Can we do markers?" Nina says, "What a good idea." Jackie opens a favorite color and rotates the tube on the fingers of his right hand as he marks on the tube with his left hand. Shea watches him between picking more stickers and rolling her tube to put the stickers on.

Note how Nina allowed Shea her own discovery of how to stop the tube from rolling. Nina asks an open-ended question in response to Jackie's looking for something else. Jackie's coordination was further challenged when he could use markers with the stickers to decorate his tube.

Eyedroppers

Toddlers' love of water motivates them to practice with the eyedroppers to move the water from one section of the ice-cube tray to another. Colored water adds interest and helps make the results of their actions more visible.

What You'll Need

- Plastic eyedroppers.
- Ice-cube trays.
- Water colored with washable tempera paint.
- Other water-moving materials, such as pump bottles (optional).

What to Do

- Provide one eyedropper and one ice-cube tray per toddler. Provide colored water in small pitchers.
- Gather a small group of interested toddlers (no more than four).
- Let the children squeeze the eyedroppers and get the feel of them.
- Pour colored water into a couple of the sections of each child's ice cube tray. If you have a group of older toddlers who are proficient at pouring, you can let them pour the water.
- Invite the children to squeeze their eyedroppers in the water. Ask them, "What happens when you squeeze the end? What do you see?" Listen to their comments and responses. Point out the bubbles that rise through the water as the air comes out of the eyedroppers and the water that gets sucked into the eyedroppers when they release the bulb. This may fascinate the children for a long time.
- When they are ready for a new challenge, invite the children to move the water from one section of their ice-cube trays to another using the eyedropper. It may make sense for you to have your own ice-cube tray so you can model for children who are confused.

- Some children may be content to continue to squeeze and release the eyedropper without the additional step of moving the water. If children get frustrated, help them to problem solve by talking them through the process and helping them pay attention to the effect of their actions.

Limits

- "Try to keep the water in the trays or containers."

- Provide sponges so children can help clean up.

- Ask the children to work with their own sets unless invited to trade or work with someone else.

Other Things to Think About

- Use washable tempera to color water (food coloring stains skin and clothing).

- Plastic pipettes may also be used.

- Appreciate the toddlers' efforts as they learn to control getting the water into and out of the eyedropper.

- This experience can lead to several other art experiences once toddlers are accustomed to the eyedropper. For example, using this skill, toddlers can transfer thin paint to a paper towel, coffee filters, or art paper to make colorful designs.

- Add pump bottles that can be pumped into the ice cube trays, and ask children, "How long does it take to fill one section?"

Supporting Play

Use these strategies to support children's learning during this experience:

- Make room for trial and error and repeated investigation

- Allow innovative use of materials

- Facilitate problem solving with observation and open-ended questions

Two-and-a-half-year-old Galen grasps the eyedropper with both hands. He uses his fist to squeeze the rubber top. Ruth, the caregiver, notes, "Galen, you've found your own way to make the eyedropper work; nice job." Across the table, thirty-three-month-old Sunita practices squeezing the submerged dropper in the water. Ruth reflects, "Look at the bubbles you are making."

Older toddlers are capable of finding different ways for things to work. In this story, Ruth notices (and honors) Galen's practice. She does not have to correct his approach since using his fist works just fine. Ruth also respects Sunita's practice of repeatedly squeezing air into the water to make bubbles.

Swinging on a Knotted Rope

Toddlers love to experiment with swinging from, climbing on, and moving with a knotted rope hanging from a tree.

What You'll Need

- A strong, thick, soft rope. A cotton lead rope for horses, about 8 feet long, works great. It is very soft to hold on to and comes with a substantial slip hook for easy hanging from a tree.

What to Do

- Safely hang at least two ropes from an overhanging tree branch or a swing framework. They need to be far enough apart that two toddlers swinging on them can each have their own swinging space, yet close enough that toddlers can observe each other and interact. About 6 or 8 feet apart should do it.

- Knotting the ropes makes them easier to hang on to. Knots spaced apart on the rope will give handholds for different-sized children. Some children may also use them to climb up the rope.

- As with any experience where children can get even a little way off the ground, be sure that there is cushioning material beneath the ropes (8 to 10 inches of sand is best, or spread 8 to 10 inches of hay beneath them if the swings are to be temporary). The cushioning material should extend far enough around the ropes that a child falling from a rope that is swinging would still land on it— at least 6 feet from the bottom of each rope in all directions. A grassy yard or lawn is not enough cushioning to protect children from a fall.

Limits

- One at a time on each rope unless two toddlers are working it together.

Other Things to Think About

- Be sure that swinging toddlers can't swing into anything that might hurt them.

- Let toddlers discover the open-ended play potential of the rope.

- Place various knots for hand- and footholds.

Supporting Play

Use the following strategies to support children's play, as shown in the scene below:

- Provide opportunities for practice at varied levels of skill

- Promote body awareness by coaching

- Allow for innovative use of materials

Westley, who is nearly three, shouts, "Yay, the ropes are hanging!" He runs to one, grabs it and runs with it until it goes taut. Nearby, caregiver Merwyn notices and coaches: "Remember how to reach up high to hang on the top knot. Now lift your feet and pull with your arms." Westley beams as he swings a bit before letting his feet down. Two-year-old Sarah approaches the other rope and practices running with it. Then she stands and "throws" the rope, catching it as it swings back to her.

Note how Merwyn reminds Westley how to hang and swing. Westley does it on his own with coaching. Sarah is intrigued and practices at her own level, and she also finds a new approach of throwing and catching the swinging rope.

Hoops

Various-sized hoops offer opportunities for toddlers to practice spatial skills in open-ended play. Children roll hoops, put themselves inside them, and use them to make tracks in the sand. Open-ended materials such as hoops can be used in many ways at various skill levels to investigate spatial and gravitational relationships.

What You'll Need

- Plastic hoops at least 18 to 30 inches in diameter. Hoops in various colors and sizes are available in catalogues.

What to Do

- Seed yard with hoops, placing them strategically around the yard. Use at least six to eight hoops for ten to twelve toddlers.
- Allow the children to discover the hoops, investigate them, and explore uses for them.
- Refrain from showing the toddlers how to use the hoops or what to do with them, but respond to their questions and requests.

Limits

- "Hoops are for holding or rolling, not throwing or hitting."
- "Try to keep the hoops low to the ground when other people are close by."

Other Things to Think About

- Model rolling a hoop across a flat, smooth surface (grass or cement).

- Help children think about how to work together to move the hoops.

- Try hanging some hoops from various locations out of toddlers' reach, such as suspended from a low branch of a tree so a ball can be thrown through. (The larger the hoop and the smaller the ball, the greater the success!)

- Tie two hoops together to suspend from a tree.

- Offer hoops to crawling infants; they will pull them around and crawl under and through as they manipulate them.

Supporting Play

In the following story, can you see how Elizabeth uses the strategies below to extend children's learning?

- Provide opportunities for practice at varied levels of skill

- Promote body awareness by coaching

- Allow for innovative use of materials

Elizabeth has put out various sizes of hoops in the yard and hung two of the biggest ones in a tree. The toddlers emerge outdoors from snack time. Megan picks up a ball from the grass, eying the hoop in the tree. Elizabeth suggests, "Throw the ball up to get it through the hoop." Megan gives it a try but misses, and Elizabeth says encouragingly, "Almost, try again." Fourteen-month-old Polle picks up a small green hoop. "Look how you can hang that green hoop over your shoulder," Elizabeth comments. Eighteen-month-old Christy steps into a hoop on the ground and pulls it up to her shoulders. "Oh, you fit inside!" Elizabeth says. She goes over to Matthew, who is spinning with his hoop, and says, "I like how safely you're using that hoop near the other kids. I see more space over there if you need it."

Locking Hardware Outside

Toddlers love to manipulate a variety of real locking hardware, challenging their small-muscle control and problem-solving skills. Hasps, slide bolts, door chains, and other locking devices can be mounted on the fence in pairs so they are always available in the outdoor environment.

What You'll Need

- Hasps.
- Slide bolts.
- Door chains.
- Other single locking devices.

What to Do

- Visit the hardware store and think about which locking devices the toddlers could manipulate and would have fun figuring out.
- Mount at least two of each kind of hardware side by side (depending on group size) either right on to the fence or onto a board attached to the fence. You can also mount them onto smaller boards for use indoors.

Limits

None needed

Other Things to Think About

- Since these devices are fixed, they are very safe. Watch for parts to become rusty or sharp, and replace as necessary.

- Take advantage of the parallel setup (two of the same thing mounted next to each other) to suggest that toddlers work together, trade places, or take turns.

- Avoid using hardware that is used in the center as a real locking device!

- Spacing is important. On the fence, pairs of identical hardware should be 1 foot apart; "stations" of hardware pairs could be at least 10 feet apart, depending on available space.

- Try to allow the toddlers to discover these "real" objects instead of showing them how they work. Allow the toddlers to experiment with them. Over time, the process of fiddling with them will lead to mastery.

Supporting Play

Use the following strategies, as demonstrated in the scene below, to support children's development of coordination while they use the locking hardware:

- Provide opportunities for practice at varied levels of skill

- Make room for trial and error and repeated investigation

- Facilitate problem solving with observation and open-ended questions

> *Twenty-two-month-old Rohan approaches a slide bolt mounted on the fence. At first he slaps at it; then he fingers the knob part. Nearby, Cara observes and says, "Can you see how that slides and turns to open?" Nineteen-month-old Hillary hears this interchange and observes Rohan's investigation. Cara says to Hillary, "You can watch Rohan or try to figure out the other lock here or the one over there," and she points to other available hardware.*

Even though Rohan slapped or hit the locking device, Cara let it happen and then offered him information about the lock. As he practices moving the parts, Cara sees Hillary observing and encourages her investigation on another device.

Outdoor Maze

Younger toddlers especially are intrigued by the spatial challenges offered by a maze constructed with various outdoor equipment. They will try to figure out what sized openings they fit through, where they need to stand or crawl or climb, and what they can carry through the maze. Older toddlers also enjoy helping to plan the construction of the maze.

What You'll Need

- Snap-together wall blocks.
- Rigid or fabric tunnels.
- Blocks.
- Tires.
- Walking boards (2 inches by 12 inches by 3 to 6 feet).
- Sheets or tarps.
- Rocking boats (turn upside down and use as "bridges").
- Tumbling mats.

What to Do

- Construct a maze using whatever large-motor equipment you have with which you can construct walls, tunnels, passageways, bridges, balance beams, etc.

- Provide a variety of kinds of spaces, sizes of openings, and changes in level. Think, too, of building the maze in such a way that it requires different kinds of motion to get through: climbing, crawling, scooting, walking on a balance beam, jumping onto a mat, etc.

- You may want to provide several entrances and exits to the maze or more than one way to get through it.

- Be sure that the equipment is solid enough to withstand pushing and climbing.
- Allow the toddlers to discover the maze on their own.

Limits

- "It is safe to climb only on rigid portions of the maze."
- "It is safer to take turns going through tunnels."

Other Things to Think About

- Plan the maze setup to be stable, with many possibilities, in order to minimize how much you have to say no to children.
- Plan the maze to be interesting for children at the various developmental levels in your center. Use your observation of the children in your program, and provide for the kinds of movement they are especially interested in or that you see them practicing.
- Crawling infants enjoy tunnels too.
- Allow the toddlers to discover the maze, then talk about it as they experience it.
- Caregivers can encourage infants and toddlers to move through the tunnels by appearing at the opposite end.
- Set up a maze and keep it for a week or more, adding to it daily or every other day.
- Take a maze apart a bit each day.
- Build a similar maze indoors.
- Build a maze scaled for infants.
- Incorporate other equipment, such as slides.
- Large cardboard boxes could be used with small groups.
- Children can help plan, paint, and decorate boxes used in the maze.

Supporting Play

Can you see how this experience makes room for you to use the following strategies to support children's growing coordination?

- Provide opportunities for practice at varied levels of skill
- Promote body awareness by coaching

> *Atticus and Grant, both two years old, crawl through a snap-wall opening and out the other side through a fabric tunnel joined to another snap-wall triangle. Fifteen-month-old Adele watches the moving lumps as they crawl through the tunnel. She walks to the opening and peers in. The caregiver, Abby, notices her curiosity and says, "You see Atticus and Grant going through that tunnel; you can try it too." Abby goes to the opposite end and peers back at Adele. Tentatively at first, Adele begins crawling through the tunnel with her eyes fixed on Abby. She gets all the way through, and Abby says, "Did you feel the tunnel all around you?" Meanwhile, Grant pops out of the maze at the other end and runs down the walking board, looking behind him to see Atticus' progress.*

Note how much practice toddlers can get squatting, crawling, turning, and following each other through this maze. Abby promotes Adele's body awareness in the tunnel as she discovers a new experience.

Scissor Skill Practice

Older toddlers love to practice with scissors, perhaps because they are "real" tools that adults use. The concentration necessary to be successful is perfect "optimal stress" for many two and a half year olds. Interested and able younger toddlers could also try. The strength and control of muscles developed during this practice will be valuable in learning to write.

What You'll Need

- Blunt-ended scissors with edges sharp enough to cut paper easily.
- Early-learning scissors that work by squeezing.
- Playdough.
- Holed edge of computer paper.
- Paper scraps.

What to Do

- If this is a toddler's first experience with scissors, plan to start with playdough. Provide paper scraps for more experienced cutters; cutting from hole to hole on the computer paper edges is the perfect challenge for some.

- Gather a small group of toddlers (no more than four) who are interested in practicing cutting.

- After toddlers are seated at the table, hand out the scissors.

- Allow them to explore with the scissors and the playdough. Sit with them and model rolling a playdough rope to cut.

- Respond to requests for help by putting your hands over theirs and getting them to hold the scissors in one hand, with the thumb in one hole and two fingers in the other. Describe the "open-closed, open-closed" action of the scissors while moving the handles. Another analogy might be to say that the "scissors will take a bite out of the paper: open up, then bite down; open up, bite down."

Limits

- Toddlers must sit or stand next to the table while holding the scissors. They may not walk around with scissors.

- Only paper and playdough are for cutting.

- Offer alternative play or other art media to those who lose interest. They can try again another time.

Other Things to Think About

- There are a variety of small scissors commercially available for toddlers. Some are attached at the handle with a spring, so that after the toddler squeezes, the scissors open again on their own. These work well for some children.

- Many children start out using two hands on the scissors. Honor whichever hand the toddler chooses to use; he may switch.

- Quite often, toddlers will resist the one-handed approach. They'll ask for help when they're ready.

- Honor their goal of just cutting the paper. This practice often results in "fringe": single cuts made all around the edge of the paper.

- Offer the experience for a few days in a row, or by request, in order to allow skill practice.

- Have envelopes ready to collect scraps if the children want to keep them to show or take them home. Envelopes for scraps can be made by folding paper and taping; older toddlers will want to do it after you model how to do it.

- Add markers or crayons to the experience if children want to color before or after cutting.

Supporting Play

Use these strategies to support children's development of coordination through cutting practice, as shown in the scene on the following page:

- Promote body awareness by coaching
- Make room for trial and error and repeated investigation

Shannon has invited four toddlers, ranging in age from twenty to thirty-five months old, to the art area to practice cutting with scissors. Angela, the youngest, tries to squeeze her spring scissors against the edge of the paper. Shannon suggests, "Hold your paper in the air so the scissors can take a bite." Angela successfully makes a cut, drops her scissors, and gleefully tears the paper into two. Two-year-old Jerry is using both hands to open and close his scissors. Shannon says, "Can I show you about holding the scissors?" "No, no, no," Jerry says, trying to capture the paper with the scissors. "Let me know if you need help," Shannon says. Thirty-five-month-old Heather is adept at cutting; she requests "bigger paper," which Shannon is happy to supply. He recognizes the continuum of development and feels no need to hurry it.

Sewing Cards

Threading yarn or string through holes punched in cardboard squares offers toddlers practice at small-motor coordination. They can practice holding and manipulating two objects simultaneously, one in each hand.

What You'll Need

- Sewing cards: make your own from cardboard or Styrofoam, or buy plastic canvas from a craft store.

- Yarn or thick string in a variety of colors, cut into 12- to 15-inch lengths.

- Masking tape.

- Scissors.

What to Do

- Make sewing cards by punching holes about 1 or 2 inches apart in pieces of cardboard or Styrofoam. The holes can be arranged in a grid or other pattern or punched randomly. Make some of each kind, if you like. If you use Styrofoam meat trays, be prepared for some children to want to break them apart.

- Make enough cards to have more than one for each toddler in the group.

- Cut enough yarn or string to be able to offer each toddler a choice of colors. Make a tape "needle" at one end of each piece with the masking tape by laying the yarn diagonally on the sticky side of a short piece of masking tape and rolling it up. Cut excess tape on a slant to make a pointed end.

- Gather a small group of toddlers who want to sew (no more than four).

- Offer each toddler a choice of sewing card and yarn color.

- Tape the free end of the yarn (the end that doesn't have the tape "needle") to the back of each card to start, and then let the toddlers investigate. Don't worry about whether they're doing it "right"—just let them explore.

- Use phrases like this one to comment on children's work with the sewing cards: "Your thread went under, across, through."

- Offer toddlers a choice of new strings when their first ones start to get short, saying something like "Let me know when you want a new string or yarn."

- You can display finished pieces or let children take them home. Often the process is more important to the toddlers than what they make.

Limits

- Have enough materials to facilitate toddlers trading with one another if they want to.

- Offer a choice of other toys in the room when a toddler is finished sewing.

Other Things to Think About

- A child who has strung beads previously will probably put the needle through the holes.

- Help children who are frustrated by the difference between what they intend and what they can do. Talk through the problem, asking gentle questions like "Are you ready for another string?" or "Is it doing what you want?" Describe the designs resulting from their efforts.

- Plastic canvas has the advantage of showing the whole design from either side.

Supporting Play

Use these strategies, as shown in the scene below, to support children's coordination through sewing:

- Make room for trial and error and repeated investigation

- Allow for innovative use of materials

Four toddlers ranging in age from twenty-four to thirty-five months are sitting at the table. The caregiver has let them choose the color of yarn to use in their sewing cards. "Oh, Peter, you remember this from last time. You're putting the needle up and down in the holes," caregiver Eduardo says. Turning his attention to CristiAna, he notices that she is making an extra wrap before each "stitch." She is concentrating very hard and doesn't look up. Suddenly and loudly, Sean says, "I can't do it! I can't do it! I can't…." Eduardo kneels by his chair and says, "Sean, isn't it working the way you want? Let's see what we can do." Sean says, "No" and looks back at the card in his hands. Eduardo backs off and gets another child a new color and length of yarn. Returning to Sean, Eduardo suggests, "Poke the needle end through the hole (pause) and then pull it out on the other side." Sean does it twice, says, "I don't want to," and goes to play with the farm animals on the shelf. CristiAna holds up her card, covered with yarn. "More, more, please," she says.

Soft Objects to Throw Indoors

When caregivers provide soft objects that can't hurt anyone, toddlers are able to exercise their throwing muscles while experimenting with their power indoors.

What You'll Need

- Soft balls: for example fleece or felt balls.
- Balled-up socks.
- Pieces of nylon stockings stuffed with quilt batting and tied into various-shaped balls, or cover foam balls with nylon.
- Fabric flying discs.
- Nylon-net puffs (usually intended for bathing).

What To Do

- Have a variety of soft throwing objects accessible in each room. Have them out on toy shelves accessible to children.
- Offer them as an alternative when you sense that toddlers need some physical outlet or when a toddler throws an inappropriate toy.
- You could set up a target to throw the soft balls at or a basket to throw them into. You could hang a hoop from the ceiling and invite children to try to throw their balls through the hoop. Be prepared for some children to be uninterested in these more structured opportunities, and let that be okay.
- These may be especially useful on rainy or inclement days.

Limits

- Point out the logical consequences of a toddler's actions: if the sock is thrown over the door or out the window, it's "lost" or "gone." This is not a game of caregiver fetch!

Use new or interesting language (hard, soft, safe, hurt, fly, throw, roll) to describe the situation and set up the principles underlying the limits. For example, "I can't let you throw the truck. It's hard and would hurt somebody. Here, you can throw this sock or roll the truck on the floor."

Try to observe and understand why a child is throwing toys so that you can respond specifically to his need. Is this child throwing because she can't say "I'm finished"? Is he testing previously set limits? Is she simply experimenting with a new toy?

Other Things to Think About

Expect that toddlers will unball the socks and use them for dress-up or hand puppets. This is okay, innovative, and fun!

Supporting Play

Can you see how this experience gives you opportunities to use the following strategies to support children's growing coordination?

Provide opportunities for practice at varied levels of skill

Promote body awareness by coaching

Allow for innovative use of materials

Twenty-two-month-old Nasser lifts a wooden block above his head to throw. The caregiver, Clara, intervenes: "Please, Nasser, stop yourself from throwing the hard block. It would hurt someone. I see a sock ball and a nylon ball over there to throw." Nasser runs to pick up the sock ball and launches it across the room. Clara says, "Look how far you can throw; nice throwing the socks." Thirty-month-old Nannette sits on the floor and tosses a nylon ball towards a basket. It hits the rim and bounces in. "You made a basket; nice tossing the ball into the basket," says Clara as Nannette beams. Thirteen-month-old Shannon pulls at an end of two balled-up socks and works at pulling them apart. She waves one in the air with a smile.

Note how Clara redirects Nasser towards a soft object that is okay to throw indoors. Throwing is such a natural developmental toddler task that it is easier for everybody in a child care setting to make it available rather than constantly saying "No throwing indoors." However, this experience not only prevents conflict but offers opportunities for toddlers to develop their coordination, as in the above example when Nannette coordinates her hand-eye skill by tossing a ball into a basket and Shannon coordinates her small muscles to pull the socks apart.

Spray Bottles

This is a fun, safe outdoor experience that builds coordination. The squeezing action needed to operate a spray bottle strengthens the arm and hand muscles that toddlers will use to cut with scissors and write. Toddlers are very interested in this opportunity to use an adult item, because they see caregivers use spray bottles at other times.

What You'll Need

- Spray bottles with trigger handles, filled with water. Have at least four to six bottles for eight toddlers.
- Tubs or pitchers of water to refill spray bottles.
- Smaller containers for toddlers to fill by spraying into them.
- Washable tempera paint to color the water (optional).
- Towels for clean-up.

What to Do

- Fill bottles and place them strategically around the play space.
- Let toddlers discover them, and observe how they respond.
- Remove toddlers' clothing if they are spraying one another and if the weather allows.
- If using spray bottles inside, cover the floor with a plastic tarp and establish what it's okay to spray.
- Prepare colored water (optional) by mixing small amounts of tempera paint with water. A few drops of paint are sufficient to color 6 to 8 ounces of water. Tempera works better for this than food coloring, which will stain skin and clothing.

Limits

- State the limits clearly as the toddlers discover the bottles, using phrases like these:

  "Not everyone likes to be sprayed. Please ask first or spray your own feet."

  "You can spray yourself; not others."

  "You can spray fences, walls, sidewalks, trikes, or other toys."

Other Things to Think About

- Provide various-sized bottles and triggers for various-sized toddler hands.

- Provide enough bottles for the group so that waiting time is short, or make it a small group experience indoors with tubs and plastic covering the floor.

- If a child asks for help, suggest using two hands to squeeze.

- Place large sheets of paper on fences or walls, dissolve tempera paint in the water, and invite toddlers to spray the paper.

- Clean, empty shampoo bottles with flip-tops may be easier for younger toddlers to use. There's no trigger mechanism; toddlers can squeeze the body of the bottle.

- Allow toddlers to spray your hands. The turnabout experience is very empowering and fun for toddlers.

- This experience may be combined with other projects, such as watering plants that like misting or washing toys or equipment. Use nontoxic soap and water or plain water for rinsing. Toddlers love to be part of "real" chores.

Supporting Play

Can you see how spray bottles give you the opportunity to use these strategies to promote toddlers' developing coordination? See the scenario on the following page.

- Provide opportunities for practice at varied levels of skill

- Make room for trial and error and repeated investigation

The caregiver, Paul, has gathered a selection of spray bottles for toddlers to practice manipulating. He has hung large sheets of paper on the fence outdoors. The bottles are filled with colored water. Gleefully, thirty-three-month-old Christian discovers a bottle and begins pumping one-handed. "Look how you aim the spray at the paper," Paul notices. "Can you see where you spray?" Sixteen-month-old Orr is carrying a large shampoo bottle in both hands. He is content with this level of involvement. Annie joins Christian, and they trade bottles, then spray at the paper, standing side by side. They trade back and repeat. Paul notices, "Nice trading bottles and playing together, Annie and Christian."

Stickers

This experience provides opportunity for the development of small-muscle and hand-eye coordination, as well as problem solving.

What You'll Need

- Self-stick stickers (usually on backing paper), commercial or homemade.
- Various textured and colored papers to place stickers on.

What to Do

- Collect a variety of commercial stickers, or make your own. Simple colored dots and labels of various sizes can be found at stationery stores and are as interesting to young children as fancy printed ones. If you have more time than money, stickers may be made from adhesive paper. Cut patterns or simple shapes from contact paper. You can pull the backing from an 8- by 10-inch piece of contact paper, cut the shapes out of the sticky part, and place the cut-out shapes back onto the backing paper.

- Prepare enough supplies to be able to offer each child a choice of two sheets of fewer than ten stickers to start with and a choice of paper to stick them onto.

- Gather a small group of toddlers (no more than four).

- Offer the children a choice of paper. The choices could vary in color, in size or shape, or in texture.

- Give each child a partial sheet of stickers on backing paper. These could vary by size, shape, theme, or color.

- Allow the toddlers to experiment with techniques to remove stickers from the backing paper and apply them to the paper.

Limits

- "Stickers are for the paper, rather than the floor or the furniture."

- Toddlers will probably stick some on their clothing or bodies; caregivers should decide ahead of time if this is okay in order to be consistent and have alternatives ready to suggest. For example, you could offer one alternative by saying "This a small piece of paper; you can put stickers on it and then put it in your pocket."

Other Things to Think About

- For toddlers who need help getting started, model the technique of taking the stickers off the paper sheets rather than doing it for them: give little hints, such as if you gently bend the sheet, the edges of the stickers sometimes pop up.

- This is a good opportunity to observe individual children's approaches to problem solving, tolerance for frustration, and communication skills with adults and peers.

- Stickers come in lots of patterns. Many of them are realistic enough to be useful for following children's interests.

- Office supply stores carry colored dots, rectangles, and labels in bulk that work well.

- Stickers may be combined with other media, such as markers. Children may notice if the marker doesn't "work" on shiny stickers or other differences.

- Offer textured paper and observe and respond to children's efforts to make stickers stick.

Supporting Play

Use these strategies to support children's play with stickers, as in the scene on the following page:

- Provide opportunities for practice at varied levels of skill

- Make room for trial and error and repeated investigation

- Allow for innovative use of materials

Nineteen-month-old Uri focuses intently as he grasps the edge of a round sticker. It folds over on itself. He releases his hold, then tries again. The caregiver, Gene, observes, "Uri, look at how you figured out how to get that sticker off. You can do it when you take your time." Across the table twenty-eight-month-old Bridget peels each round sticker quickly and efficiently sticks one on top of another to make a small stack of stickers on the paper. Gene notes, "You're making a pile of stickers, one on top of another." Thirty-two-month-old Scott quickly places six stickers in a row on his paper. "Markers?" he asks. Gene says, "You'd like to use markers too?" Scott says, "Yeah," and Gene gets out baskets of markers. Twenty-three-month-old Jessica gratefully receives the markers, abandoning her efforts to get a sticker off her shirt.

Notice how Gene observes Uri's concentration on the task and supports his efforts. If a toddler gets easily frustrated when the stickers "don't work the way he wants," the caregiver can acknowledge that "You seem frustrated when the sticker sticks to itself. Let me know if you want help, or "You can try again another time....Take your time." In the above scenario, Gene allowed Bridget her own approach of stacking the stickers in one spot on her paper and responded to Scott's request for markers.

Streamers

Toddlers are exhilarated by having streamers to wave, pull behind them, or twirl. The variety of movement possible with streamers allows toddlers to use their large muscles in many ways.

What You'll Need

- Fabric streamers, made from old linens, approximately 2 inches wide by 2 to 4 feet long.

What to Do

- Make streamers by cutting or ripping up old linens or other pieces of fabric.
- Have more streamers than the number of toddlers in the group.
- Place the streamers around in the indoor or outdoor environment for toddlers to discover, or pass them out to interested children.
- Use a streamer yourself to experience the possible motions!

Limits

- Limit tying streamers to children's *own* body or clothing, and watch to be sure they are safe.
- Never allow anyone to tie a streamer around a child's neck.

Other Things to Think About

- Windy days make this experience especially fun.
- Toddlers will instinctively wave and run with the streamers.
- Toddlers could color the streamers with markers.

- Repeat this experience for a few days to enable the children to fully explore the possibilities of the streamers.

- Show toddlers how to dance around a Maypole by tying four to six long streamers to a pole, post, or tree so that the ends hang within their reach. Then walk around the Maypole singing this song:

  "We're winding round in a circle, a circle, a circle;
    we're winding round in a circle on this bright May day!"

  You can unwind by going in the other direction and substitute *unwinding* for *winding* in the song. You can also substitute other, more active verbs, such as *running, skipping, hopping,* or *jumping,* if there are few enough children in the circle that you can be sure they will not run into one another.

Supporting Play

Use these strategies to support children's play with streamers, as shown in the following scene:

- Promote body awareness by coaching

- Allow for innovative use of materials

> *Four thirty-month-old toddlers each grab a streamer and run with them across the grass. Yael and Zachi wave theirs above their heads. Lettie and Barry watch their feet running, then spy their streamers behind them. When the running toddlers slow down, the caregiver, Deanne, promotes another bodily movement by tying four of the long streamers to a post and inviting children to join her in dancing around the Maypole.*

String Painting

Dipping strings in paint or colored glue and setting them on and off paper results in multi-lined designs and offers toddlers practice in two-handed manipulation and hand-eye coordination.

What You'll Need

- Lengths of string about 12 inches long for each color of paint used; have extras available. (A "handle" may be made by taping one end of the string, but be aware that the toddlers may try to paint with it; it can draw attention away from the string manipulation.)

- Washable powdered tempera paint in various colors.

- Glue.

- Liquid starch.

- Paper of various sizes, shapes, and colors.

- Wax paper or plastic lids to place strings on between uses.

- Spray bottles and towels for clean up.

- Smocks or paint shirts.

- Shallow bowls or trays for the paint.

What to Do

- Mix the washable powdered tempera with water, glue, or starch to a fairly thick (pudding-like) consistency. The first time you do this experience, you may have to experiment a bit to find the thickness that works for you.

- Put each color of paint in a shallow bowl or pan so it's easy to dip strings into it.

- Set up space for four toddlers to paint at a table. Have several lengths of string and colors of paint and paper available so you can offer each toddler a choice of materials.

- Have smocks or paint shirts ready, or plan to take children's clothes off to keep them from getting paint-smeared.

- As children come to the table to paint, explain that painting with string is another way to put paint onto the paper.

- Allow the toddlers to choose the paint color, string, and paper they want to begin with.

- Instead of trying to show them how to paint with the string, let them experiment and watch what they do.

Limits

- Remind children that "Paint and strings are for the paper."

- Facilitate trading and taking turns with the paint colors and strings.

Other Things to Think About

- Give lots of reflective feedback, using comments like these:

    "Oh, you dropped the string. What mark did it make?"

    "You're dragging the string across the paper. What happens when you do that? How else can you move the string on the paper?"

- Have wax paper ready as a place to put strings when finished. Be sure to follow through and discuss what happened to the strings as a result of being dipped in the paint.

- Let paint-soaked strings dry on the wax paper or plastic lids, then hang the dried strings as mobiles. (String mobiles work best when the paint is mixed with starch or glue.)

- Older toddlers may be able to fold their paper over their string and hold down the paper while pulling the string out from between the folded paper. This process makes another interesting pattern.

Supporting Play

Use these strategies to support children's learning, as in the scene below:

- Make room for trial and error and repeated investigation

- Allow for innovative use of materials

- Facilitate problem solving with observation and open-ended questions

Twenty-seven-month-old Hamilton loves to paint. He is surprised when caregiver Mary shows the strings they will be painting with today. At first he scrunches the string up and rubs it on the paper. Looking around, he watches Marjorie carefully dipping the string in paint and pulling it across her paper. "More string," he says to Mary. "Do you want red or yellow?" she asks. Settling on yellow, he drops the string into the paint. Lifting it up with a little tail, he drags it across the paper. "You made a thin line," Mary observes. "More," he says. "How can you do more?" she asks. He pulls the tail on his string, dips it in the paint, and pulls a line across his paper. Mary returns his smile of satisfaction that she let him do it his way.

Three-Dimensional Painting

Toddlers integrate skills of observation, cause and effect, and coordination to investigate and solve problems presented by painting on vertical or other odd-shaped surfaces.

What You'll Need

- Large boxes: one or two for each group of four toddlers. (Appliance boxes, such as those from large TVs, refrigerators, washers, or dryers, work well for this.)
- Small boxes or cardboard tubes (one for each toddler).
- A tarp or sheet of plastic or newspaper to protect the floor.
- Paint cups and brushes.
- Tempera paint.
- Smocks or paint shirts to cover clothes.

What to Do

- Set up the large boxes where you want to have the painting experience take place, or set out small boxes and tubes on a table. You may want to cover the floor or the table with a tarp or newspapers to protect it.
- When children come to paint, put on paint shirts or smocks or take off their clothes if it's warm enough.
- Offer each child a choice of paint color, noting that they can trade with each other if they want to.
- Facilitate the toddlers' movement around the box and their trading of paint colors.
- Discuss the painting process with them: if the paint drips, for instance.

Limits

- Each child uses one color and brush at a time.

- Paint goes on the box, not on children or furniture.

Other Things to Think About

- Facilitate problem solving and experimentation. For example, ask children to describe what they see, encourage their use of language, and ask them questions to illuminate their intentions in order to facilitate any of these possibilities:

    working side by side

    painting the inside of the box

    painting the top of the box

    moving around the box

- It helps to have a small table that children can set the paint cups on when they are ready for a new color. If you have one or two more paint cups than children, every child will always have a choice, and the table facilitates trading for younger children who might have a hard time physically managing the trading.

- Older toddlers may trade colors by directly handing them to one another without setting them on the table if they are coordinated enough to manage it without spilling.

- It is possible to stuff large bags full of newspapers to make three-dimensional shapes for painting. Tape the open ends closed after you have stuffed them. Or use small stuffed sacks on the tabletop.

Supporting Play

Use these strategies, as shown in the scenario on the next page, to support children's painting experience:

- Make room for trial and error and repeated investigation

- Allow for innovative use of materials

- Facilitate problem solving with observation and open-ended questions

Four toddlers are busy painting two large boxes. Jude says, "The paint dripped again" to caregiver Bea. She says, "Didn't you want it to?" Jude says, "No." "What did you want to do?" Bea asks. "I just wanted some blue right there," he says. Bea says, "Try wiping your brush off on the edge of the cup." Jude says, "No." "Okay," says Bea. "What else do you want to try to get that blue there?"

Letting toddlers form their own approach to problem solving puts the emphasis on process rather than on the product, which helps them to gain competence.

Tire Rolling

This experience provides large-muscle challenge for older toddlers: lifting a tire to a rolling position and pushing, balancing, and turning it while negotiating gravity and the tire's balance.

What You'll Need

- Used, rimless automobile tires of various sizes. (Tire stores will often give away old tires. Check each tire for embedded nails or other unsafe objects.)
- Duct tape.
- A smooth surface for successful rolling.

What to Do

- Tape two tires of the same size together so they roll easily.
- Make multiple sets, depending on the size of your group, so that toddlers can practice simultaneously, separately or together.
- Place the tires in the outdoor environment, near a paved or otherwise smooth surface where they can be successfully rolled and won't knock anyone down.
- The tires are heavy; toddlers may need help to balance and lift them to get started. Together, with each toddler, model how to lift the tire into rolling position by placing fingers and palms under the tire and lifting. Allow the toddler to feel the weight and lift it himself as much as possible for challenge and success.

Limits

- Observe and encourage safety, using phrases like these to help children pay attention to safety:

  "Tires are not for running into people."

  "Roll the tire around her or stop while she goes by."

  "Nice waiting."

- Set up an area where it is safe to let tires roll away until they fall over.

Other Things to Think About

- This experience is especially useful for older toddlers who are strong and active.

- A single extra-wide tire may work fine all by itself.

- Investigate narrow, wide, flat, rounded, large, and small tires with the children. How do they work?

- Encourage and facilitate two toddlers rolling the tires together.

Supporting Play

Can you see how tire rolling gives you the opportunity to use these strategies to support children's developing coordination?

- Provide opportunities for practice at varied levels of skill

- Promote body awareness by coaching

- Make room for trial and error and repeated investigation

> *Thirty-month-old Lauren has a lot of energy today and has been expressing it by pushing kids, then running off. Caregiver Lasana has been observing this and redirects Lauren by saying "Lauren, try pushing these tires instead of people." Lauren excitedly approaches the taped-together tires as Lasana says, "Help me lift them—like this" as he places his fingers and palms under the bottom tire. Lasana models an easy groan as he allows Lauren to feel the tire weight while they lift together. He says, "Look how strong you are, Lauren." She smiles as the tires begin to roll. Lasana coaches, "Nice balancing the tire as it rolls. Can you steer it around that trike? Take your time. Ooo, it's falling—hold it up." The tire falls flat to the sidewalk. Lauren points and yells, "Get it." Lasana says, "Let's do it together" as they both bend to pick up the tires and begin the experience again.*

Note how Lasana calmly redirects Lauren's high energy to a challenging experience. He encourages her to practice as they lift the tire together, acknowledges her body awareness of her strength, and coaches her through her first experience of negotiating gravity and balancing the tire.

Index

Note: *c* indicates a chart.

A

"activities" vs. "experiences," 3, 58
alternatives, offering. *see* Choices, offering
    (caring strategy)
anger
    acknowledging children's feelings, 34
anticipation
    caring strategy, 36–37
    needs of children, 113, 115
    skills, providing practice opportunities, 188
    during transitions, 125
articulation of needs and wants
    caring strategy, 37–38
    open-ended questions, use, 193
autonomy
    and anticipation, 36–37
    and caregivers as "islands," 116
    choices and decision making, 39–40
    modeling behavior, 16
    needs of children, meeting, 114
    security built on trust, support for, 107
    and self-doubt, modeling "can do" behavior, 193

B

birthdays, reflecting cultural differences, 112
biting, behavior and response, 127–28
body language
    communication methods, learning and
        teaching, 12–14
    feelings, labeling or naming, 35
    and toileting, 199
    and transitions, 199
books, encouraging curiosity, 48
Bos, Bev
    life is a conversation, 14
brain development, first three years, 6–7
Bread Bread Bread (Morris), 113

C

caregivers
    assistance, toddlers in simultaneous distress, 116
    attitudes, and transitions, 125
    attitudes reflected by children, 24, 53
    caring strategies. *see* Comprehensive caring
        strategies
    coaching, to promote body awareness,
        189–90, 195, 200
    commitment to caring interactions, 23–27
    and conflict. *see* Conflict
    defined, 4
    emotional investment in children, 11
    gender issues and cultural basis, 22
    honest feelings, expression, 15–16, 35–36
    "I" messages, 15
    inner conflicts, awareness of, 118, 121–22
    "islands" for physical connections, 108, 115–17
    learning about selves from children, 24–27, 118
    modeling behavior. *see* Modeling behavior
    patterns and routines, teaching trust, 17–18, 121
    paying attention to children, 23, 192
    personal beliefs, and personal care routines, 123
    personal interests, sharing to encourage curiosity,
        49–50
    predictable and consistent actions, 113–15, 123
    relationship with children and parents,
        10, 20, 112, 114
    responsive vs. reactive actions, 113–14
    staff rotation system, 7, 9–11
    talking out loud. *see* Self talk (caregiver talking
        out loud)
    "thinking like a kid," fostering independent
        learning, 19
    verbal/nonverbal communication, 13
caregiving routines. *see* Routines
caring (attitude), defined, 23
caring interactions, 23–27
caring responses to hurtful behaviors, 126–28
caring strategies. *see* Comprehensive caring strategies

Note: *c* indicates a chart.

The Case for Mixed Age Grouping in Early Education
    (Katz, et al.), 9
celebrations, reflecting cultural differences, 111–13
charts and charting, 31–32
    child's action/child's need/respectful response, 13*c*
    comprehensive caring strategies, 42*c*, 56*c*, 131*c*, 201*c*
    infant room procedures, 32*c*
    materials for infants and toddlers, 45*c*
    needs of children, meeting, 113
child care centers. *see also* Palo Alto Infant-Toddler
        Center
    child information profiles, 21, 111, 113
    choosing, parents' needs and concerns, 20–21
    connections with families, 111
    environment, planning by function, 7–9
    family age grouping, 7, 9
    organization of, authors' beliefs enumerated, 7
    traditional school model, drawbacks, 7–8
child care programs
    authors' beliefs enumerated, 7
    connections in, 108–9
    written philosophy, importance of, 5
child development. *see also* Cognitive development
    acknowledging children's feelings, 35
    autonomy. *see* Autonomy
    caring interactions, effect of, 26–27
    concern for quality in each stage, 18–19
    curiosity and extended exploration, effect of, 47
    emotional connections. *see* Emotional connections
    emotional stages of, Erikson's theory, 5, 18
    for every no, give two yeses, 40–41
    everyday experiences, reflecting, 6–7
    failure to thrive syndrome, 7
    family age grouping and, 7, 9
    faster not necessarily better, 18
    how thinking develops, Piaget's theory, 5–6
    independent learning, fostering, 7
    "is," "is not" naming, 48
    "okay" actions, 38, 40–41
    PACCC program philosophy, 2
    physical connections, 108, 126
    physical development and coordination, 186–87
    physical stages, 18, 186
    record keeping. *see* Record keeping
    self-directed play, 46
    support for vs. preparation for, 18
    understanding, importance of, 5–7
child information profiles
    and cultural differences, 21, 111
    individual schedules, developing, 113
    use during mealtimes, 121
children with disabilities, use of materials
        reflecting, 113
child's experiences, validation of
    coaching, to promote body awareness, 189
    curiosity, encouraging, 46
    during mealtimes, 51–52

sensory experiences, 12, 52
    during transitions, 54–55
child's interests
    exploration, and encouraging curiosity, 46–47, 55
    offer additional information, 47–48
choices, offering (caring strategy), 38–40
    biting, response to, 127–28
    curiosity, encouraging, 45–46
    decision making, 39–40
    hurtful behaviors, caring responses, 126–27
    materials, innovative uses, 191
    during mealtimes, 122
    needs of children, meeting, 115
    providing in the environment, 39, 45
    respecting children as individuals, 38–39
    setting consistent limits, 40–41
    during transitions, 125
cleaning up. *see* Personal care routines
coaching, to promote body awareness, 189–90
    during naptimes, 195
    during transitions, 200
cognitive development. *see also* Child development
    and curiosity, 43–56
    and trustful connections, 107–8
comfort level and curiosity, 43–44
communication methods
    action/need/respectful response (chart), 13*c*
    biting, 127
    body language. *see* Body language
    learning and teaching, 12–14
    "misbehaviors," 13
    modeling behavior. *see* Modeling behavior
    reflecting children's awarenesses, 49
    verbal/nonverbal communication, 13
comprehensive caring strategies, 28–42
    acknowledging feelings, 33–36
    anticipating transitions, unusual events, or changes
        in routine, 36–37
    articulating needs and wants, 37–38, 193
    charting, 42*c*, 56*c*, 131*c*, 201*c*
    enumerated, 28
    for every no, give two yeses, 40–41
    modeling behavior, 32–33
    observation and optimal stress, 28–31
    offering choices, 38–40
    setting consistent limits, 40–41
conflict
    caregivers' feelings about, 109–10, 118
    caregivers' inner conflicts, awareness of, 118, 121–22
    and connections with others, 109–10, 118–20
    facilitating as learning opportunities, 20
    vs. mutual interest, 118
    resolution, essential skills, 119
    resolution at ITC, 22, 112
    turn taking and trading skills, 120
    when to intervene, 119, 126

Note: *c* indicates a chart.

connection with others (strategies), 107–31
    charting, 131c
    in child care, 108–9
    and conflict, 109–10, 118–20
    emotional connections, importance of, 107, 113
    family culture, including, 111–13
    hurtful behaviors, caring responses, 126–28
    inner conflicts, caregivers' awareness of, 118, 121–22
    interdependence. *see* Interdependence, facilitating
    "islands," 108, 115–17
    list of, 110
    during mealtimes, 121–22
    meeting individual needs, 109
    meeting needs predictably and consistently, 113–15
    mutual interests, affirming, 117–18
    names, introducing peers and adults, 110–11
    during naptimes, 124
    observation, promoting through, 29
    pace of movement, slowing down, 115–17
    during personal care, 122–23
    physical connection, 108, 126
    planned play experiences, 132–84
    during routines, generally, 121–25
    during transitions, 124–25
    turn taking and trading skills, 120
coordination, encouraging (strategies), 185–201
    charting, 201c
    coaching, to promote body awareness, 189–90
    developmental sequence, 186
    list of, 187
    materials, innovative uses, 191–92
    during mealtimes, 194–95
    milestones of coordination, 185–86
    during naptimes, 195–96
    observation, promoting through, 29
    and open-ended questions, 193
    during personal care routines, 196–99, 200
    physical coordination, 186
    planned play experiences, 202–52
    problem solving, facilitating, 192–93
    process, focus on, 191
    during routines, generally, 194–200
    self-discovery, 190–91
    sensory experiences, feedback, 185
    and skills. *see* Skills, providing practice opportunities
    toddlers' levels of meaning, 186–87
    during transitions, 199–200
    trial and error, repeated investigation, 190–91, 193
Cross Cultural Child Development, A View from the Planet Earth (Werner), 10
cultural differences
    child information profiles, contents, 21, 111
    environment, reflecting, 21
    family culture, including, 111–13
    and gender issues, 22
    and personal care, 123

practices and celebrations at ITC, 21, 112
    and toileting, 197
curiosity, connection, and coordination. *see* Three Cs
curiosity, encouraging (strategies), 43–56
    caregivers' interests, sharing, 49–50
    charting, 56c
    child's experience, validating, 46
    cognitive development and, 43
    exploration, child's interest as guide, 46–47
    helping children feel comfortable, 43–44
    information, offering, 47–48
    list of, 44
    materials, providing choices and time for manipulation, 45–46
    during mealtimes, 51–52
    modeling behavior, 32–33
    during naptimes, 53–54
    observation, promoting through, 29
    during personal care routines, 52–53
    planned play experiences, 57–106
    during routines, generally, 50–55
    say what you know, 47–48
    say what you see, 46
    say who you are, 49–50
    self-awareness, promoting, 48–49
    during transitions, 54–55

D

decision making, offering choices, 39–40
Demonstration Infant Program, 2, 11
diapering. *see* Personal care routines
Dooley, Norah, 113
dressing. *see* Personal care routines

E

emotional connections
    with adults, 7, 107, 113
    and short story time, 124
    verbal/nonverbal communication, 13
environment
    choices, providing for, 39, 45–46
    cultural differences reflected, 21
    independent learning, fostering, 19–20
    planning by function, 7–9
    pockets of play (areas for small group interactions), 19
    safe exploration, experimentation, and practice, 19–20
    skills, opportunities to practice, 187–88
    skills, reinvestigation of, 191
Erikson
    security built on trust, supporting autonomous exploration, 107

Note: *c* indicates a chart.

theory of emotional stages of development, 5, 18
theory of trust/distrust, 17
Everybody Bakes Bread (Dooley), 113
Everybody Cooks Rice (Dooley), 113
everyday experiences
    and child development, 6–7
    three Cs, strategies for, 3
"experiences" vs. "activities," 3, 58
Eyer, Dianne Widmeyer, 11

F

failure to thrive syndrome, 7
families
    respect and nurturing, authors' beliefs
        enumerated, 7
    respect from caregivers, 20–22
    values, conflict resolution at ITC, 22
family age grouping
    connections, introducing peers and adults
        by name, 110
    generally, 7, 9
    interdependence, encouraging, 118
    and staff rotation system, advantages, 10–11
feelings, acknowledging (caring strategy), 33–36
    appropriate expression, 33–34
    helping children feel comfortable, 44
    honest expression by caregivers, 35–36
    hurtful behaviors, caring responses, 126–27
    labeling or naming, 34–35
    and learning manners, 128–30
    needs of children, meeting, 115
    physical expressions, 36
for every no, give two yeses, 40
Forrest, Dr. Tom
    and Demonstration Infant Program, 2
frustration
    acknowledging children's feelings, 34–35
    and biting, 127
    needs and wants, helping articulate, 37–38

G

gender issues, at ITC, 22
gentleness, modeling behavior, 32
Gerber, Magda
    and Demonstration Infant Program, 2
    Ten Principles of respectful caregiving, 7
Gonzalez-Mena, Janet, 11, 21, 197
    cultural differences, exploring through dialogue, 21
    for every no, give two yeses, 40
    on holding infants, 197
    optimal stress, challenge of, 29
    Ten Principles of respectful caregiving, 7, 11

Greenspan, Stanley, 7
The Growth of The Mind, (Greenspan), 7

H

Hats Hats Hats (Morris), 113
home care model, at ITC, 7
House and Homes (Morris), 113
house with invisible walls metaphor (setting limits), 41
humor, use of, 41, 48
hurtful behaviors, caring responses, 126–28

I

"I'm sorry," 129–30
individualizing children
    choices, offering, 38–39
    connections, meeting individual needs, 109
    names, introducing peers and adults, 110
    during naptimes, 124
    observation, 29
    quality time, investment, 12
    respect for, 38–39
    Ten Principles of respectful caregiving, 11–19
infant experiences
    Babies Love Balls (connection), 133
    Boxes for Babies (coordination), 203
    Experience Table or Tubs (connection), 135
    Floor Pictures (curiosity), 60
    Gathering Table (connection), 139
    Infant Massage (connection), 141
    Peeking and Hiding (connection), 137
    Pillow Mountain (coordination), 205
    Scarf Box (curiosity), 63
    Wind Chimes and Windsocks (curiosity), 66
infants
    action/need/respectful response (chart), 13c
    attention from caregivers, effects, 23
    calming selves, practicing, 195
    caregivers learning from, 24–27
    comfort level and curiosity, 43–44
    crawling and physical connections, 108, 115–16
    defined, 3
    first connections, physical touch, 116
    individualizing (observation), 29
    involvement in things concerning them, 12
    personal care routines, involvement in, 52
    problem solving. *see* Problem solving
    reflecting caregivers' attitudes, 24
    relationship with caregivers and parents, 10
    sitting up, physical stages of learning, 18–19
    trust. *see* Trust
    validating experience, 46
Infants, Toddlers, and Caregivers (Gonzalez-Mena and
        Eyer), 11

Note: *c* indicates a chart.

infant/toddler development. *see* Child development
infant/toddler experiences
    Bird Feeding (connection), 152
    Bubbles (curiosity), 68
    Cameras From Home (connection), 154
    Classic Rhymes (connection), 145
    Clear Tubes (curiosity), 71
    Experience Bottles (curiosity), 74
    Fingerpainting (curiosity), 77
    Musical Instruments (connection), 149
    Photo Display (connection), 143
    Puzzles (coordination), 207
    Water Play (curiosity), 80
information, offering
    curiosity, encouraging, 47–48
    during mealtimes, 52
    needs of children, meeting, 115
    during personal care routines, 53
    during transitions, 54–55
interdependence, facilitating, 108–9, 117–18, 193
    during mealtimes, 122
    during naptimes, 124
    toileting, 197
introductions, using names of peers and adults, 110–11
ITC. *see* Palo Alto Infant-Toddler Center

K

Katz, Lilian, 9
Kurcinka, Mary Sheedy
    traits, expression of temperament, 48–49

L

language development
    absorbing more words than can be used, 119
    biting, response to, 128
    charting, 42*c*, 56*c*, 131*c*, 201*c*
    child's experience, validating, 46
    connections, introducing peers and adults
        by name, 111
    feelings, labeling or naming, 34–35
    honest feelings, expression by caregivers, 16
    hurtful behaviors, caring responses, 127
    "is," "is not" naming, 48
    manners, learning, 128–30
    needs and wants, helping articulate, 37, 193
    offer additional information, 48
    during personal care routines, 52
    say what you see. *see* Say what you see
    self talk. *see* Self talk (caregiver talking out loud)
    skills, reinvestigation of, 191
limits, consistent setting of (caring strategy), 40–41

M

Mama Zooms, 113
manners, learning, 128–30
materials, choices and manipulation
    chart, 45*c*
    curiosity, encouraging, 45–47
    family cultures, including (connection strategy), 113
    guidelines, 45
    innovative uses, 191
    planned play experiences. *see* Planned play
        experiences
    providing in the environment, 39
    during transitions, 55
mealtimes. *see also* Routines
    connections, promoting, 121–22
    coordination, opportunities for, 194–95
    cultural differences, reflecting, 112–13
    curiosity, supporting, 51–52
modeling behavior
    attitudes reflected, 24, 53
    "be a balloon," 196
    caregivers' interests, sharing to encourage
        curiosity, 49–50
    caring strategy, 32–33
    cultural differences, 112–13
    hurtful behaviors, caring responses, 126
    manners, 128–30
    during naptimes, 196
    during personal care routines, 53
    self-doubt and "can do" behavior, 193
    Ten Principles of respectful caregiving, 16
    during toileting, 199
    during transitions, 199
Morris, Ann, 113
Multicultural Issues in Child Care (Gonzalez-Mena), 21, 197
mutual interests, affirming (connection strategy), 117–18

N

names, introducing peers and adults, 110–11
naptimes. *see also* Routines
    connections, promoting, 124
    coordination, opportunities for, 195–96
    curiosity, encouraging, 53–54
    infants, calming selves, 195
National Association for the Education
        of Young Children
    materials, guidelines for choosing, 45
needs of children, meeting
    articulation of needs and wants, 37–38, 193
    individual needs, 109
    during mealtimes, 121
    predictable and consistent actions, 113–15

Note: *c* indicates a chart.

O

observation and optimal stress (caring strategy), 28–32
  biting, response to, 127
  goal of learning specific information, 29–30
  individualizing children, 29
  providing optimal stress, defined, 29
  record keeping, 30–32
  and self-discovery, 190
  skills, providing practice opportunities, 188
  and toileting, 198
  during transitions, 54, 200
open-ended questions, and problem solving, 193
optimal stress. *see* Observation and optimal stress
     (caring strategy)

P

PACCC. *see* Palo Alto Community Child Care
pace of movement, slowing down, 115–17
  during personal care, 122
  during transitions, 125
Palo Alto Community Child Care, 1–2
Palo Alto Infant-Toddler Center.
     see also Child care centers
  attitude, caring and commitment, 23
  child care philosophy, generally, 5
  child information profiles, 21, 111
  conflict resolution with families, 22
  cultural practices and celebrations at, 21, 112
  diaper changes while standing, 197
  environment, planning by function, 7–9
  establishment, 2
  family age grouping, 9–11
  gender issues, 22
  home care model, use, 7
  house with invisible walls metaphor, 41
  materials, innovative uses, 192
  parents' participation at, 21
  registration procedures, 21, 111
  relationship among children, caregivers,
     and parents, 10
  staff rotation system, 3, 7, 9–11
  teaching directors, 3, 10
  tours, 111
parents
  defined, 4
  relationship with children and caregivers,
     10, 20, 112
  toileting, involvement with, 199
  verbal/nonverbal communication, 13
personal care routines. *see also* Routines
  connections, promoting, 122–23
  coordination, opportunities for, 196–99, 200

  curiosity, supporting, 52–53
  diaper changes, 40, 52, 196–97
  hand-washing, modeling behavior, 32
  involvement of children in, 12, 52, 200
  predictable and consistent actions during, 123
  toileting, 52, 123, 197–99
physical coordination. *see* Coordination,
    encouraging (strategies)
Piaget
  theory of how children's thinking develops, 5–6
Pikler, Emmi
  philosophy of child care, 2–3, 11
planned play experiences
  common characteristics, 58
  connection, encouraging, 132–84
  coordination, opportunities for, 202–52
  curiosity, encouraging, 57–106
  defined, 58
  guidelines for use, 59
  infants. *see* Infant experiences; Infant/toddler
     experiences
  reasons for use, 58
  toddlers. *see* Infant/toddler experiences;
     Toddler experiences
"please" and "thank you," 130
pockets of play (areas for small group interactions), 19
politeness, modeling, 128–30
preferences, promoting self-awareness, 49
problem solving
  for every no, give two yeses, 40–41
  facilitating with observation and open-ended
     questions, 192–93
  feelings, acknowledging, 35
  and interdependence, 193
  learning opportunities, recognition as, 16–17
  matter-of-fact approach, 196
  modeling behavior, 33, 35
  self-doubt, dealing with, 193
  and skills integration, 187, 197
  Ten Principles of respectful caregiving, 16–17
  during transitions, 199–200
purpose of book, 3

R

Raising Your Spirited Child (Kurcinka), 48–49
record keeping
  anecdotal records, 31
  birthdays (connection strategy), 112
  charting. *see* Charts and charting
  needs of children, meeting, 113–14
  running records, 30–31
  and staff rotation system, 10

Note: *c* indicates a chart.

reflecting children's awarenesses, 49, 51
relationships. *see also* Social relationships
    among children, caregivers, and parents,
        10, 20, 112, 114
    among children and adults, 108
Resources for Infant Educators, 2
respect for children as individuals
    choices, offering, 38–39
    Ten Principles of respectful caregiving, 11–19
    three Cs, 3
    during toileting, 199
    as worthy people, 14–15, 39
respect for families, 20–22
RIE. *see* Resources for Infant Educators
routines. *see also* Mealtimes; Naptimes; Personal care
        routines; Transitions
    changes, anticipating, 36–37
    connection, promoting, 121–25
    coordination, opportunities for, 194–200
    curiosity, supporting, 50–55
    involvement of children in, 121
    manners, learning and modeling during, 128–30
    regular schedule provides security, 36
    and teaching trust, 17–18, 121

S

say what you know
    curiosity, encouraging, 47–48
    during mealtimes, 52
    during personal care routines, 53
say what you see
    accidents and saying "I'm sorry," 129–30
    biting, response to, 128
    curiosity, encouraging, 46
    and open-ended questions, 193
say who you are
    curiosity, encouraging, 49–50
    during naptimes, 54
scripting
    modeling "please" and "thank you," 130
    needs and wants, helping articulate, 37–38
self talk (caregiver talking out loud)
    child's experience, validating, 46
    coaching, to promote body awareness, 189
    hurtful behaviors, caring responses, 127
    modeling behavior, 32
    reflecting children's awarenesses, 49
    verbal reflection, 47
self-awareness, promoting
    curiosity, encouraging, 48–49
    during naptimes, 53–54
    during personal care routines, 52–53
    during transitions, 54–55
self-discovery, supporting, 190–91, 194
separation anxiety, and caring interactions, 26

sharing (learning manners), 128–29
Shoes Shoes Shoes (Morris), 113
skills, providing practice opportunities
    coordination strategies, 187–88
    dressing, undressing, 200
    integration of, 187, 197
    during mealtimes, 194–95
    pouring from a pitcher, health concerns, 194–95
    "practicing gravity," 191
    reinvestigation of, 191
    toileting, 198
    during transitions, 200
    turn taking and trading, 120
social relationships
    and interdependence, 117
    and mealtimes, 122
    and personal names, 111
    during short story time, 124
staff rotation system, 7, 9–11
stranger anxiety, and caring interactions, 26

T

talking out loud. *see* Self talk
    (caregiver talking out loud)
teaching directors, at ITC, 3, 10
teasing vs. humor, 48
temperament, traits expressing, 48–49
Ten Principles of respectful caregiving, 11–19
    communication methods, learn and teach, 12–14
    development, quality of each stage, 18–19
    enumerated, 11
    honest feelings, expression by caregivers, 15–16
    involvement of children in things concerning
        them, 12
    modeling behavior, 16
    problems, recognition as learning opportunities,
        16–17
    quality time, investment, 12
    respect children as worthy people, 14–15
    security, build by teaching trust, 17–18
    strategies for applying, 28–42
    total persons, building, 14
    "whole child," concentration, 14
three Cs, 3
    connection. *see* Connection with others (strategies)
    coordination. *see* Coordination, encouraging
        (strategies)
    curiosity. *see* Curiosity, encouraging (strategies)
toddler experiences
    Beads, Strings, and Nail Boards (coordination), 210
    Bug Study (curiosity), 85
    Cardboard Binoculars (curiosity), 83
    Cardboard Tubes for Construction (curiosity), 88
    Cardboard Tubes or Cylinders, Decorating
        (coordination), 213

Note: *c* indicates a chart.

Cars and Trucks (connection), 157
Collage of Faces (connection), 160
Colored Glue (curiosity), 90
Drumming (connection), 163
Eyedroppers (coordination), 216
Farm Animals (connection), 166
Flannelboard (connection), 169
Hoops (coordination), 221
Ice Chunks (curiosity), 92
Implement Painting (curiosity), 97
Locking Hardware Outside (coordination), 223
Ooblick (curiosity), 101
Outdoor Maze (coordination), 225
Painting (curiosity), 94
Paper with Holes (curiosity), 99
Photo Albums (connection), 172
Rock Game (connection), 174
Scissors Skill Practice (coordination), 228
Sewing Cards (coordination), 231
Soft Objects to Throw Indoors (coordination), 234
Spray Bottles (coordination), 237
Stickers (coordination), 240
Story Time (connection), 177
Streamers (coordination), 243
String Painting (coordination), 245
Swinging (connection), 179
Swinging on a Knotted Rope (coordination), 219
Three-Dimensional Painting (coordination), 248
Tire Rolling (coordination), 251
Watercolors (curiosity), 104
Weather (connection), 181
Wheelbarrow (connection), 183
toddlers
    action/need/respectful response (chart), 13*c*
    attention from caregivers, effects, 23, 117
    caregivers learning from, 24–27
    comfort level and curiosity, 43–44
    conflicts, facilitating as learning opportunities, 20
    conversation, involvement in, 14–15
    defined, 4
    diaper-changing, involvement in, 123
    individualizing (observation), 29
    interest and abilities, acknowledging, 14
    interest in peers, 120
    involvement in things concerning them, 12
    manners, learning, 128–30
    "misbehaviors," 13

    "perform" assumptions, 14
    problem solving. *see* Problem solving
    reflecting caregivers' attitudes, 24
    relationship with caregivers and parents, 10
    relaxing, to sleep, 195–96
    simultaneous distress, caregivers' assistance, 116
    toileting, involvement in, 199
    trust. *see* Trust
    walking and physical connections, 108
toileting. *see* Personal care routines
traits, expression of temperament, 48–49
transitions. *see also* Routines
    anticipating, 36–37, 55, 125
    connections, promoting, 124–25
    coordination, opportunities for, 199–200
    curiosity, supporting, 54–55
    introducing peers and adults by name, 110
    meeting individual needs, 109
    transitional objects, helping children feel
        comfortable, 44
trust
    caregiver relationships with infants/toddlers, 6
    infants, attachment to others, 107, 116
    stranger/separation anxiety, caring interactions, 26
    teaching through patterns and routines, 17–18, 121
    theory of trust/distrust, Erikson, 17
    during toileting, 199

U

unusual events, anticipating, 36–37
using this book, 4

V

vocabulary-building. *see* Language development

W

Weber-Schwartz, Nancy
    patience and understanding, 27
Werner, Emmy Elisabeth, 10
Where's Chimpy, 113

Other Resources
from Redleaf Press

Prime Times: A Handbook for Excellence in Infant and Toddler Programs
By Jim Greenman and Anne Stonehouse
An essential guide to establishing a high-quality program for infant and toddler care.

More Than Counting: Whole Math Activities for Preschool and Kindergarten
By Sally Moomaw and Brenda Hieronymus
Unusual and new manipulatives, collections, grid games, path games, graphing, and gross-motor play for a complete math experience.

More Than Magnets: Exploring the Wonders of Science in Preschool and Kindergarten
By Sally Moomaw and Brenda Hieronymus
More than 100 activities for life sciences, physics, and chemistry.

More Than Singing: Discovering Music in Preschool and Kindergarten
By Sally Moomaw
Over 100 activities and ideas for songs, instrument making, music centers, and extensions into language, science, and math.

Big as Life: The Everyday Inclusive Curriculum, Volumes 1 & 2
By Stacey York
From the author of *Roots and Wings*, these two curriculum books explore the environment of a child's life and the connections that make life meaningful.

The Kindness Curriculum: Introducing Young Children to Loving Values
By Judith Anne Rice
Create opportunities for kids to practice kindness, empathy, conflict resolution, and respect.

Making It Better: Activities for Children Living in a Stressful World
By Barbara Oehlberg
Offers bold, new information and activities to engage children in self-healing and empowerment.

800-423-8309
www.redleafpress.org